GITCA GOLF

MAKING GOLF FUN FOR THE OTHER 99 PERCENT OF US

KELLEY PETER

Copyright © 2021 Kelley Peter
All rights reserved
First Edition

PAGE PUBLISHING, INC.
Conneaut Lake, PA

First originally published by Page Publishing 2021

ISBN 978-1-64628-004-9 (pbk)
ISBN 978-1-64628-005-6 (digital)

Printed in the United States of America

This book is dedicated to all those heroes near and far who have sacrificed so much in order for all of us to be so blessed. To all the military and first responders who keep us safe and aid us in times of need, we cannot thank you enough. I also cannot begin to repay my family, friends, coaches, and teachers, who have always been there for me through thick and thin. All of you are constantly in my thoughts and prayers, and your spirit lives on in my heart forevermore.

CONTENTS

Introduction 7

Opening Hole: We Need to Make Golf Much More
Appealing for the Masses 21

Hole Number 2: Playing GITCA GOLF Will Give
Everyone a New Outlook on Golf and Life 30

Hole Number 3: Prioritizing and Counting Blessings 41

Hole Number 4: What in the World Is GITCA? 44

Hole Number 5: Just Imagine a Better Way to Play Golf 50

Hole Number 6: A Lifetime Pursuing Ultimate
Enjoyment out on the Links 72

Hole Number 7: The Eight Simple Rules of GITCA GOLF 96

Hole Number 8: Learn to Become a Master of Your Domain 122

Hole Number 9: Golf Myths That Need to Be Eradicated 137

The Back Nine: How the Idea for GITCA Was Hatched
and Developed 153

Hole Number 11: Why Do We Really Even Bother with
This Game Anyway? 177

Hole Number 12: Introducing the Most Ardent Golfer in
the Family to GITCA GOLF 180

Hole Number 13: The Passing of a Dear Golfing Buddy
and a Lifelong Mentor 186

Hole Number 14: Inherent Problem with Traditional
Golf Scoring System 188

Hole Number 15: A Boyhood Dream of Mine Comes to
Fruition Getting to Meet Jack Nicklaus 195

Hole Number 16: Focusing on Family and Friends 207

Hole Number 17: What Defines a Good GITCA Score? 288

The Final Hole: Tragic Passing and the Reevaluation of
Our Priorities 314

Addendum to Gitca Golf 323

INTRODUCTION

This book is a wake-up call for everyone who loves and appreciates golf. Golf courses around the world are being forced to close down their operations due to a lack of customer support. The demand for this once immensely appealing sport has been waylaid by an oversaturation of the market, high prices, slow play, and an absence of gratification by most of its participants. Dreadful scoring, nitpicky rules to try and discern, needless arguing, and few moments of actual enjoyment out on the links have led many golfers to give up the game for their own sanctity. Everyone who cares about the health of the sport must learn to think outside of the box if we hope to garner new participants while making the game far more appealing for current golf enthusiasts.

The main objective whenever you play golf is to get the ball in the hole in the least amount of strokes possible. With this being the premise, it behooves you to play a fairly forgiving course from distances that you can easily traverse. Golf is much more enjoyable when you are not getting embarrassed by your playing partners or the course. The key to not letting this happen is to play from those tee markers which allow you to stay competitive with both the course and your opponents. If everyone is playing from distances that allow them to find approximately the same number of greens in regulation with their approach shots, then the match is likely going to be highly competitive. Unfortunately, most golfers are bullied by one or two other golfers or their own ego into playing from distances that they can't possibly score well from, and as a result, the matches are not very competitive at all. Golfers who are playing from distances that far exceed their capabilities are going to be fortunate to make bogeys on most of the holes they play. Now attaining a bogey on certain holes is not a bad score, but once again, we have been conditioned to believe that any score above par is a blemish. Thus, most scorecards are left with a ton of blemishes, and the jovialness that was there to begin the day is usually squelched by the end of the round. Certainly, the professionals would never be content to shoot scores worse than par, yet the golfing world has placed most amateurs in situations where attaining par on most holes is extremely challenging. Of course, the professionals are asked to traverse the course from much farther distances than most amateurs, but proportionately speaking, most recreational golfers are forced to hit much longer clubs for their approach shots than their professional counterparts. How ludicrous is it that the typical weekend hacker is asked to try and pull off much more difficult shots than the pros on most of the holes that they attempt to play? Due to this degree of difficulty usually resulting in a greater dispersion of where the ball might end up in relation to the hole, scores of ninety or worse are commonplace, and the desire to play more in the future wanes with every poor round played. Something must be done to change these dreaded outcomes, or the future of recreational golf is in grave danger.

If golf can be made more enticing to those on the outside looking in while making actual golfing venues more rewarding for all participants, then the popularity of this sport will likely grow by leaps and bounds. *Topgolf* has done a wonderful job of marketing hitting golf balls to golfers and nongolfers alike. The entire experience is positive as it combines family, friends, drinking, eating, and hitting balls to targets from pristine lies without much regard for poor shots. In other words, the blemishes are not brought to the forefront as only the good shots are remembered and recorded. Now the trick is bringing a similar enthusiasm from these friendly confines to actual golf courses. The key is getting people hooked on playing golf from the get-go by greatly reducing the negative moments while accentuating the positive ones.

In order to greatly reduce the embarrassment factor, it is imperative that all new golfers start their quest into golf by receiving proper instruction from certified golf instructors and working their way backward from the hole to the tee. Most beginning golfers should live on the putting green as they learn to get competent at putting, chipping, and pitching. Once these short game basics have been taught and learned, it is crucial that all novice golfers attempt to play par 3 and executive golf courses prior to embarking on much longer and harder courses. Playing these shorter courses allows for much greater proficiency and much better scoring opportunities. Once a good level of expertise has been demonstrated on these shorter courses, golfers should attempt to play regulation-length courses only from the most forward of tee markers until they have demonstrated sustained excellence. By putting themselves in a position to achieve moderate levels of success, all golfers should be enthused to continue to play and get better incrementally without ever feeling overwhelmed. The next big step to making recreational golf fun for everyone is to reward any score of bogey or better on a hole. Since we don't do this for a living, it is okay to accept the fact that a bogey on certain holes is a pretty respectable score for most amateurs. All recreational golfers should be encouraged to adopt the mindset that achieving a par or bogey on most holes is to be lauded and applauded. If we can put most golfers in position to achieve mostly pars and bogeys, then the average score for the avid golfer is apt to be much better and the rounds far more enjoyable for everyone. When the average avid golfer's score is in the low 80s, instead of pushing 90, every foursome will play infinitely faster and attain far more gratification.

Only by making golf extremely more enjoyable for everyone are golf courses going to see a return to the golfing boom that we saw in the late 1980s and early '90s. There needs to be some wholesale changes to the way that the game is being marketed, or nearly every golf course will have to contemplate shutting down their doors for good in order to make way for more profitable real estate ventures. The days of making the golf courses as long and penal as possible are over as we need to start catering golf to the masses rather than just the top 1 percent of all golfers. Nearly every course record is being easily shattered by the professional golfers out there. So why then are we still insistent on making the game as difficult as possible for the nonprofessionals? No matter how difficult you make your course, the pros are still going to score extremely well, while the average avid golfer is going to be torn to shreds trying to play from distances that are far beyond his/her capabilities.

For golf to see a huge resurgence, certain paradigm shifts must occur in the way the game is currently played by a majority of its participants. Since 99.9 percent of us will never play in a sanctioned golf tournament, we need to adapt the rules so that the game is far simpler for the recreational player to understand and do reasonably well at throughout their golfing career. By allowing for better scoring opportunities while greatly increasing the pace of play, we are greatly enhancing the golfing experience for recreational golfers around the world. Golf must be made more user-friendly for the majority of its participants, or the future of golf will continue to be very bleak. Gerald Celente, publisher of *Trends Journal*, states, "People are working longer and harder just to stay even. It's a virtual world and golf has no place in that world. Playing golf used to be an integral part of climbing that corporate ladder, but the practice has gone the way of the 'three martini lunch'" (MarketWatch, March 29, 2017).

There are three entities responsible for the decline of golf around the world. Number 1 are the powers that govern golf proclaiming that there is only one set of rules and that everyone must follow them. Certainly, this is not true as there are different sets of rules for scrambles, match play, alternate shot, and best-ball competitions. Secondly, golf course designers and management teams have set up a majority of their clientele for extremely trying days out on the links. By making most golf courses too harsh and too long for the majority of their patrons, the powers that run these courses have unwittingly dug their own grave. Golfers like to challenge themselves from time to time, but only when the moments of gratification actually outweigh the negative ones. If we don't reward our ego periodically, then eventually we will cease repeating that particular activity. Even if the golf course management team has set us up for failure, we still have the power to remedy this situation ourselves. By moving up a tee box or two and giving ourselves more opportunities to be successful, we can turn what oftentimes would be a dreadful experience into a very memorable one. So if we can get everyone on board with making golf easier and more enjoyable for all recreational golfers, most golf courses have a chance to survive and possibly thrive.

    Several years ago, I almost gave up the game for good. Playing golf was bringing me so little satisfaction that the thought of never playing again was very tempting. No matter how hard I tried or how long I practiced, the results were often sporadic at best. I'd have a couple of nice holes and a few really good shots, but in the end, it always felt as though I could be spending my time doing much more productive things with my life. Fortunately, I have been extremely blessed to have an amazing family and truly special friends who have always been there for me in my darkest hours. Thankfully, one of my buddies convinced me to stick with golf and use it as a medium to spend more quality time with those closest to me. That five-minute conversation was just the impetus to change my perspective on golf and life. It gave me renewed hope to give golf another chance and to inspire others to do the same. I realized at that moment that I needed to come up with a solution to make golf much more enticing for everyone. For the last few years, my buddies and I have developed a system that allows golf to be much more positive in nature and far more ego-gratifying. By following our simple changes, every recreational golfer will be far more motivated to play golf far more often with those closest to them. I am so thankful that my support system inspired me to stick with golf and help me develop a much more enjoyable way to play this wonderful game. My friends, family, and I have had so many iconic moments out on the links it is too hard to recount all of them. What a tragedy it would have been to miss out on any one of these magical moments. My goal is to invite all of you to think outside the traditional norms so that you too can enjoy many more of these indelible moments golfing with your beloved friends and family.

    Father Time takes its toll on all of us, robbing us of speed, flexibility, and strength. Many people quit playing their beloved sport altogether because they can no longer play at the high level in which they once competed. Even with all the accumulated knowledge we have acquired by playing a sport most of our lives, we still are limited in our ability to compete against those who are in their prime athletically. This can be very depressing watching more youthful athletes far surpass our current best efforts. Fortunately, golf can negate these large discrepancies by properly distancing the space between the various tee markers. The key then is to get everyone on board with playing from distances that allot every participant the opportunity to record good scores. If every golfer who plays is hitting their approach shots with roughly the same scoring iron, then the probability for everyone to score well is improved significantly. With every golfer hitting far more greens in regulation and recording better scores than they ever believed possible, the enjoyment factor will be off the charts. The pace of play will be brisk, and golfers everywhere will be much more enthralled to play golf far more often.

In the minds of most golf historians, Arnold Palmer, Jack Nicklaus, Lee Trevino, and Gary Player are four of the greatest ambassadors the sport has ever known. These four icons took the game of golf to a whole another level with their inspired play on the course and, more importantly, with all of their goodwill off the course. Televised golf came to the forefront with the rise of these great heroes, and their legacy has lifted golf and the rest of us to a much better place. I had the privilege to watch these great men play several times in person and numerous times on television. These four beloved figures always had the biggest crowds, and there were always magical moments to be had inside and outside of the ropes. They didn't always win the tournament, but they were always extremely gracious to their throngs of fans. When the world lost perhaps the most beloved sports figure of all time in the "King" several years ago, a void was left that can never be replaced, but his legacy has left an indelible impression for all of us to try and emulate for the rest of our own lives.

Mr. Nicklaus, Mr. Trevino, and Mr. Player have certainly carried on this mantle with their worldly missions as well as their everlasting passion for golf. These childhood heroes of mine are precisely the role models the rest of the golf world should rally behind. Certainly none of these legends can play at the level that they once did in their prime, but if you ever get the chance to watch them play together now, don't miss it for the world. The three of them usually get together for the Masters Par-3 contest and several other scramble tournaments throughout the year, and undoubtedly, one or two magical moments are still produced by their trademark swings. Playing par 3 courses and scramble events from the white tee markers as they all are close to eighty years old, these three beloved figures are still extremely competitive as they continue to impress golf fans of all ages. To see these living legends still battling it out against their often much younger compatriots is something that you could never witness in any other sport. It is for this reason that I continue to watch and play golf every chance I get. If three of the greatest ball-strikers the game has ever known are not too proud to move up to the correct tee boxes for their abilities, then why should any recreational golfer ever be questioned for moving up to tee markers which greatly increases his/her chances for sustained success?

Golf is truly the only sport that one can be competitive at all ages. Tiger Woods has been shooting near-par golf since about the age of two, and there are many senior golfers out there who continually best their age with their eighteen-hole score. Now certainly, these are the exceptions rather than the rule, but all of us can be quite competitive if we choose circumstances that promote golden opportunities while taking into account our limitations. Few of us have the power and precision to take on really difficult golfing venues from the distances from which the top golfers in the world so easily traverse, but we can choose to play far less treacherous courses from distances that give us ample opportunities to have moderate levels of success. Unfortunately, most golfers have fooled themselves into trying to play far too difficult treks from distances that statistically set them up for disappointment a majority of the time. If some of the greatest golfers of all time are reaping the benefits from playing in scrambles from distances they can handle while continually amazing all of us with their scoring irons on the par 3 courses, then why in the world should the rest of us continue to put ourselves in situations that leave us few moments of actual joy out on the links?

Most recreational golfers have been set up to fail by the golfing industry as well as themselves. The majority of championship golfing venues have their black tees around 6,800 yards, their blue tees around 6,500 yards, and their white tees around 6,100 yards. Many of these clubs have rules that state that all male golfers between the ages of sixteen and seventy must choose to play from one of the aforementioned tee boxes. Armed with the latest and greatest technology, the majority of golfers try to challenge themselves by playing from tee boxes that offer them little chance to achieve any sustained success. What my research has found is that each of these tee markers is 300 to 400 yards farther back than they should be if the golf course hopes to promote relatively good scores and an enjoyable time for a majority of its clientele. Most of these championship courses have had a difficult time attracting and keeping new playing members because the brutality of their venues combined with the limited tee box options have left most golfers gasping for air. Even with all the latest golfing gear, the majority of the participants have little chance to reach a majority of the greens in regulation. The frustration level usually reaches such a boiling point that most golfers eventually give up playing the game for good.

Provided that most of the top PGA professional golfers are well over 100 yards longer with their driver and over four clubs longer with their other clubs than most recreational players, getting to play perfectly manicured courses on the PGA Tour that average around 7,300 yards is a breeze for most of the top professionals. Following a good drive, most of the best players in the world are hitting short scoring irons for a majority of their approach shots. Hence, if these top players are on with their tee shots, then most of their approach shots are likely to find the putting surfaces a high percentage of the time. For the average golfer to have a similar scoring iron in their hands for their approach shots following their typical 210-yard drive, the average recreational golfer would have to play from a total distance of no more than 5,100 yards. Since the average championship course forces most recreational golfers to play from at least 6,100 yards, proportionately speaking, the typical hack recreational golfer is now faced with the unenviable task of trying to bite off 1,000 or more yards than the best players on the planet. Since most recreational golfers have neither the time nor the skill to keep up with the much longer and much more talented professionals, is it any wonder why the disparity gap between the two is greater than any other time in golf history? While most professionals are averaging in the 60s, most avid recreational golfers are lucky to break 90. Given this huge discrepancy in the scoring averages, it is easy to discern why more and more recreational golfers are choosing to play far less. We need to make the scoring opportunities much more plentiful for all recreational golfers, or the mass exodus from golf is likely to continue.

At most charity golf events, the usual format is a four-person scramble. A ton of money is usually raised and a great time is had by all participants, as the rules are usually very liberal and the course is usually set up for almost every group to score extremely well. Since everyone had such a great time out on the links, the donations to the charity are often very big and everyone can hardly wait to tee it up again next year for this worthy cause. Everyone in your group contributed to your great team score, while the bad shots were quickly forgotten as the next player in line would usually step up and carry the load for that hole. (In a scramble format, your team gets four attempts at each shot, so the likelihood of someone coming through with a decent shot is very high.) The team orientation format encouraged everyone to help one another with strategy and reading the greens properly. There was a concerted effort for everyone to pull together in order to see just how many under par your team could record. High fives were given on nearly every hole as one magical shot after another brought a sense of bewilderment to the entire round. You all played off one another's momentum and sense of camaraderie to record a score that would make Tiger Woods envious. Since only the best shot was taken, the pace of play was very brisk, and many exuberant screams of joy were heard throughout the round. Wouldn't it be great if everyone felt this giddy out on the links every single time they teed it up?

Professional golfers spend most of their lives continually honing their craft just so they have the opportunity to shoot par or better for most of their playing careers. The pros practice nearly every day as they know that they have to be darn near flawless in order to stay competitive and keep their playing credentials. They almost always play in great weather on courses that have been groomed to perfection so that the conditions are consistent and extremely playable. The average golfer is fortunate to get out and play a few times a month on far-from-perfect courses and oftentimes in far-from-ideal weather. Since they only get out sporadically and they often play in less-than-ideal circumstances, the average golfer must be willing to accept the fact that their games and the courses they play are likely going to be less than perfect. It is extremely difficult to have all aspects of your game in sync when you play and practice so infrequently. As a result, most amateurs must play under parameters in which "bogey golf" or slightly better is about as good as they can hope to achieve on a consistent basis. The pros would never put up with having to play so infrequently in such sparse conditions or with having to play from distances that make scoring well darn near impossible. It is high time that all recreational golfers band together and agree to follow protocols that give them much greater opportunities to post far better scores and have a far more enjoyable time out on the links.

The USGA and the R&A set up the intricate rules for the professional golfers to abide by, and they make certain that there are plenty of rules officials standing by to clear up any rule ambiguities throughout their tournament proceedings. Whenever you and your buddies go golfing, it is the group consensus and not the USGA that ultimately decides the protocol for how the round is going to proceed. Each group has their own guidelines that they generally follow, but usually the rules are not followed that stringently and there oftentimes is a lot of leeway. I am certain that there are some groups out there that try and follow the exact letter of the USGA rule book, and I am quite certain that I have no desire to ever join these groups for a round of golf. Having to follow the standard stroke-play protocol from distances that are above most amateurs' pay grade on largely unkempt courses doesn't allow for many instances of sustained gratification. Being very complicated and extremely penal in nature, the rules do not lend themselves to the majority of participants leaving the course feeling very good about themselves or golf in general. Most amateurs simply don't have the carry distance to hit many greens in regulation, nor do they generate the amount of spin needed to hold many of these greens with their approach shots. Playing "bogey golf" is about the best that most amateurs can hope for even after bending some of the rules that the USGA institutes for strict tournament play.

Following the strict tournament stroke-play format offers very little latitude as a golfer must be darn near perfect on nearly every hole in order to post a respectable score. Unless you are a professional, the odds of having several blow-up holes that ruin your entire round is highly probable. With no one to back you up, it can get very lonely out on the course as various aspects of your game start to betray you. Things can go sideways literally and figuratively very quickly. Not only is it extremely embarrassing to hit shots far into the woods and into many water hazards, you then must check the rule book for how to properly proceed. Oftentimes, arguments arise between participants as to the proper procedure to follow, and the scores that are finally submitted are often highly questioned. When handicaps are added, this only adds to the misery as every golfer becomes further scrutinized as to the validity of their stated handicap. Being any good at golf is hard enough; we don't need these petty rules or our integrity being questioned to further bring us angst out on the links. For 99 percent of the people who play it, golf is for recreational purposes only. It should be a way for us to get out with our friends and family and knock the ball around and have one hell of a good time. Unfortunately, most golfers set their expectations way too high, and as a result, they really can't let loose and enjoy themselves. The parameters need to be changed so that everyone can score better, play faster, and have many more memorable moments each and every time they hit the links.

My buddies and I feel that we have come up with a perfect compromise between the standard stroke-play format and a scramble format, and we have labeled our system GITCA GOLF. Following our guidelines allows all golfers to play from distances that are much more conducive to scoring well, and the need to be perfect on every single hole is no longer warranted. We have streamlined the rules down to eight basic tenets that make the round highly competitive for all participants from beginning to end without any controversy whatsoever. By getting rid of all the gray areas and allowing leniencies which greatly increase the probability of striking the ball cleanly from manageable distances, we are almost assuring every group of playing faster and having far more fun than they could ever imagine as they post some of the best scores of their lives.

My foursome has fully embraced the GITCA guidelines for the last four years, and we are excited for the rest of the golfing world to get on board. Being out in the sunshine with our dear friends and soaking in all the camaraderie interspersed with a lot of great scoring opportunities, we all know that it doesn't get much better than that. Our mindset is that we live in the greatest country in the world, and we are fortunate enough to have the freedom to be playing golf with our friends whenever the course beckons us. Unfortunately, most golfers don't implore this eternally grateful mindset or a system that gives them many opportunities to succeed. Golfers around the world have been shamed into playing from tee markers which allot them few opportunities to be successful out on the links. By the time they reach the end of their round, most of them have not enjoyed the journey at all. They are often so full of rage that they rarely acknowledge all the wonderment presented to them along the way with their friends and family. The majority of golfers only allow themselves to experience fleeting moments of joy and only when their scorecard is in tact with their often grandiose expectations. Most of these golfers are so filled with performance anxiety that they can't truly enjoy themselves until after the final putt has been holed and only when their score is up to snuff. Let's stop this madness by providing everyone a much higher probability for success and, ultimately, a much better experience out on the course. It is time to embrace a new way of playing so that all golfers can relish every opportunity they get to tee them up with those closest to them.

If I had magical powers and I could grant three wishes, I am betting that almost all avid golfers would have similar requests. Without a doubt, all of them would love to add another twenty to thirty yards or more of straighter distance to their arsenal. This is the main reason why the market is flooded with clubs, balls, tees, and the latest instructional techniques that promise to deliver on this wish. Try as hard as they might to buy a better game, most golfers go unfulfilled in cracking this code and, as a result, never achieve their lifelong desire to post scores around par or better. So invariably, most golfers would then use their second wish to guarantee scores near even par or better. Many of these avid golfers would insist that if you simply grant the first wish, the second wish would come to fruition most of the time. Not everyone may agree on this assessment, but the third wish of being able to play golf one more time with a loved one from heaven is almost universally agreed on. How amazing would it be to snap our fingers and be able to get back just one special day out on the links with a family member or beloved friend? Knowing that this was a once-in-a-lifetime dream come true, we would certainly treat it with much greater respect than the normal Saturday afternoon round that we far too often take for granted. Now unfortunately, I don't have the power to fulfill this last request, but hopefully, I can inspire all of you to no longer take your typical weekly round with your buddies in such a cavalier manner. Once we acknowledge that these special occasions may not last forever, we start to really appreciate them. This change in mindset allows us to see with much more clarity all the wonderful moments that our friends and family members have provided us with throughout the years. This new perspective will greatly alter our priorities as to what is truly important out on the golf course.

Fortunately, I can help most of you gain another twenty to thirty yards or more on each hole by encouraging all golfers to simply move up at least one tee box with no guilt or remorse whatsoever. By granting all golfers a "hall pass" to these much more manageable tee boxes, the likelihood of hitting more accurate shots and posting scores much closer to par increases dramatically. By closely following all the GITCA guidelines, every golfer will have even more opportunities to improve their scoring chances. With every golfer in your foursome scoring much better and fully embracing all the wonderful interactions, each golf outing will be much more treasured.

My main goal in writing this book is that I hope to inspire each of you to embrace each precious moment that you have been given on and off the golf course. Ask almost any avid golfer, and they will tell you that some of their most cherished moments happened on a golf course with a family member or beloved friend. With GITCA

GOLF, we have greatly reduced the embarrassment factor while granting far more opportunities to succeed. By making the scoring and the experience far more positive, we allow each participant to achieve contentment almost every time out on the links. No longer will there be needless arguing about rule interpretations or the validity of one's score. Every golfer who embraces the GITCA guidelines will experience far more positive energy before, during, and after each round. Even though the rules are much less rigid than the traditional stroke-play scoring method used in professional tournament settings, the competition and the camaraderie will be greater than you ever believed possible. The main premise with GITCA GOLF is that we want you and your buddies to thoroughly enjoy your entire golfing experience from beginning to end. In fact, we want you to enjoy it so much that you can barely wait to go out and do it again as soon as possible. Once you and your buddies make GITCA GOLF the staple for how you play golf on a regular basis, you will have a much greater appreciation for life's truly memorable moments on and off the course.

OPENING HOLE

We Need to Make Golf Much More Appealing for the Masses

Golf is often viewed as a very difficult sport that lends itself to many opportunities to embarrass oneself while offering few instances of actual gratification. While most professional golfers make the game look relatively simple, most recreational golfers are inherently frustrated by this ever-maddening game. The hidden secret is that the professionals have been set up to succeed most of the time, while most recreational golfers have been set up to fail. Most avid golfers greatly overestimate how far and how well they hit a majority of their shots while greatly underestimating how much further and more skilled most of the professionals are in comparison to their own games. Having to play with a mishmash of clubs on less-than-stellar courses from distances that far exceed their capabilities, most amateur golfers leave the course angry at themselves, the course, and/or their playing companions. Meanwhile, the people who do this for a living have the best equipment, play perfectly groomed courses, and usually only tee off in rather temperate weather conditions. In addition, they are asked to play from distances that promote great scoring opportunities on almost every hole they play. Most pros are scoring better than they ever have in their career and are having a ball setting one record after another. On the other end of the spectrum, very few recreational golfers are garnering much enjoyment at all out on the links. This reality has to change dramatically if recreational golf is going to stay relevant for the next century.

In the late '90s we saw the rise of Tiger Woods's dominance, and the sport of golf took off like never before. Suddenly, everyone wanted to emulate this incredible athlete who transcended all sports and who made golf immediately appealing to the masses. Money became no object as more and more extremely difficult and often tricked-up courses were built to meet the supply brought on by this overnight demand for more golfing venues everywhere. The game seemed simple enough: simply hit the crap out of this little white ball just sitting there asking to be mutilated. Golf instructors became booked like never before as everyone wanted to become the next Tiger. However, reality soon hit as most people readily learned just how frustrating this seemingly benign game can be. The eagerness soon wore off as people became more and more frustrated with this game no matter how much they paid for new equipment and endless lessons. These people learned what most of us who have been playing for most of our lives have reluctantly come to accept: that this game is damn hard and darn near impossible to master with any sustained consistency, especially from the distances that most golfers are trying to navigate the course from and still hope to score well.

After watching Jack Nicklaus win the 1965 Masters, Bobby Jones declared, "Nicklaus played a game with which I am not familiar." The incomparable Mr. Jones was referring to just how much longer Mr. Nicklaus was in comparison to his own game. Several decades later, Jack paraphrased that quote when watching a young Tiger Woods dismantle the field at Augusta National. In comparing my somewhat limited golfing prowess to the pros, I can honestly surmise that all of you professionals play a game that I am unfamiliar with. The statistics show that even with all the advances in technology, the average golfer fails to break the century mark on a regular basis. While all the technological advances have made the probability to hit better shots much more likely for almost everyone, the scoring differences between the best players in the world and the average amateur golfers are astronomical. The average carry distance between the top players in the world and most of the baby boomers still playing this game is immense. Most golf courses have failed to take this large disparity between the varying groups into account, and as a result, there is often a huge discrepancy in the scoring opportunities. While most professionals are hitting short scoring irons for a majority of their approach shots, the average golfer must often use a long hybrid or fairway wood in a desperate attempt to reach the putting surface on most holes. Nearly every golfer has had fleeting moments of success, but sustained excellence is hard to harness for very long for the majority of golfers trying to score well with these often cumbersome clubs. Most golfers can have a few good holes a round, but to keep up this consistency for an entire round is very challenging except for the truly gifted players. As a result, frustration and despair end up ruling the day, and most golfers eventually lose their passion for the game.

Unfortunately, the trends show that this scenario is playing itself out around the world as a majority of aging golfers are simply putting their clubs in the closet for good. Likewise, younger golfers are overly apprehensive about participating in golf as they find the game far too intimidating and often very embarrassing. In between these age groups, we are finding the "Generation Xers" and the "Millennials" growing far too disenchanted with golf to continue participating with any regularity. As a result of this mass exodus, many golf courses are not remaining productive enough to keep their doors open. In the United States alone in 2018, 298.5 courses closed down their operations, while only 12.5 new courses were built (*Sports Illustrated*, November 2019).

So now that the rose is off the bloom, so to speak, what can we do to make recreational golf infinitely more appealing to the masses once again? What can we do to spark the mainstream interest to make golf a much more desirable activity for the vast majority of people who attempt to play it? How can we lessen the frustration factor so that people can experience far more joy than sorrow out on the links? The major detractions from modern golf is that it takes too long, it is inherently frustrating, and it is way too hard to sustain any sort of positive vibes while attempting to master it. If we don't want to see this stark downtrend in golf participation continue, then everyone in the golfing community must be willing to adopt some paradigm shifts that differ from the traditional manner in which golf has been played for the better part of four centuries. The avid amateur golfer must no longer have to overcome such long odds in order to find contentment out on the links.

With 9.3 million golfers only partaking in driving range and simulator-type activities (National Golf Foundation, 2019), the next step is to get them out on an actual golf course and make certain that they have a thoroughly entertaining outing. If we can lure this large market share out to the links and greatly increase their probability of having a great time and wanting to come back, then many golf courses around the world will naturally increase their revenue for years to come. The beauty of Topgolf is that it is fast-paced and ego-friendly as points are accumulated for good shots, while points are never subtracted for less-than-stellar shots. What if we could move introductory golfers from these mostly enthralling activities to equally enjoyable experiences almost every time they get to tee them up on an actual golf course? The key is to put all golfers in situations where they have a reasonable chance to reach a majority of the holes they play in regulation. This dream is not so far-fetched if every golfer has a scoring iron in their hand for most of their approach shots. These shorter clubs impart far less sidespin and far more backspin than the longer playing clubs that are far too often used by recreational golfers for a majority of their approach shots. As a result, the shots struck with these scoring clubs find their mark much more frequently and are able to hold the greens with much more regularity. Thus, in order for this dream to become a reality, nearly all recreational golfers must be encouraged to play from much shorter yardages than they currently are being subjected to. Now certainly, the pros are going to have much tighter dispersion radiuses than most amateur golfers in relation to the flagstick, but at least most recreational golfers will now have a fighting chance to record far more greens in regulation than ever before. If nearly every golfer is getting on or near the putting surface in regulation, then recording bogey or better on many holes is going to be the norm. Scores of double bogey or worse should be rare occurrences on most golfers' scorecards, and as a result, most recreational golfers are going to be far more anxious to get out and play much more often.

The bottom line is that the rules of golf must be made far more user-friendly for the recreational player, or the entire industry is in big trouble. Let's streamline these down to a few basic, easy-to-interpret rules that allow everyone to be on the same page and have ample opportunities to post some decent scores. If you look at the back of most golf course scorecards, it states that "play is governed by USGA rules." In reality, there are only rules officials dictating the day's play during actual tournament settings. For the rest of us, we pretty much set our own rules based on our group's desired form of play. Most groups allow first tee mulligans, which immediately goes against the USGA guidelines. Since there is no set standard, the scoring and playing deviations are usually decided by each group's personal interpretations. What if we could standardize recreational play so that everyone played infinitely faster and scored much better with far less controversy? What if all golf courses got on board by setting their clients up for better scores and faster play by shortening the rough, adding many more tee box options and making the greens much more forgiving and user-friendly?

Back when Tiger was shattering almost every single record in the book, more and more courses tried to "Tiger proof" themselves in order to prevent the new age golfers from making a mockery out of their beloved course. Most course designers have tried to one-up one another by so much that only the top 1 percent of all golfers can post scores that leave them with any satisfaction. Now certainly the modern pros are making a mockery out of almost every golf course in the world, but the rest of us are now forced to try and conquer these brutal courses from insane distances. Trying to stretch these courses out and making them as difficult as possible is usually a very expensive undertaking and often results in some very high green fees. Thus, the majority of us are now paying an arm and a leg to try and play golf on courses from tee box lengths which give us few shining moments. If people are feeling guilty about all the time and money it takes to play golf and they aren't having a really good time, then rest assured this is not a scenario that is going to be repeated very often. As a result, many of these magnificent courses have been forced to close their doors for good, and all these wonderful holes have become nothing more than spectacular homesites.

In order to prevent this scenario from happening more and more frequently around the world, steps must be taken immediately to make golf faster, cheaper, and inherently more enjoyable. In today's fast-paced world, long-standing golfing traditions must be altered if we hope to see the game thrive once again. The first thing that needs to be done is to make nine holes the norm for most golfers. Most golfers don't have four to five hours to spend on golf, so let's cut this time and cost in half and entice people to play much more often. If we can get everyone excited to play a quick nine holes with much greater regularity, then golf courses around the world should see a sharp uptick in their rounds played and revenue brought in. The USGA has been promoting the "Play Nine" protocol for several years, and it has been a rousing success. The next key step is to fully embrace the GITCA guidelines so that every participant has ample opportunities to score well while minimizing the embarrassing moments no matter what type or length of golf course they choose to play. By providing a higher probability for success for most of their clientele on a majority of the holes they play, the golf course management teams are almost assuring themselves of many repeat customers. Making golf more enjoyable for everyone should be the goal of the entire golfing industry. Allowing everyone to play faster and score better at a reduced cost is going to incentivize golfers of all ages and abilities to play much more frequently.

I feel that an all-out marketing campaign must be done to promote all the wonderful experiences that can take place on the shorter and less extravagant golfing venues. As the baby boomers continue to age and the length of their game starts to decrease, par 3 and executive courses should become the preferred venue. Being distance-challenged is often not an issue on these shorter venues as most participants have ample opportunities to reach most of the putting surfaces in regulation. As a result, many golfers are able to post some really incredible scores. Firing at close range at these often defenseless pins is a treasure that too many ego-driven golfers miss out on. These shorter courses could have patrons pay an annual fee, which would entitle them to play unlimited rounds of golf. Once people realize just how enjoyable playing these shorter and less expensive courses can be, foursomes of all ages will be lining up to play these hidden gems throughout the year.

For those golfers who continue to play only the "championship golf venues," they must learn to take their ego out of the equation and play from tee boxes that give them a much better chance for sustained success and faster play. We need to get rid of the negative connotations often associated by moving up a tee box or two on these championship courses or by playing shorter and perhaps less arduous golfing venues. What harm can come from posting some of the best scores of your life? No one ever bats an eye when scramble scores are posted. GITCA allows individuals to post way better scores than they ever believed possible as well. Playing on a scramble team or following the GITCA guidelines, each golfer is going to have far more opportunities for truly remarkable golf outings. With everyone's ego being stroked throughout each of these outings, the likelihood to want to repeat these experiences on a regular basis increases dramatically.

What everyone in the golfing industry must learn to embrace is proportional math. Failure to properly align all participants with their appropriate tee boxes will result in most golfers eventually leaving the game far too prematurely. As we all know, golf is already hard enough. We don't need the average golfer to have to overcome odds, which would make even the top professionals extremely discouraged. Putting golfers in situations where they are inadequately prepared to handle is akin to putting a nonadvanced skier on a black diamond run. Having either group of participants getting "too far out over their skis" is only going to lead to disaster and a reluctance to ever return to the scene of such horror. Let's reverse this trend by allowing all golfers to have the same tools of the trade in their hands as the pros do for their scoring opportunities. This can only be accomplished if everyone learns which tee markers give them the same proportional distances that the pros must face. By determining how far a professional golfer hits his driver and his 8 iron and the total distance that they must traverse during their round, any golfer can then put in his/her own driver and 8 iron distances in to our proportional equation in order to best estimate which tee markers would provide an equivalent challenge.

Comparing J. B. Holmes's overall golfing abilities to mine would be ridiculous, but knowing his exact distances (driver distance 310 yards, 8 iron 165 yards, *Golf Magazine*, May 2017) would allow me to properly gauge which tee boxes would allow me to have an equal proportional test of my own abilities against his. Now since he is one of the top pros on the PGA Tour year in and year out, I certainly would expect him to blow me away a majority of the time. But due to the beauty of proportional math, I no longer have been set up by the course management team or myself to fail miserably. By calculating that J. B. Holmes's combined driver distance plus his 8 iron distance equals 475 yards and that the average course on the PGA Tour measures approximately 7,300 yards, I then plug in my own driver distance of 230 yards and my 8 iron distance of 130 yards in order to determine that I should be teeing off on most golf courses that I play from an average distance of approximately 5,500 yards. Since this is several hundred yards less than I currently play from, I am going to be using much shorter irons for all my approach shots. As a result of using my much more forgiving scoring irons on nearly every hole, I am much more likely to find more greens in regulation and post much better scores than usual. If every golfer around the world would simply offer to give themselves a fair fight against the incomparable J. B. Holmes, then scores around the world would be markedly better, and the pace of play would be infinitely faster. When most golfers plug in their corresponding distances, they are often dumbfounded as to how short the distances are that they are now being asked to traverse. "This will be way too easy," they all say. For perhaps the first time in their lives, they now have an idea as to how the pros feel nearly every time they get to tee them up. My rule of thumb is that if you are not averaging at least six greens hit in regulation for every eighteen holes played, then you are trying to play from distances that are out of your jurisdiction, or you really need to improve your proficiency with your scoring irons. Simply move up to the correct proportional tee box for your abilities so that you are not straining your capabilities or having to hit career shots on every hole. When everyone in your foursome finally buys into the GITCA protocol, the scoring opportunities will abound, and everyone will want to play this way as often as possible.

HOLE NUMBER 2

Playing GITCA GOLF Will Give Everyone a New Outlook on Golf and Life

There is nothing more sacred in our lives than our family, friends, and the personal liberties that have been bestowed upon us. Unfortunately, these precious things are often the very things that are taken most for granted. Many brave women and men have paid the ultimate sacrifice to ensure our protection and our freedom. Remember this the next time you see military personnel or first responders and go out of your way to thank them for their service. It is our duty to repay them by never ever taking our liberty or those closest to us for granted. The best way to honor those who gave everything is by not wasting a single opportunity to make the world a better place.

"Ask not what your country can do for you, but ask what you can do for your country" (President John Fitzgerald Kennedy, January 1961).

Every single time that you are fortunate enough to hit the links, please play with a sense of decorum and gratitude. Be thankful that you have been given this freedom and don't take it for granted for a second. Know that you may have some less-than-stellar shots and some bad holes, but don't let this tarnish your overall enjoyment. Realize that the course you have chosen to play may have some shoddy greens, some unfilled bunkers, and even a few holes that you despise. Once again, don't let this rain on your parade. There are literally millions of people who would trade places with you in a heartbeat. Be grateful that you are blessed with the opportunity to be playing golf, while many others are literally fighting for their lives or wondering where their next meal is going to come from.

I am extremely thankful for every day that I am on this side of the soil. To be given another day to enjoy my family and beloved friends is truly a gift from above. Some days I am fortunate enough to get the opportunity to play golf with those nearest and dearest to my heart. Even though some of the courses my buddies and I choose to play are in less-than-perfect condition and the weather is oftentimes less than desirable, you can rest assured that we cherish every single one of these special outings. None of us know for certain when this will be our last chance to golf together, so our goal is to make the most out of each of these often-too-rare occasions. We follow the GITCA rules to a tee so that the scoring opportunities and laughter abound. Everyone has such an enjoyable time that we all make a pact to do this again as soon as possible.

Compare all these positive vibes my foursome engenders with all the negative ones that most golfers find themselves subjected to almost every time they play. For these participants, golf feels more like a final exam than the fun recreational activity that it is supposed to be. It becomes a test of one's abilities to see how little they can screw up rather than an enjoyable way to let off steam and have some fun. My mission is to make golf far more exhilarating for everyone who has the privilege to play this grand old game. This can only be achieved if we are willing to loosen the reins a little bit and allow nontournament golfers to have far more leeway with the rules and regulations. By invoking general guidelines instead of rules that are written in stone, all golfers are clear on how to proceed, and no one is ever accused of breaking the rules.

Because of the fact that I have made all six of my hole-in-ones on par 3 and executive golf courses, the USGA will not sanction any of them. Even though the powers that be might put an asterisk next to them, in my book, they are all legit as they all found the bottom of the cup in one swing. Try as they might, the USGA cannot take these wonderful moments away from me, nor can they discourage me from following the GITCA GOLF guidelines every single time

I tee them up. Adhering to the GITCA doctrines allows me to have many more memorable moments than I would have trying to follow the "official doctrines of professional golf." Certainly, the GITCA scores I post would never be confused with actual scores posted in official stroke-play sanctioned events, and that is made abundantly clear to all participants. Believe it or not, we are not getting paid to play, so why should we bow down to what the USGA dictates for tournament play? GITCA GOLF promotes the same nonsanctioned benefits for all of its participants so that the game can be universally enjoyed by all recreational golfers without any disputes. Utilizing all these liberties certainly disqualifies GITCA disciples from posting any official course records, but recording better scores than they ever thought possible now becomes the norm. Leave the official scoring records for the professionals. Every recreational golfer's goal should be to see how much fun they can have out on the links as they try and accumulate as many GITCA points as humanly possible. By allowing every golfer to find and excel in their proper niche, GITCA GOLF gets everyone excited to repeat these joyous experiences again and again. It is my bold prediction that once all golfers get acquainted with playing GITCA GOLF, they will never return to the far-less-enjoyable ways in which they used to try and conquer golf courses.

Brandel Chamblee just commented prior to the 2017 US Open at Erin Hills that the difference between the average golfer and the top professional golfers has never been greater. Most of the top golfers on the PGA Tour are carrying the ball in excess of 290 yards with their drivers, while the average golfer is barely carrying it 190 yards. In addition to carrying the ball so much farther with their driver and every other club in their bags, these top professionals create so much clubhead speed and ball spin that holding most of these greens is a relatively simple task for them on a majority of the holes they play. For most of us rank amateurs, these professionals are playing a game that is far beyond our wildest dreams. They are amazing to watch, and I am completely spellbound by just how far they are able to hit the ball and then make it stop on a dime like a magician. To kid myself into thinking that I could ever play the game as they do would simply be setting myself up for a colossal disappointment.

What I have done, and what I hope to inspire all of you to do, is to play a game that allows me to have ample opportunities for sustained success out on the links even with my somewhat limited golfing prowess. In other words, I have built a better mousetrap for myself and others to follow. I have done away with the notion that I will ever be so inclined as to drive the ball over 300 yards, or even 250 yards, on a regular basis. Rather, I have accepted my golfing limitations, and I now only tee off from tee markers that give me a realistic chance to hit a majority of the greens in regulation following my average 230-yard drive.

By finally admitting that I am in fact a "white or green tee marker player" or somewhere in between, I have allowed myself to have many great opportunities to score well on a regular basis. Playing most of the golf courses that I play from these tee markers allows me to reach most of the greens I play in regulation with my scoring irons and thus has afforded me numerous opportunities to post some outrageously good scores. My friends who are much longer than me will move back to their appropriate tee markers, while those who are significantly shorter than me will move up a tee box or two so that we all have ample opportunities to hit a fair amount of greens in regulation. By playing from our proper tee boxes, everyone in our foursome has roughly the same number of good scoring opportunities, and thus, the need for having handicaps is no longer needed or warranted.

We utilize a scoring system similar to the original Stableford scoring system in which only positive integers are used to keep track of everyone's tally. Any score of bogey or better is recorded with a corresponding positive integer so that scores are easy to record and any sort of negativity is quickly erased from one's mind and the actual scorecard. Essentially, each golfer is playing against the course on each and every hole, and with our system, salvaging a bogey is now deemed to be a respectable score and consequently is rewarded with a point. Failure to record a bogey or better leads to the course being declared the winner for that hole as the golfer must mark a zero on his/her scorecard. Of course, every golfer is trying to accrue the most points on the day in order to receive the top honors for the day, but almost everyone is going to have a far more enjoyable time than they have ever thought possible out on the golf course with their colleagues with our simple-to-follow and very forgiving system.

In order to increase everyone's scoring opportunities throughout the round, our system also allows many leniencies rarely granted to those who try and earn a paycheck each week out on one of the professional tours. We have eliminated the need for varying rule book interpretations by simply making all golfers adhere to the same eight basic golf tenets of our system. This way, everyone is playing under the same auspices, and as a result, everyone gets far more opportunities to hit great shots and thus greatly increase their overall enjoyment out on the links. If every nontournament golfer in the world would adopt our simple-to-follow general guidelines, then golf around the world would be played at a much brisker pace, and everyone would be having more fun than they ever imagined out on the course. By motivating golfers of all ability levels to play far more often, most golf courses around the world will see a huge increase in their profit margins.

"Sport has the power to change the world. It has the power to unite people in a way that little else does. Sport can create hope where once there was only despair" (Nelson Mandela).

Uniting People by Making Golf More Enjoyable for Everyone

Life is both precious and fleeting at the same time. How many of us really embrace all the wonderful things in our lives each day? Most of us live our lives in a stupor simply trying to survive day to day instead of really thriving and living each moment to its fullest. I truly believe that by changing our perspective and embracing our differences as well as our commonality, we can change the world around us and make it a much more enjoyable place for everyone.

Jack Nicklaus is widely regarded as the greatest golfer of all time as the record books are filled with all of his amazing accomplishments. Mr. Nicklaus is always quick to point out that his greatest accomplishments are what Barbara and he have achieved outside of the ropes. Their marriage, their children and their grandchildren, and all their incredible charity work are without a doubt their greatest legacy. What their foundations have been able to do to bring hope, love, and compassion to so many is nothing short of miraculous. Certainly, the Golden Bear has inspired countless golfers around the world with his phenomenal play on the course, but it is his family's charitable work that will continue to positively impact lives for many generations.

As Americans, we have so much to be thankful for. While we are busy enjoying our day-to-day liberties without a care in the world, there are many unsung heroes from the past as well as the present who have continually made sacrifices to ensure our freedom and safety. Many have made the ultimate sacrifice, while many others have suffered debilitating injuries that have greatly affected their lives. As a result of these tragic events, many families of these brave patriots have been left devastated.

Personally, I have been so inspired by both the Nicklaus family's efforts and our military's resolve to protect and serve all of us that I am donating a large percentage of the proceeds from this book to many worthy charitable causes that can help these distraught families. It is my hope that together, we can raise millions so that we can help lift the spirits of all those in need of assistance. By giving hope to those who need it most, all our spirits will be raised.

Living in today's society has the potential to be one of the greatest periods in recorded human history. We have the ability to go almost anywhere and to be connected with people from all over the world. Technology has improved the lives of millions, and yet many people are still largely unfulfilled. Instead of embracing all the wonderful moments available to us, many people have chosen to tune the rest of the world out. It is far easier for most people to stay holed up from the rest of the world, then risk breaking down the barriers that we often let come between us. So even though we are "connected" now more than ever, there is a growing disconnect among people of all ages.

One of my dear friends from college recently passed away, and this has left everyone who knew him with a huge void in our hearts.

This young man was extremely bright and extremely gracious with everyone he came in contact with. His never-ending kindness and thoughtfulness made an indelible impact on my life and hundreds of others. As I was posting how much I was going to miss my beloved friend, I wondered aloud if he fully comprehended the profound impact he had on so many of us. I am guessing not as he became quite withdrawn during the last several months of his life. I regret the fact that I didn't reach out to him in his time of need. I wish I had known just how much he was hurting so that maybe I could have said something that could have turned his perspective around. Most people greatly underestimate their self-worth and the amount of positive influence that they can provide to others. A five-minute phone call or sending a positive message can often provide that little spark of optimism that can literally transform another's life. My heart is deeply saddened by my beloved friend's passage, but my life has been infinitely enriched by the unconditional love he constantly provided to all of us who were lucky enough to know him.

Sports, entertainment, food, and drink have a way of bringing us all together and allowing all of us to appreciate the commonality that makes us all human. A rousing round of golf followed by an awesome home-cooked meal with some fine spirits is often just the ticket to bring people from all walks of life closer together. If we can find more ways to break down the barriers between us, the world has a much greater chance to come together and achieve a more peaceful coexistence. No matter what nationality we are or where we fall on the political or religious spectrum, we all ultimately desire love and compassion from one another and for one another.

Getting out and golfing with those closest to you should be a refreshing respite from your day-to-day struggles, and more importantly, it should be a golden opportunity for you to reconnect with those nearest and dearest to your heart. It is a chance for you to give and receive encouragement from your beloved friends and family members. A kind word or pat on the back can go a long way to inspiring those closest to us to never give up on themselves and their dreams. Almost everyone greatly underestimates the differences they can make throughout the world. Reassuring those closest to us that you believe in them can literally make all the difference in their belief system. "If you think you can, or you think you can't, you are always right" (Henry Ford).

The bottom line is that we need to quit making excuses as to why we can't get together more often and simply make it our number 1 priority. We never know when we are going to see a dear friend or loved one for the last time. Almost everyone regrets the fact that they didn't play golf with one of their loved ones at least one more time prior to their passing. The question that has to be asked is, "Why didn't you?" Usually, the answer is that life got in the way and that we all thought that there would be many more opportunities to remedy this situation. The more truthful answer is that the last time everyone played golf together was not that enjoyable or memorable. What if we could alter the way in which golf is currently played by most constituents so that it is far more gratifying for everyone? Only then would everyone be far more likely to quit making excuses and get out and play golf far more often with those closest to us.

Playing golf can be a very spiritual event, or it can be a kick in the teeth. The key is to put yourself in an environment that is conducive to maximizing your enjoyment. You must surround yourself with positive golfers who exude enthusiasm for playing and having a great time out on the links. Secondly, you must choose to play a course that you don't have to be perfect on and from distances that don't overextend your capabilities. By adapting the guidelines that I have put forth with GITCA GOLF, you and your foursome will have many more opportunities to succeed in a far-less-threatening environment.

If golf courses want to flourish and remain profitable, then they must make their accommodations much more forgiving for the vast majority of their participants during nontournament weeks. Certainly, it is okay to make the course as devilish as possible for the tournament settings, but make the conditions much more playable for the other fifty or so weeks of the year so that the recreational golfer can have a much more rewarding experience every time they hit the links. Many more forward tee boxes must be put in place so that every golfer has ample opportunities to score well. Those members and course management teams that brag about the severity of their course conditions may be temporarily stroking their ego and tooting their own horn, but in reality, they are driving the majority of their clientele away due to far-too-many unsatisfactory experiences. It is this illogical way of thinking that is forcing many wonderful golf tracks to eventually lose most of their ever-aging clientele, and many of them are ultimately closing their doors for good. If an expensive round takes a long time to complete and the scores are astronomical, then most golfers are not going to want to play this course on a regular basis. Sometimes, you only get one chance to make a good impression. If golfers have a dreadful experience playing a golf course, then rest assured they will be in no rush to ever return to the scene of such carnage.

The GITCA bylaws that I have put forth strongly suggest that course management teams get in line with making the game easier, faster, and more enjoyable for all their golfing patrons. Everyone must adapt to the changes I am suggesting if golf hopes to rebound and far exceed the current demand. Golf has always acknowledged that there needs to be varying tee box lengths. The problem has always been that these designations were often based solely on one's gender and age rather than one's actual golfing prowess. What I am proposing with GITCA GOLF is that the tee marker assignments be based solely on one's overall golfing abilities with an emphasis on one's total carry distance deviations. By having every golfer tee off from tee boxes that give them excellent scoring opportunities, each participant should have ample chances to score well and play much faster than they ever believed possible. With the pace of play as well as the scoring opportunities being greatly enhanced for everyone, golfers of all skill levels and abilities are going to be more enticed to golf much more often.

With the baby boomers getting more advanced in age and much of their golfing prowess waning from what it once was, course management teams must add more forward tee boxes, or they risk losing the largest portion of their clientele base forever. The days of having only three or four set of tee boxes need to be augmented so that every level of golfer is properly tested but not overwhelmed. I recommend that each championship level course have six or seven different tee markers all spaced approximately four hundred total yards apart. I then suggest that combination tee boxes be the standard protocol so that there are at least eleven different yardage allocations so that every golfer can find their appropriate GITCA tee box niche. With these disparities in yardage differences, every single player in your foursome should be able to find a comfortable tee box marker that will allow him/her to be competitive with every other golfer in the group.

 If everyone in your group is playing quickly and having more enjoyment than they ever thought possible out on the links, then naturally, everyone will be motivated to repeat this wonderful experience as often as possible. By offering multiple tee markers and making their courses less penal, golfers are much more likely to experience magical moments out on the links. The easiest way to make a golf course infinitely more playable for all participants is to simply make the current farthest back tee boxes the "tournament tees" and then simply move every colored tee marker forward one designation. Doing so immediately knocks off about four hundred yards from each colored tee marker, which should equate to far more greens hit and hence far better scores for every single golfer. After posting some of the best scores of their lives, these golfers can still proudly boast that they did so from the same colored tee boxes that they have always played from. The truly prodigious hitting golfers can play from the "tournament tees" and be challenged with attacking the greens with the same scoring irons as everyone else who is playing the course that day. It becomes a win-win as every golfer will play much faster and no longer feel overwhelmed by the course or their playing companions.

 The course management team also must make certain that all tee times be spaced ten minutes apart, and then the pace of play must be strictly monitored to make certain that every group is keeping up with the group in front of them. The golf rangers must be pleasant, but they must be firm in their convictions that the pace of play be carefully monitored. Failure to enforce four hour or less eighteen-hole rounds will lead to much disdain from everyone. The most important task for the starter is to ensure that every golfer is teeing off from their properly designated tee box. Local golf pros should be forced to sign off on a player's ability so that the proper tee marker assignments are strictly adhered to. With every golfer in your group adhering to their proper tee marker designation, the competition should be brisk and thrilling right down to the final few holes.

So if golf is going to flourish in the future, then everyone must get on board with the doctrines that I am laying out with GITCA GOLF. The golf course management team must make their courses much more user-friendly and provide tee boxes that properly accommodate all their golfing patrons. These varying tee markers must be adequately spaced so that everyone has roughly the same scoring iron in their hand for their approach shots on most holes. It is then the responsibility of the various golf organizations to properly verify the correct tee boxes that are suitable for each golfer. It is then up to each individual golfer to honor their proper GITCA tee marker allocation. If everyone will implement these suggested guidelines and the other ways in which GITCA expedites the speed of play, then everyone should be posting far better scores and having far more memorable moments out on the links with their beloved friends and family.

HOLE NUMBER 3

Prioritizing and Counting Blessings

To dream the impossible dream!

If I told you that you only had one week to live and in that time you were only allowed to play one round of golf, where would you choose to play and whom, besides family members, would you choose to play with? If you are like me, then without a doubt, you would choose your regular golfing buddies to join you for your final eighteen holes of golf ever. You would choose your golfing "regulars" for the same reason you choose to tee it up with them throughout the year: you enjoy their company, and you want the camaraderie to be flowing throughout the final round of your life. Knowing that this is the last time you all are ever going to tee it up together, you would want to choose a great course that is stunningly beautiful and that challenges all of you but not one that is so difficult that no one can enjoy themselves. My foursome would probably choose Stonehedge North in Battle Creek, Michigan, as we have all played this course numerous times. It is fair and challenging, and it is always a spectacular setting at sunset. Cost is no expense, so you readily hand over the money as you get to tee it up with your beloved friends for the very last time. As you walk to the first tee, a loving sense of awe overcomes you as you realize just how blessed you have been to have shared so many wonderful memories out on the links with your dear golfing buddies. Since you want to get one more crack at playing with each of your dear friends, you all gladly decide to rotate partners every six holes so that the competition can be as fierce as ever and that the good times will be flowing freely. Since you all want the thrill of seeing the ball land on the green for the majority of your approach shots, you all would play from tee markers which makes this highly probable. In other words, you would all be following the GITCA guidelines to a tee. The banter and the laughter will be abundant as you all fully cherish this final jaunt around the links with one another.

You play these last eighteen holes of your life with quite a different outlook than your standard Saturday game, however, as you really take in all the wonderment that your friends and this great game of golf have provided you with throughout the years. Each shot taken is relished, and you all wish this day and this round would never end. Naturally, each match is decided by the final putt taken, and the wonderful feelings as well as all the harassing are soaked in by each golfer fully. Handshakes and warm hugs are freely given as the sun is setting, and everyone can now sense the utter finality of your last foray out on the links. Tears are freely flowing in each golfer's eyes as we all salute our great friendships and camaraderie one final time.

What if we embraced this thought process during every single round of golf? To play every round as though it were our last. Our mindsets and our priorities would certainly change as to what is and what isn't important. We would be far more focused on our dear friendships and just how blessed we all are rather than being overly concerned about some trivial score. Laughter and overall jovialness would far surpass the moments of despair and anger that we normally allow to rule the day in our usual golf outings. We would all see just how fortunate we are to live in a free country where we can play golf with our beloved friends whenever the moment strikes us. We would no longer take anyone or anything for granted, and we would all cherish the precious time spent out on the links with our dear friends. No matter what the scorecard read at the end of the day, no one would ever leave the course dejected or disappointed.

If only we could have a similar paradigm shift in the way that golf is currently played by most people, maybe we could have far more satisfied customers who would be more excited to tee it up as often as possible. The purpose in writing this book is to foster several paradigm shifts from the way in which golf is currently played by most of its participants so that everyone can have many more enjoyable moments out on the links. By changing the scoring system as well as every golfer's overall mindset, I hope to foster far more positive experiences out on the golf course. I want everyone who ever picks up a club to be so enthused that they can hardly wait to tee it up again as soon as possible.

HOLE NUMBER 4

What in the World Is GITCA?

The first question that I always get asked is, "What in the world does GITCA stand for?" Originally, GITCA was an acronym for "Get in the cart already." It was an expression I used to urge my fellow golfers to give up on a hole that was clearly getting the best of them. In order to speed up play and ease one's pain, I made a double bogey the maximum score that a golfer could receive on a hole, with no negative points being accrued. My intent was that golf should be a mostly positive experience and that there needs to be a mercy rule so that a golfer's entire day is not ruined by a few bad holes. In other words, let's move on from this less-than-stellar hole so that we can shift our focus to all the positive opportunities that the future holes might bring us. The original goal was that I simply wanted everyone who plays golf to have the positive moments far outweigh the negative ones. I wanted to provide a pathway in which all recreational golfers can achieve at least moderate levels of satisfaction. Thus, my buddies and I got together to devise a way to play golf that is far more ego-gratifying throughout the round.

Our system acknowledges that none of us are tour material, but that should not preclude us from having the ability to post good scores from distances we can handle and have the time of our lives every time we are fortunate enough to tee them up. Provided that the majority of golf courses are not nearly as well maintained as those venues on the professional tours and the fact that most recreational golfers are not nearly in the same stratosphere as the top players in the world, GITCA GOLF allocates several other rules that greatly improve all golfers' chances for a satisfying experience almost every time they hit the links. With these rules being uniform for all the participants, there is never any controversy as the scoring opportunities are enhanced for everyone. Not only do these GITCA rules greatly speed up the pace of play, they also allow golfers of all abilities to be less than perfect and still score well and ultimately have one heck of a good time out on the links.

The time-honored and sacred rules of golf certainly have their place in sanctioned stroke-play tournament settings, but the majority of recreational golfers (about 99 percent) will never enter an actual stroke-play tournament. Although many golf traditionalists are likely to scoff at the bylaws that I am laying down with GITCA GOLF, I simply encourage them to embrace them for nonsanctioned tournament play, or we are likely to see the golfing numbers continue to dwindle on a grand scale. Furthermore, many of the regulations that I have put forth with GITCA GOLF have already been fully embraced by most recreational golfing foursomes for decades. With the implementation of GITCA GOLF for all nontournament play, we are simply proclaiming that these long inherent practices are to be fully accepted and uniformly implemented by all recreational golfers. It is high time the golfing industry starts making golf much more enjoyable for its constituents who will never earn a nickel by playing it.

GITCA is more than just a newfangled way to play golf and keep score; it is a different mindset altogether that allows everyone to fully embrace each golf outing. What we will take away from our GITCA GOLFING rounds is the undeniable joy of getting to spend quality time out on the links with those closest to us. Under this premise, GITCA could also stand for Golden Instances to Cherish All. By adopting an eternally grateful mindset, golfers will have their eyes open to all the glorious opportunities that have been presented to them out on the golf course with their beloved friends and loved ones. Essentially, GITCA allows all golfers to have many more opportunities for success while instilling a much more positive mindset throughout their round. So in essence, GITCA could be seen as Golfing in Terms where Contentment Achieved.

"Ego says: Once everything falls into place, I will find peace.
Spirit says: Find peace and everything falls into place."

As you can see, GITCA can mean many different things to many different people. Essentially, GITCA has evolved into a microcosm for life in that it is a "rally cry" that means this: quit waiting for perfection to get off your butt and start striving for excellence. How many of us talk ourselves out of our best intentions because the situation wasn't ideal? How many great ideas get discarded as we let doubt and negative feedback rain on our parade? I used to be that guy. I would have many wonderful plans get waylaid by negative people who would talk me out of pursuing my hopes and dreams. Those days are over. Life is too short to sit on the sidelines and watch golden opportunities pass us by. Hopefully, this book is a wake-up call for many to no longer let your dreams get dashed. Listen to your heart and live with passion and supreme confidence as you no longer let anything deter you from pursuing greatness. Regret is a terrible burden to have to bear. Failure to follow through on your best intentions will haunt you throughout your life. So get in the cart already and get on the path to fulfilling your life's ambitions. Today is the first day of the rest of your life, so climb aboard and enjoy the journey. The road might be rocky at times, and there may be occasional setbacks, but never stop believing in yourself. Fully embrace the GITCA mindset so that you can lead a rich and fulfilling life on and off the golf course.

What Brings Us Contentment out on the Golf Course?

Certainly, shooting a good score is going to bring contentment, but what constitutes a "good score"? For many golfers, breaking 100 is quite an accomplishment and can often signify a landmark achievement. Whereas barely breaking the century mark would leave many golfers on the brink of quitting the game altogether. Many golfers only dream about shooting in the 70s, whereas the top pros and amateurs often lament the fact that they didn't score much better. Most people erroneously presume that those golfers who shoot the lowest scores achieve the highest level of contentment out on the links. I have seen many people literally cry tears of joy the first time they break a 100 or record their first birdie. Likewise, I have seen many golfers break their clubs for missing a short putt that would have given them the course record. So one's score is a relative term to one's expectations. The greater one's expectations are, the more difficult it often is to achieve any level of satisfaction out on the course. Even for the greatest players on the planet, luck and fortuitous bounces can play a big part in ultimately determining one's final score. If a golfer adopts the mindset that they will only receive contentment after they have finished posting a certain score, then all the opportunities for enjoying the journey will often be relinquished. As a consequence for not stopping to smell the roses, this type of golfer often brings no levity to the foursome. Every little thing sets them off, and they rarely stop to enjoy the beauty and tranquility during any part of their round or any of the amazing friends who surround them. By the time they figure out why no one wants to play with them, many wonderful opportunities will have been vanquished.

So the lesson learned is to quit worrying so much about some arbitrary score and find other ways to maximize your satisfaction. Step 1 is to acknowledge how fortunate you are to live in the greatest country in the world that allows you to play golf at a moment's notice. Step 2 is taking time to appreciate all the wonderful friends and family that you also have been blessed with. Everyone seeks acknowledgment, and the more positive you are with your attitude and your comments, the more positive the experience will be for everyone in your foursome. Laughter and positive vibes are contagious, and making the experience as delightful as you can is simply going to add to the level of contentment and overall satisfaction for your entire group. Certainly, keeping score is important and definitely heightens the experience, but at the end of the day, people are much more concerned with how you treated them rather than what score you posted.

Abiding by the laws that I have put in place with GITCA GOLF will allow every golfer in your foursome to have a higher probability to score better than they ever thought possible. Due to the leniencies that we provide, the playing conditions and the golfers no longer have to be perfect for everyone to find harmony out on the course. By having each golfer play from tee markers which ensure many good looks at par and the occasional birdie, spirits will be high throughout the round. With our format, each hole is its own entity. Thus, every hole is a new opportunity to achieve success while not letting the previous bad holes tarnish the entire day. Our system is much more user- and scoring-friendly than the traditional stroke-play method, and as a result, most golfers leave the course filled with contentment every time they are fortunate enough to tee them up.

Putting Everything into Perspective

I doubt that on one's deathbed, too many people are going to lament the fact that they didn't get to play more golf. Most, however, will be filled with regret that they didn't get to spend more time with their beloved friends and family members. It is my hope and dream to kill two birds with one stone by inspiring more people to spend more quality time with those most endearing to them out on the links. Some of my most treasured memories have occurred out on the golf course with my closest friends and family members. Playing golf with my buddies is very therapeutic for all of us. It is often a sacred time for us to commiserate about anything and everything as we chase that ball around the course in the fewest strokes possible. The final tallies are often secondary to the camaraderie and funny moments that are indelibly etched into our hearts and souls forevermore. We let loose on the golf ball as we talk about our families, our jobs, and our overall state of happiness. Whatever land mine has gotten in our way, golf seems to be just the medicine to soothe all our souls. The dew on the grass, the freshly manicured fairways and greens, the whiteness of the sand traps, and the beautiful fall leaves remind us of how truly blessed we are to be fortunate enough to be on this side of the soil golfing with our beloved friends in the greatest country in the world. By adhering to the GITCA GOLF guidelines, the enjoyment factor for everyone has increased exponentially. Bickering has become a distant memory, and we all are scoring much better and feeling much better about ourselves and our games. Everyone tees it up from their properly assigned tee box, and the competition is often thrilling right down to the final putt holed. If no one is there to hold us up, our foursome can usually play nine holes in ninety minutes or less, and we cherish every second of it. Thanks to the simple-to-follow GITCA GOLF rules, the atmosphere is delightful and devoid of controversy, and we can hardly wait for the opportunity to do it again as soon as possible.

We are confident that our new way of playing golf will be readily embraced by the rest of the golfing world. What golfer out there doesn't want to play faster and have a much more enjoyable time every single time they tee it up? Who doesn't want to hit far more greens in regulation and record the best scores of their life? It is time for a golfing revolution to unfold. No longer be content to tee off from tee markers which offer few opportunities for success and overall enjoyment. Let's give every golfer ample chances to score well and play faster so that the desire to play increases dramatically. Start embracing the GITCA GOLF guidelines today so that you and your foursome have a memorable time every time you are fortunate enough to hit the links.

HOLE NUMBER 5

Just Imagine a Better Way to Play Golf

The object of golf is to have as much fun as you possibly can out on the links as you are trying to master both the distance and direction that the ball must fly for any given shot. This seems like a simple enough premise, but less than 1 percent of golfers can truly hit it prodigious distances while still maintaining some semblance of where the ball might actually come to rest. Only a select few, most of whom have devoted the majority of their lives to achieving this conquest, can truly play from distances that measure over seven thousand yards and be able to laugh about it. For the rest of us, it is but a pipe dream that almost always goes unfulfilled, leaving us bewildered and often frustrated that we will never be able to reach that summit. We often kid ourselves into thinking that someday we might actually break through this glass ceiling, but after many years and often decades of futility with the latest and greatest new clubs, we finally surmise that that day is never coming.

Why do we beat ourselves up for not being able to play like the professionals? Certainly, the majority of us cannot compete with the professionals in any other sport. We cannot touch a ninety-mile-per-hour fastball or dunk a basketball in traffic. We cannot line up against a three-hundred-pound lineman in football or play competitive tennis against Roger Federer. So why on God's green earth do we kid ourselves into thinking that we should be able to hit a golf ball as far and with the same often marvelous results as Rory McIlroy and Tiger Woods? We devote endless hours trying to squeeze out the best of our abilities, only to find ourselves largely unfulfilled with varying aspects of our game. Try as we might, the various parts of the game never seem to come together at the same time. If we do ever catch lightning in a bottle, it is often for a few fleeting rounds at best. Then we often spend the rest of our waking hours trying hard to replicate this magic, only to be disappointed a majority of the time. This eternal frustration often leaves us longing for more from ourselves and the game of golf. As a result, many golfers give up the game for good as they can no longer achieve much satisfaction from their time logged out on the links.

In order for this scenario to be dramatically reduced, a paradigm shift must occur throughout the golf world before more and more courses become bankrupt due to lack of demand from the general public. My simple solution is to make golf far easier for the 99 percent of us who don't have "pro distance" and who simply want to get more bang for our buck each and every time we tee it up. By making a few little tweaks to the scoring and playing norms, I believe that I have found a far easier way for far more positive vibes to be emanating from each and every golfer who tees it up. My system allows the game to be played much faster and with much more latitude. A golfer no longer has to maintain near perfection in order to have a positive experience on the course. In fact, we embrace the fact that "to err is human," and thus, we allow many liberties, which keeps the pace of play brisk and the competition lively right down to the final putt being holed. Once all participants acknowledge that they are not likely to earn a living playing this game, they learn to not take themselves or the game too seriously and, in turn, have much more fun out on the links.

For years, the golfing world has been enamored with making golf courses as challenging as possible in order to maximize the gratification that comes from successfully tackling these extremely difficult venues. Unfortunately, few golfers in the world have the true capabilities to master these devious courses playing from the lengths we try and play them from. Even after a great drive, choosing to play from tee markers that are way above our abilities will result in very few opportunities to hit many of the greens in regulation. Unless we are fantastic at getting up and down from off the green, playing bogey golf or slightly worse is about as good as we can hope to score on any given day. On most days, this means that we are destined to rarely break 90. Thus, if you and your golfing buddies choose to play difficult courses from distances that exceed your abilities, then you should expect to be disappointed almost every time you tee them up. On the other hand, if your foursome were to begin to play easier golfing venues from distances that are well within everyone's capabilities and the rules that you followed offered more latitude for success, then achieving golfing blissfulness is well within every participant's grasp.

GITCA GOLF forces every golfer and every golf management team to rethink the way in which golf for the recreational player is presented. Rather than making golf for the recreational golfer so difficult that few ever want to pursue it for very long, steps must be taken so that every nonprofessional golfer sets themselves up for sustained success out on the links. Gone are the days where a golf course can only get away with a few sets of tee boxes spaced a mere ten yards apart. Under the auspices of GITCA GOLF, it is recommended that each championship golfing venue has at least six different tee markers with at least twenty yards spaced between each succeeding tee box. With many accomplished golfers hitting the ball prodigious distances while many of the baby boomers continue to age and lose a little more distance each year, more tee boxes must be added and be spaced farther apart so that the competitive balance is not lost. The ultimate goal is for everyone in your group to have roughly the same scoring iron in their hand for their approach shots so that a high percentage of greens may be hit in regulation by all the participants.

Provided that the GITCA guidelines allow for lift, clean, and place from anywhere, the odds of hitting the ball cleanly and onto the green are further enhanced. To further aid golfing success for most of their clientele, golf course management teams can help out by reducing the length of their rough and reducing the speed and severity of their greens so that the odds of finishing on the putting surface are increased significantly. If there is a preponderance of greens hit in regulation, then the pace of play will improve substantially as well as the overall mood of your golfing foursome. By greatly increasing each golfer's likelihood for success, golfers around the world are going to be more motivated than ever to get out and golf more often. Naturally, every golf course will reap the benefits of more green fees accrued. So by abiding by the GITCA GOLF guidelines, there will be far more enthused golfers out on the links, and golf courses everywhere will benefit financially from this renewed golfing boom.

Certainly, we all want to challenge ourselves from time to time by playing more challenging courses from distances that occasionally stretch our capabilities, but after getting humiliated time and time again, most golfers are ready to quit. By following the GITCA GOLF protocol a few times, our egos will readily acknowledge that the real gratification in golf comes from sticking our approach shots and putting for birdie on many of the holes that we are fortunate enough to play. Nothing beats hitting a good drive and then following it up with a well-struck 8 iron that allows you to pinpoint your ball close to the flagstick. Having an 8 iron left for your approach shot can only be made possible if you have correctly identified the tee markers which allow this to be a possibility following a decent drive. Professional golfers have an 8 iron or less in their hands for most of their approach shots on most par 4 holes. As a result, they find the putting surface a majority of the time and are in prime position to record a par or better on most of the holes they play. Yet the average golfer almost always chooses to play far-too-difficult golfing treks from distances that leave nearly impossible odds to reach many of the greens in regulation. Thus, most recreational golfers achieve only a few fleeting moments of actual gratification. Is it any wonder that more and more golfers are putting their clubs away for good and that more and more golf courses are closing? Golfers and golf courses alike need to get with the GITCA program so that these trends don't continue. Putting golfers in position to be successful on most of the holes they play is the key to assuring a great time for all and a ton of repeat business. Every single one of the professional tours puts their players in positions to succeed on most of the holes they play throughout the year. Why do most golf courses and golf clubs set up the majority of their clientele to have less-than-satisfactory experiences most of the time? It is this backward way of trying to provide customer satisfaction that is in fact leading to the demise for most courses.

How Do We Measure Ourselves against Other Golfers?

The first question asked every golfer after they play is, What did you shoot? This sounds like a simple enough question, but many variables must go into answering this seemingly straightforward question, none more important than, What course did you play, and from what tee markers did you play from? Did you all roll the ball or play it down? Did you take first tee mulligans? Were you conceded any putts? Were the greens rolling well, or had they recently been aerated? Was the rough thick, or had it recently been thinned out? Were the conditions wet, or was the course fairly dry? Was it really windy, or were the conditions rather benign? Did you play off your handicap, and was every stroke counted? Was everything played as a lateral hazard, or were you forced to go back to the tee if you discovered your ball was out of bounds?

Obviously, all these factors come into play in determining the exactness of your given response. Since there are no universal ways for amateur golfers to play this grand old game, many variables go into ultimately determining your true score. In other words, a very good golfer and a not-so-great golfer can both say with the same level of certainty that they both shot an 85 playing golf over the weekend. The first golfer might have played from the tips at *Bethpage Black*, while the second golfer might have played from the white tees at his local municipal course. Being a strict follower of the USGA rule book, the first golfer recorded every single stroke, abided by the same rules that the professionals must adhere to, and was by and large excited by his fine round. By the same token, the average golfer took several liberties never granted to the true professionals and was very excited to shoot an 85 by his own standards. Now if both of these golfers were forced to switch places and play under the auspices of the other's rule interpretations and tee markers, the scores would likely be vastly different. Allowing the much longer golfer to play from the white tees on a local municipal golf course and have many generous liberties never granted in tournament play, his score is likely to be dramatically better. Likewise, forcing the average golfer to tee off from the tips at *Bethpage Black* and be forced to follow the exact letter of the USGA handbook is most likely going to result in a recorded score well north of the century mark.

    Which golfer is going to play faster, score better, and have the more enjoyable time out on the links? Certainly, it would be the better golfer playing from the white tees and taking several liberties. If my calculations are correct, he might grow quite accustomed to shooting in the 70s on a regular basis and might even have a chance to post his best round ever. After averaging about ten strokes better than his previous attempts, this excellent golfer will hopefully learn that this is a much more enjoyable way to try and tackle most golf courses. It is a nice feeling knowing that you no longer have to continuously hit career shots just to try and stay in the 80s. By moving up several tee boxes, you will quickly ascertain that you are a pretty good golfer when placed in the proper parameters. On the other hand, the second golfer will quickly realize that he is in over his head and will be in no hurry to ever try and repeat this diabolical challenge. Unfortunately, most golfers set themselves up for failure a majority of the times that they tee them up due to their overinflated egos. As a result, a disappointing round is almost a foregone conclusion. Certainly, there is a small minority of golfers who truly are gifted enough to handle some of the most challenging golf venues in the world from the tips, but that number is minuscule compared with the throngs of golfers who would be miserable trying to score well given this scenario. GITCA allows everyone to have far more opportunities to score well and have a great golfing experience almost every time out. By adhering to the proper GITCA guidelines, most golfers should average at least eight strokes less for eighteen holes. Thus, your foursome is going to be taking about thirty-two less strokes per round as you all learn to play much more efficiently and have infinitely more fun!

My Goal When I Play Any Sport Is to Give Myself Ample Opportunities to Succeed

My ultimate goal is to be competitive on the tennis court and the golf course while not embarrassing myself. Choosing tennis players of like ability assures this objective, while choosing the correct tee markers for me and my opponents assures a competitive match out on the links. The beauty of golf is that I can play with golfers of all abilities and ages as long as we all tee off from our properly designated tee markers. The distance disparity between the tee boxes should account for the disparity between the clubhead speed being manufactured. If everyone plays from the correct tee markers for their abilities, then everyone should have a similar scoring iron in their hands and roughly the same statistical probability to hit about the same number of greens in regulation.

Provided that I am a fifty-two-year-old teaching tennis professionally and that I have played the game pretty well since the age of three, everyone wants to know how I would do against the top touring tennis professionals. Simple answer: I would be humiliated! Even though I know how to hit almost all the shots that they do, I simply do not have the foot speed or racket head speed to be able to give these top players any competition whatsoever. I would be lucky to win any points at all, and not much fun would be had by anyone. It would be similar to me trying to tee off from the championship golf tees against Tiger Woods. Tiger's swing speed would dwarf mine by so much that there is no way I could play the course from the distances he is easily traversing. Eventually, he would get tired of waiting around for me and having to continually watch me struggle. I would be so embarrassed that I would quickly find an excuse as to why I could only play nine holes with him.

Then everyone asks me how I would do against some of the local young tennis pros who compete for the city championship each year. Again, not well. Even with all the knowledge that I have accrued over the years, my lack of quickness and racket speed would doom me from the start. It would be akin to me trying to combat the young local golf pros from the blue tees. It wouldn't be a fair fight, and they would quickly grow weary of me lagging behind them. I would be so thoroughly embarrassed trying to "compete" with them that I would be in no hurry to ever subject myself to this humiliation again.

Now against other fifty and older tennis players, I feel that I would definitely be very competitive as most of us possess about the same amount of foot and racket speed. Likewise, I feel that I could be very competitive with all golfers, including Tiger, as long as we all are hitting roughly the same scoring iron for most of our approach shots. By quickly moving up from the backward tees to the much more scoring-conducive white and green tee markers, I feel that I could hang with almost any golfer out there. So simply by moving up several tee boxes, I went from an embarrassing hack to a very good golfer who knows how to negotiate himself around the links. So it is not that I am golfing challenged but rather distance challenged in relation to these long-hitting professionals. By playing from my appropriate tee markers, I now have a chance to prove that I am far better than I was previously given credit for. If given the right opportunities, I may prove to myself that I am far better than I ever thought possible and that playing golf under these circumstances is infinitely more enjoyable. This is my main premise for GITCA GOLF: to give nonprofessional golfers advantages that allow them better scoring opportunities so that they can play faster and achieve much more contentment out on the links with their buddies in a friendly, nontournament setting.

Why Is Everyone Afraid of Making the Game More User-Friendly?

Turn on any golf tournament on any week, and you are likely to see at least one golfer shooting in the very low 60s with a good chance to break into the 50s. This would be a rare feat thirty years ago on any tour, but today, in almost any professional tournament, you are apt to see some extremely low scores if the weather is cooperating and the greens are holding. Just three decades or so ago, everyone was using actual wooden drivers and balata balls. As a result, the ball did not go near as far as it does today, and it was far more difficult to control. A great round of golf usually hovered right around par or just under it. Today, however, with all the modern equipment and overall better course conditions, a professional golfer must average at least three under par for all four rounds in order to be in the hunt. Even with all the lengthening the tours have done to try and defend themselves against these onslaughts, if the conditions are benign, a golfer must post a final score of at least twelve under par to be in contention. I know all the golf historians and golfing immortals are probably turning over in their graves when they see these low scores posted, but I have yet to hear a golfer complain that a course was too easy. Even though on many of these courses these long bombers are hitting an 8 iron or less for most of their approach shots, I have yet to hear one of them declare that the course was too short for them.

So if the greatest golfers in the world have no problem going extremely low on a regular basis on these immaculately groomed golf courses, then why in the world should any amateur be dismissive to moving up a tee box or two so that they can have the same club in their hands that the pros do for their approach shots? Why would anyone put up an argument to improving their scores substantially by playing the course from distances that are well within their capabilities? Wouldn't it be refreshing to not have to come out of your shoes on every single swing in a desperate attempt to try and reach most of the greens in regulation? Wouldn't it be nice to be putting for birdie and par on most holes rather than bogeys and doubles? Why make golf eternally frustrating when we have found a way to make it eternally gratifying almost every time you tee it up? If the best players in the world are not afraid to break all the course records, the least you and your foursome can do is to have the gumption to move up a tee box or two so that you can post scores that were previously reserved for your dreams.

Justin Rose just finished winning a golf tournament by posting a final score that was twenty-nine strokes under par. In two of the four rounds, he posted matching scores of ten under par. In all likelihood, it will not be long before someone shoots ten under in all four rounds and shoots an even forty strokes under par. Forty years ago, very few pros were hitting their drives over 300 yards, whereas today, nearly all of them are on a consistent basis. The technology has gotten so good throughout the bag that most of the top professionals are easily breaking par almost every time out. The average PGA tour set up measures just around 7,300 yards for a majority of the tournaments played throughout the year. Although this seems like a tremendous length for these professionals to try and navigate, it is at least a thousand yards shorter than they should actually be playing from in proportional comparison to the average golfer who tries to negotiate distances between 6,000 and 6,500 yards. As a result, the top professionals are often left with nothing more than an 8 iron for most of their approach shots as they are continually setting themselves up for numerous birdie opportunities. The average amateur, meanwhile, is forced to hit at least a 5 iron for a majority of his/her approach shots in a desperate attempt to try and reach a few greens in regulation. In order to truly test himself like the rogue amateur does, a tour professional should be playing from tee markers that measure at least 8,300 yards. This would give the professional a fair assessment of what the average amateur has to deal with as he tries to negotiate the course from tee markers that measure over 6,000 yards.

Having to play a course that measures over 8,300 yards would certainly test the professionals as they would be forced to hit every club in their bag well and with ultimate precision. No longer would these professionals have the luxury to tee off on many of the holes with irons or hybrids for placement. Most of them would have to rear back and crank their drivers out there on nearly every hole. Certainly, this would lead to a much greater dispersion on where their shots landed and in all likelihood lead to much higher scoring averages. Hybrids and mid to long irons would replace the shorter scoring irons currently used for most of the approach shots, which would ultimately lead to far fewer greens hit in regulation and once again lead to much higher scores on average. *Welcome to our world!* If the pros wanted to get a further look into the playing conditions that most amateurs face for the majority of the rounds they play, then the PGA tournament greens keepers must do a much worse job of keeping their courses in such immaculate shape. Furthermore, these pros should try teeing it up at these courses when the weather is not perfect for golf. Let's see how they fare playing *Oakmont* in mid-November when the temperatures are hovering near forty and the greens and fairways are dormant.

Now, of course, the PGA would never allow their top players to play courses out of season and that weren't almost perfect. In addition, they would be crucified if they could somehow stretch most of their courses to lengths over 8,300 yards. The scores would be so astronomically high in comparison to what they currently are that the complaints would never cease. Most of the professionals would boycott until the conditions were improved and the length of the courses shortened to more acceptable lengths.

So if the best players on the planet are playing from distances that are 1,000 yards closer proportionately speaking than they should be on courses that are always in pristine condition, then why in the world are most amateurs choosing to play from tee markers that make it highly improbable for them to shoot decent scores on courses that are far from perfect in less-than-ideal playing conditions most of the time? It doesn't make sense, and it only adds up to much higher scores and utter frustration for most of the people who try to get some satisfaction out of a round of golf. No wonder the way golf is currently played by most amateurs is inherently frustrating and often a death blow to one's self-esteem.

In order to level the playing field somewhat and make the scores more comparable, then the professionals are going to have to move most of their tee boxes back approximately fifty-five yards per hole, or most amateurs are going to have to move forward at least one tee marker. Provided that most golf courses don't have the room to accommodate moving the professionals another fifty-five yards farther back on each hole, the only viable solution is for most amateurs to move up at *least* one and, in most cases, two tee boxes and not feel guilty about doing so. Due to the fact that the professionals practice and play much more often, other leniencies should be granted to the amateur so that they have more chances to achieve some semblance of success out on the links. Since technology is only improving and the PGA isn't about to make the playing conditions more Spartan-like for the professionals, provisions must be made to allow amateurs to score better and have more fun on the rare occasions that they get to play golf. Let's keep the harsh tournament stroke-play rules in place for the professionals, but let's relax the rules for the recreational players since they play so infrequently and often in less-than-ideal conditions.

Since we aren't playing perfectly manicured courses, we don't do this for a living, and since we barely have time to practice or play, GITCA GOLF acknowledges these differences and gives us many advantages that would never be allowed in a strict stroke-play tournament setting. For example, we are always given a mulligan off the first tee. Since we rarely have time to hit a bucket of balls prior to our round, we give you two attempts to open your round with a good drive. Once you get to your best of the two drives, we allow you to lift, clean, and place it in a favorable spot within a club length of your landing spot similar to a scramble format. We do this because we want you to have a favorable lie for your second shot so that once again you are greatly increasing your chances for achieving moderate levels of success out on the links. By removing your ball from a less-than-desirable lie, you have greatly increased your chances to make solid contact and hit far more greens in regulation. The pros play lift, clean, and place when the course conditions are not ideal. Most recreational golf is played in less-than-ideal conditions most of the time; thus, we allow everyone to lift, clean, and place from anywhere, including the bunkers. Most golf courses around the world do not have the time, money, or resources to adequately upkeep all their bunkers. As a result, GITCA makes taking a free drop out of the bunker a viable solution in bunkers that are deemed by your group as "unplayable." No golfer should ever be forced to play out of a bunker that is not properly racked or that has little to no sand. If the bunkers at the course you are playing are deemed by your foursome to be unplayable, then everyone who ends up in a bunker can simply remove the ball from the trap and play it from a good lie no closer to the hole. Once on the green, we allow "gimme putts" if most of the other golfers signal that the putt is good. Certainly, these GITCA rules and others to follow make it infinitely easier to score better-than-standard stroke-play tournament scoring rules, and that is precisely our point. These much-simpler-to-follow rules and guidelines are the same for every golfer in your group and are going to greatly increase the odds in everyone's favor of posting much better scores. If everyone in your group is having great looks at par or better on nearly every hole, then rest assured everyone will be lighting up the scorecard and having the time of their lives.

Perhaps There Is No Greater Event Than the Father-Son Golf Tournament

The 2018 PNC Father-Son Challenge combined an amazing golf course venue with a two-person scramble for both rounds. Naturally, the scoring opportunities were fantastic for all the teams as every shot was lift, clean, and place, and every team played from tee markers that allowed each team to hit nearly every green in regulation. The premise is the same as GITCA: encourage great scoring opportunities so that everyone has a memorable day out on the links. Davis Love and his son Dru made a mockery of the course as they shot an incredible 56 on the second day to win the championship going away. Every team literally had the time of their lives, including the incomparable seventy-nine-year-old Jack Nicklaus and his fifteen-year-old grandson GT, who finished the two days in the top 5. Does it get any better than being out on the golf course and competing with your grandson against some of the greatest players in the game's history and their family members? Every team completed their round in less than four hours, and there were never any controversies. Hugs, smiles, and even tears abounded as a phenomenal time was had by every participant. In fact, everyone said that this tournament is the absolute highlight of their year, and they can hardly wait to do it again next year. We all should be so lucky to tee them up with our own grandchildren when we are almost eighty. Of course, we are not likely to shoot as well as the Nicklauses, but we should embrace these opportunities every chance we get.

For this event, the professionals who are over seventy years of age tee off from the white tee markers, the high school kids or younger tee off from the blue tees, and the other players from the black tees. This allows everyone to be extremely competitive with one another, and the two-man scramble format allows everyone to contribute and almost every team to go extremely low and have about as much fun as humanly possible out on the golf course. The more seasoned golfers get a kick out of how far the next generation is hitting the ball, while the younger generation is amazed at the precision the older generation still has in their arsenal. Even though most of the seasoned golfers don't play nearly as much as they used to, they all are still amazing when playing from distances that they can handle. Needless to say, the entire event is a win-win for everyone no matter what final scores are posted. These special moments will last every participant a lifetime.

This event encompasses GITCA GOLF to a tee:

1. Golfers from every age bracket and varying distance abilities compete fiercely with one another.
2. Everyone plays from tee boxes that give them a great chance to reach most greens in regulation.
3. Handicaps are never used, and it is a two-man scramble format with lift, clean, and place.
4. Everyone posts excellent scores.
5. The pace of play is brisk.
6. Everyone will cherish every moment that they are out on the links with their family members.
7. The rules are lax, and no one has a problem with it.
8. What place everyone finishes in is often secondary to all the wonderful moments that are created.
9. Everyone can't wait to get out and do it all again next year.

Compare all the wonderful moments created in this event with the usual exasperating moments that ensue from playing your own ball in a stroke-play format from tee markers that offer you little chance for sustained success. Over the following pages, it is my goal to get more players to buy into a more user-friendly way to compete out on the links in a nonsanctioned setting. Like the father-son outings, I want to allow every golfer numerous opportunities to have the time of their lives every single time they tee it up with their family members and beloved friends. I implore golfers everywhere to open up their minds to the better golfing experiences that GITCA GOLF promotes. No longer be duped into thinking that golf has to be the slow, sadomasochistic game that your forefathers used to subject themselves to every weekend. GITCA GOLF is a much faster, less penal, and far more enjoyable way to play this grand old game.

Ultimate Goal: Seeking Nirvana out on the Links with Your Beloved Friends

The most satisfying moments out on the golf course occur when you bomb a drive right down the middle of the fairway or when you make an approach shot literally dance on the green. When you put these two together on a hole, you are most likely putting for at least a birdie, and it doesn't ever get much better than that. For me personally, if I have killed a drive and made my approach shot dance around the flagstick, then quite literally, I too will be dancing around the flagstick. It matters little if I miss my birdie putt, for if I have controlled the ball to do what I have visualized, then all is right with the world at that moment. Naturally, it is even more euphoric when I convert these birdie opportunities, but even the pros miss their fair share of birdie putts. If they didn't, rounds in the 50s would be the norm.

As far as I am concerned, a perfect golf round would include me hitting eighteen out of eighteen greens in regulation and seeing that ball dance for me on every single hole in front of those closest to me. Now this would only be possible if I was playing my approach shots from distances that would allow me to hit scoring irons into most of these greens. I am pretty confident that I might actually accomplish this goal someday if I have an 8 iron or less for all my approach shots. For this to occur, I would have to play from tee boxes that allow my 230-yard drives to leave me with nothing more than 120–130 yards for my approach attempts. Thus, I would have to play from tee markers where most of the par 4 holes measure less than 350 yards. On most golf courses around the world, this would entail me teeing it up from the green tee markers, which I propose should measure around 5,400 yards. With my distance limitations, playing from this yardage would allow me to hit the same scoring irons that the pros do playing from their usual distances out on their respective tours. Why shouldn't I have roughly the same look that the pros do for a majority of their approach shots? Certainly, I am nowhere near as talented as any of them, so why should I make my plight any more difficult than theirs?

Now if my ego or someone else's ego encourages all of us to move way back and try and tee off from the black or blue tee markers, then I am going to be hard-pressed to hit any of the greens in regulation. If I am not hitting many of the greens in regulation and getting to see the ball dance, then I am robbing myself of one of golf's greatest joys. It is really depressing when you hit one of your greatest drives and you realize that you don't have a club in your bag that will allow you to reach the green with your approach shot.

Don't deprive yourself of one of life's greatest joys. Learn to follow the guidelines I have set forth with GITCA GOLF so that you allow yourself numerous opportunities to experience golfing nirvana. Once you start hitting a majority of the greens in regulation, your scores will improve dramatically, and more importantly, your soul will be eternally satiated. No longer be suckered in to playing from tee markers that offer you few opportunities for sustained success. Be grateful to play from your properly designated tee box, and watch your spirit and your golf ball soar.

One of the easiest ways to acclimate yourself to hitting a lot of greens in regulation and getting to watch your ball dance on a regular basis is to immerse yourself in playing par 3 and executive courses. These courses can be played quickly, excellent scoring opportunities abound, and the price is usually right. The brevity of these courses allows you to reach most of these greens in regulation and to marvel at the control you can have over the ball with your short scoring irons. Even if you mess up on a few holes, the holes don't take long to play, so you can get your revenge quickly over the next several holes. Whenever my buddies and I need a golf morale boost, we almost always head to the closest par 3 or executive course so that we can remind ourselves just how much fun this game can really be when we have scoring irons in our hands. When all of us are striking the ball well, the laughter and camaraderie are second to none. Playing these shorter courses allows us to get a glimpse into what the professionals must feel like as they make their balls do magical things as they maneuver them around the flagsticks. Certainly, we will never be as skilled or nearly as long as the professionals, but that does not deter our joy one iota. A lot of golfers snub their noses at these short courses for not being challenging enough. I can only implore these golfers to open up their minds a little bit so that they can learn to appreciate the sheer and utter joy that playing these short courses can bring to every golfer smart enough to play them on a regular basis.

Every time I go to the practice green to work on my short game, I always get a kick out of watching golfers teeing off on the first tee and simultaneously watching those finishing up their round on the final hole. Prior to teeing off, there is often great optimism, and everyone agrees to play from tee markers that leave them few opportunities for sustained success. Right from the opening drive, it is readily apparent that most of these golfers are way in over their heads playing from their chosen tee boxes. Only a scant few ever reach the green in regulation, and this misery is often repeated throughout the duration of the round. So with few greens hit in regulation, it often becomes a battle of who can escape with the least amount of double and triple bogeys. Certainly, there are fleeting moments of greatness, but these become quickly lost in the bloodbath that ensues for the majority of the round. It doesn't take long before most of the participants are questioning their sanity for continuing on with this charade.

Even for those golfers who are quite proficient, the stroke-play method employed by most foursomes in the United States puts constant pressure on everyone to never screw up throughout the round, or the entire experience will be greatly diminished. A slow start can put you behind the eight ball for the rest of the round, while a poor finish can put a serious damper on the day's overall enjoyment. Likewise, a bad hole or two in the middle of the round can vanquish all the round's goodwill. In other words, every golfer must be darn near perfect throughout the round or risk having a less-than-memorable day out on the links. With limited time to practice throughout the week and oftentimes playing from tee markers that leave them little chance for sustained success, the odds of achieving near perfection during their once-a-week outing are stacked against most golfers. As I look at the long faces of the golfers finishing a round, I don't see too many happy campers as I wonder what happened to all their giddy optimism. Most of them look as though the life has been sucked out of them as they try to leave the scene of so much carnage as quickly as possible. Certainly there has to be a better way to play golf that allows its participants to experience far more joy out on the links.

The first question that comes up on the first tee and that almost always leads to raised eyebrows is, What is everyone's handicap? No matter how valid the responses may be, almost everyone immediately questions the legitimacy of everyone's stated handicap. So immediately, the mood has been darkened. For the rest of the day, everyone is going to have to try hard in order to validate the legitimacy of their stated handicap. Anyone who plays much better than their stated handicap is going to be continuously interrogated throughout their splendid round, whereas those who have a particularly bad day are going to be labeled as having a "vanity handicap." Unless you shoot just about what your stated handicap states, then you are destined to fall on either end of this spectrum, and your day is going to be far less enjoyable than it should rightfully be.

The second question that greatly influences the legitimacy of everyone's stated handicap is, What tee boxes are we playing from? Almost universally everyone usually agrees to tee off from the same tee markers in order to "speed up play." Not only does playing from the same tee box not speed up play, it actually adds at least twenty minutes to each foursome's round. Each player in your foursome who is playing from tee markers that exceed his/her distance comfort level is going to be adding at least ten more shots and a lot more time to his/her round. If you typically play from the white tee markers and you are bullied or shamed into teeing off with everyone else from the blue or black tees, then your score is likely to be far worse than your handicap deems you to be. You are likely going to be way out of your comfort zone, and you will have a hard time reaching any of the greens in regulation. As a result, you are going to be hard-pressed to keep pace with the rest of your foursome. Similarly, if you are a golfer who normally tees off from the way-back tees and you agree to play from the white tees with everyone else, then you are much more likely to score far better than your stated handicap. Given that you are playing the course from about four hundred yards less than normal, you are probably going to play much smarter off the tee and hit far more greens in regulation than you are accustomed to reaching. You are probably going to be hitting an 8 iron or less for most of your approach shots, and everyone is going to want you to be their partner because in all likelihood, you are trouncing the field. Everyone including your partner will question the legitimacy of your handicap, and you will probably feel guilty even though you are simply placing yourself in a much better position to score well.

Moving up or back tee boxes can greatly affect your "real handicap." In my conservative estimation, for every hundred-yard discrepancy, you should realize at least a one- to two-shot difference. Thus, moving back a tee box and trying to attack the course from four hundred yards farther away, your score will probably be at least five to eight strokes worse than normal. Whereas those who move up and play the course from four hundred yards less than they normally do are likely to shoot at least five to eight strokes better than normal. Say you are a 12 handicap that most often shoots around 85 from the blue tees. By moving up four hundred yards to the white tees, you are suddenly breaking 80 with ease, and everyone is going to question your integrity. Whereas being forced to play from the black tees, you are going to be very hard-pressed to ever break 90, and you are going to have a "vanity handicap."

So now that the odds have been stacked either for you or against you before a single shot has been taken and your integrity has already been questioned, it now becomes a question about how much your foursome is going to follow the USGA rules for sanctioned tournament play. Are first tee mulligans allowed? Do you lose stroke and distance for a ball hit out of bounds? Is your group playing winter rules, or is everyone forced to play the ball as it lies? Will putts be conceded, or must everything be putted out? Is there a limit to the maximum score a golfer can record on a hole, or must a golfer keep going no matter how high the stroke total becomes? In other words, are there going to be some leniencies given in order to speed up play and to impart some mercy, or is everyone going to follow the exact letter of the USGA bylaws verbatim? Not being in agreement with any of these stipulations only adds to the dismay throughout the round, and almost everyone is going to leave the course fuming.

The main questions a golfer must ask themselves at the end of the day are, Did I have fun? Am I anxious to do this again? If the answer is no to these two simple questions often enough, then eventually, the golfer is going to play much less frequently or may in fact give up the game forever. Ask yourself when was the last time you had a really enjoyable day out on the links? If you can't remember the last time you had an awesome time out on the golf course, then it is high time you give GITCA GOLF a chance. Once you and your foursome fully embrace GITCA, the pertinent question at the end of the day will be, "When can we all get together to repeat this wonderful experience as soon as possible?"

Insanity: Doing the Same Thing Again and Again and Expecting Different Results

If you keep going to a restaurant over and over again and you keep getting less-than-satisfactory meals, then eventually you will quit going to that establishment altogether. It doesn't matter if this is some fancy restaurant or some fast-food establishment. If the service and/or the food are consistently less than desirable, you will inevitably find somewhere else to spend your hard-earned money. For the last few decades, golf has seen a mass exodus among its participants. Whether it is slow play or people just becoming so frustrated with their games that they have chosen to participate far less, golf has seen such a drastic decline in its number of patrons that it is becoming an epidemic throughout the golf industry as a whole. The number of golfers and the number of rounds played have been reduced by such large quantities that the entire golf industry has felt this large pinch. Something must be done quickly to reduce this dire trend, or more and more golf courses will be turned into vast real estate developments.

In the past decade, there were forty-three million less rounds of golf played in the United States than in the previous decade (GolfLink, 2014). The PGA of America has launched initiative after initiative to try and reverse this trend, and they have announced that their goal is to reach a peak of forty million golfers in the United States by the year 2020. This would be approximately sixteen million more golfers than the twenty-four million golfers we currently have playing on actual golf courses, and this number has been diminishing almost every year. In order to reverse this trend so that we can come close to reaching this idealistic number in golf participation, drastic measures must be taken before the interest in golf falls further into the abyss. It can no longer be assumed that the game of golf is so intrinsically rewarding that people are simply going to come out of the woodwork to play the game in droves. The current direction in which golf is being sold to the public is obviously not working, or we would not see the mass exodus that we are witnessing year after year from our beloved game. In our fast-paced society where delayed gratification is a thing of the past, we must make the game much faster and infinitely more enjoyable, or we risk seeing the golf participation numbers reach an all-time low. If we don't find a way to make the game inherently more appealing for everyone, then people will continue to find reasons to vacate the golf courses, causing many of them to shut down permanently. The leaders in the golf industry must take off their blinders and see that there are alternative ways to play this game that make it faster and more enjoyable for everyone. If we continue to hold fast to the premise that there is only one way to play this grand old game, then everyone will eventually suffer as the mass exodus will continue, and there will be a strain put on the entire industry to stay afloat.

The hypothesis has always been that there are only one set of rules for golf and that they must be intently followed, or the game will deviate too much to survive. The hard-liners who embellish this hypothesis say that the game has stood the test of time for centuries, and it must not be altered in any way from what the founders intended. In fact, in its latest campaign to promote the game of golf, the USGA has highlighted how there is only one set of rules that must be followed by everyone, and that is what makes the game so great and inherently popular. If this hypothesis were valid, then the game of golf should be thriving like never before. The courses would be so crowded that there would be a great demand to build more courses just to keep up with this ever-growing demand.

Unfortunately, as the numbers bear out, this is the furthest thing from the truth as people are leaving the game at a record pace, and more and more courses are being forced to shut down their operations. For those of us who love this great game, that is a very disturbing statistic and one that must be remedied if we do in fact want this game to survive and eventually thrive. In our ever-changing fast-paced world, most people don't have the time or the patience to play golf as it has been played for the last several centuries. The eighteen-hole, six-hour escapades of yesteryear are a thing of the past as most people are no longer willing to forego their entire day on eighteen holes of drudgery. If we are not willing to make the game faster and inherently more enjoyable, then more and more people are going to forego golf altogether and more and more courses will be forced to close. We must take into account that following all of golf's sacred traditions can be very intimidating as well as would make the game infinitely longer to try and play. We must allow some variances in the way that golf has always been played, or we risk losing entire generations of golfers. I feel that we need to make the game less intimidating and much easier to play so that everyone feels less threatened by all the numerous rules and regulations. The set of rules that I have set forth are to be used by the majority of recreational golfers so that the game is less intimidating and inherently more fun. With GITCA GOLF, golfers enjoy simple-to-follow guidelines that allow golf to be far less penal and to proceed at a much brisker pace. It is my hypothesis that if the game is faster, simpler, and infinitely more enjoyable, then golfers will be lining up to tee off like never before.

HOLE NUMBER 6

A Lifetime Pursuing Ultimate Enjoyment out on the Links

Growing up, I rarely played much golf due to the fact that the game appeared so serious, and quite frankly, I was horrible. I never wanted to embarrass myself in front of anybody, and I had no idea where the ball was going to go when I swung. I had such a tremendously huge slice that I would literally aim almost straight left in a desperate attempt to get my ball to land in the fairway. The few times that I was asked to join my dad for golf were tremendously terrifying experiences for myself and anyone else who was within fifty yards of me in any direction. As a result, I was not asked to play that often, and honestly, I was never in any hurry to return to the course anytime soon. I excelled at tennis, basketball, and baseball, and as far as I was concerned, golf was a lousy game played by old men in horrible pants. Golf was eternally frustrating for me and, thus, was something to be avoided at all costs. That line of reasoning all changed during Jack's magical win at Augusta in April 13, 1986, at the ripe old age of forty-six. With his beloved son Jackie on his bag and tears in Jack's eyes, our entire house became spellbound, and there was nary a dry eye in the house. Suddenly, I wanted to become good enough at golf that I could play with my dad and make him proud to be playing with me.

Thus began a never-ending quest to once and for all lick this game. I bought and read practically every single book that has ever been written on golf instruction. Long before the advent of YouTube,

I watched every golf video that I could get my hands on via my trusty VHS. Unfortunately, all this did was create information overload, and I became so full of contradictions that I developed severe cases of paralysis due to overanalysis. My mind was so jumbled that I literally could not get myself to take a full swing at the ball. I was petrified standing over the ball once again, and I literally had nightmares about swinging and missing or continually popping the ball up for very short distances. If you have ever seen Charles Barkley's golf swing, then you have an idea into how bad my swing had become. Psychologically, I was a mess, even with my degree in psychology in hand, and once again, I was too embarrassed to play with anyone. I thought about quitting the game more times than I could remember just so I wouldn't have to continually face my demons, but the lure of the game kept drawing me back. I would hit one or two fairly decent shots a round, and I was convinced that I should be able to do this on a regular basis given my athletic prowess in every single other sport that I pursued. Plus, my friends were all really good golfers, and I longed to someday be as good as them. Thus, I continually went back to the drawing board and read the latest swing tips in a desperate attempt to find the Holy Grail to golfing excellence.

I did a thorough study of all the golfing greats throughout the history of the sport, and I came away with the profound conclusion that each of them swung uniquely, and yet they all produced magnificent results. From Harry Vardon to Bobby Jones to Arnold Palmer to Jack Nicklaus to Lee Trevino to Nancy Lopez, they all swung the club with their own unique styles and idiosyncrasies, and all of them became Hall of Famers. When Jim Furyk came along and Gary McCord described his swing as an "octopus swinging in a phone booth," I knew once and for all that I had to quit copying the latest golfing trend and simply swing the club my own damn way. I must also tip my cap to John Daly, who implored all of us to "grip it and rip it" and who shocked the world with his homemade golf swing to the tune of two major championships and who became the folklore hero for every one of us blue-collar golfers. So I finally quit worrying what I was doing right and what I was doing wrong, and I simply swung the club in my own unique way and let the chips fall where they may. Miraculously, the hitch in my swing went away, and my ball flight started to become much straighter with a heck of a lot more carry. Now don't get me wrong, I am not going to be winning any club championships anytime soon. However, I am once again having a blast out on the golf course swinging freely with my butt-ugly homemade backyard golf swing! I certainly am not going to win any long-drive contests, but I get a huge rush of adrenaline when I hit it pure, and the ball seems as though it will go for miles. Of course, it only ends up about 230 yards out most of the time, but occasionally, I will crank it out there over 250 yards. And when those moments of ecstasy happen, it feels as though you will live forever. Naturally, these moments of glee are quickly tainted when I play with really good golfers who can crank it out there well over 300 yards, and once again, I am forced to realize that I am not nearly as long as these golfers and that I most likely never will be.

This jaunt back to reality used to keep me up at night and once again would force me to question why I continued to be so passionate about golf when I had no hope of ever competing with these superhuman golfers from the way-back tees. I tried for many years to develop an excellent short game in order to try and offset my lack of distance in comparison to these extremely long hitters à la Corey Pavin, but alas, I could never ever really compete with these "super golfers" because they also usually possessed outstanding short games as well. As a result, I would avoid playing with these much longer-hitting golfers altogether, and I usually found myself playing shorter courses and even executive courses where accuracy was far more important than length. I became quite proficient at playing these shorter courses, and in fact, I posted many scores right around par. I often bragged to my longer-hitting compatriots about my feats, and they would often laugh at me and would tell me to play a "real course." Occasionally, they would relent and play me on my shorter tracks, and the competition would be fierce right down to the wire. I won my fair share of these contests on these shorter courses, something that would never happen when I would join them on their championship courses from the blue tees. Even when they would spot me a few strokes, I almost always got my shirt handed to me trying to compete with them on these championship courses from the blue tees. Even when I would occasionally "win," it was only because they were feeling so sorry for me that they gave me an inordinate amount of strokes to try and make it fair. These "victories" were not satisfying to me at all. They were an assault on my ego, and even when I "won," I felt hollow inside. As a result, I often steered myself to playing the executive-type courses or playing easier courses from the white tees. Whenever my buddies would try and get me to play with them, I would often find an excuse not to play with them and then would go find someone else to play the shorter courses with me. Whomever I got to join me would also have an incredibly enjoyable time out on the links, and we would all admit that this was in fact much more enjoyable than hacking it around on the "big courses" from tee boxes that often overwhelmed us.

The beauty of playing the shorter courses is that they allow you to have ample opportunities to make par or better on nearly every hole. The par 3 holes are short enough that you almost always have a short iron in your hand for your tee shot, and thus, you have a high probability of hitting most of the greens in regulation. On the short par 4 holes, my 230-yard drives allow me to reach many of these greens with my tee shots or be so close that I am left with but a short pitch to the flagstick. Thus, I have ample opportunities to record many pars and birdies on these delightful short par 4 holes. My buddies and I feel like we are suddenly Babe Ruth playing in a Little League ballpark. We fire at the pins at will and are often disappointed when we don't make par or better on nearly every hole. This is the same mindset the pros must have as they record par or better on darn near every hole they play on the PGA Tour. So in essence, this is our chance to get a glimpse into what golf must feel like for the best players on the planet. Certainly, we are doing so on a much smaller stage, but that doesn't dampen our enjoyment one bit. We almost always feel triumphant whenever we are finished playing these executive courses with our scores hovering around par or better. Whenever we get up the moxie to tee it up from the blue tees on truly "championship courses," we once again return to our bogey golfer at best status and often feel so thoroughly defeated that we really have to talk one another out of quitting the game altogether.

Harnessing all our goodwill from playing these shorter courses, my buddy Bob and I decided once and for all that we would never again kid ourselves into thinking that we were in fact long enough to score well from the blue tees on most of the championship courses that we play. Both of us average about 230 yards on our tee shots, and thus, we were often left with shots of over 170 yards for our approach shots on most of these holes from the blue tees. By swallowing what little pride we had left and once and for all moving up to the white tees, our 230-yard drives were now leaving us with 140 yards or less for most of our approach shots. Since both Bob and I are pretty proficient with a 7 iron or less in our hands, we both began hitting a high percentage of greens in regulation. As a result, both of us began having a much higher tally of pars and an occasional birdie or two and were once again having the time of our lives out on the golf course. So essentially, Bob and I put our egos aside and decided to give ourselves a realistic chance to record par or better on a significant number of the holes we played. We no longer had to swing out of our shoes on our drives to try and get close enough to give ourselves a reasonable chance with our approach shots. As a result, we have been able to swing within ourselves and hit many more fairways and far more greens in regulation than we ever have before. We are having more fun than we ever have had out on the links, and we don't care if the other golfers in our foursome are dead set on continuing to tee it up from the blue tees. "Go ahead," we implore them, "you are way longer than us with your tee shots and your irons, so we know that we can't compete with you all from back there. We will play you straight up, no strokes whatsoever given to anyone. You all tee off from the blue tees while we tee off from the white tees. May the best golfer win! Game on!" Thus, the idea for GITCA GOLF was hatched. No handicaps taken into account. No strokes given whatsoever. Everyone simply finds the tee box that is right for them, and then may the golfer who records the best score be declared the winner.

We played this way for a while and had a lot of fun, but inherently, arguments would still ensue as to what score one would give oneself when they hit a wayward ball or two into the woods or water hazard. Numerous confrontations would come up when someone would award themselves a "7" when they clearly had gotten at least a snowman. Nearly everyone we played with had varying degrees of latitudes on golf's traditional scoring and rules interpretations, and therefore, numerous arguments would often ruin any goodwill that had been established that day between "friends." My buddies and I got together, and we all decided that we needed to streamline the rules and in fact make a standardization of the rules for all nontournament golfers. We all acknowledged that traditional golf purists would never go along with these modifications to their sacred game, and that was fine by us. Our intention was to make the game as enjoyable as possible for everyone else who is not so "anal retentive" about following the strict rule interpretations about how golf should be played. We all had witnessed firsthand just how emotional it can get between friends when everyone is on a different page about how the game should be played and scored. These emotional confrontations had caused many rifts in friendships and had in fact caused certain people in our group to no longer join us in our regular golf outings.

How ridiculous is it that lifelong friendships can be tarnished by varying opinions of rules interpretations? Thus, we all put our heads together so that we could streamline the majority of all the varying golf interpretations down to a few simple and understandable bylaws that everyone could easily interpret and that would hopefully become universal for nonsanctioned play. We also put into play the standard golf leniencies that the majority of amateur golfers already abide by and declared them to be universal. Therefore, it is no longer a question of whether or not your group gets a first tee mulligan; we have declared it to be an accepted part of GITCA GOLF. Likewise, "gimmes" are also now decided upon by the majority of the golfers' discretion in your group. This speeds up play on the greens and makes for a much more enjoyable experience for everyone who is on the receiving end of one. We have also taken a major leap in our nonsanctioned rules that every shot hit out of bounds or into a hazard will be deemed a lateral hazard with no loss of distance and only a one-stroke penalty. Again, this speeds up play dramatically and, more importantly, takes away the arguing and bickering that normally ensues about what is the proper ruling and action to be taken. We have made a double bogey the maximum score that you can receive on a hole, and our modified Stableford scoring system simply records any score higher than a bogey with a zero on the scorecard. Thus, if anyone in your foursome is having one of those god-awful holes, they simply pick their ball up when a bogey is no longer attainable and head to the cart to regroup before the next hole. Hence, the term *GITCA (Get in the Cart Already)* was hatched.

Since fully embracing GITCA GOLF as the only way I play golf, I have rarely been disappointed out on the links. In fact, I am scoring much better than I ever thought possible, and I have even had a walk-off hole-in-one and a walk-off "par buster double eagle" to win matches that everyone thought were already over. Although I could never beat really long-hitting golfers playing from the same tee boxes that they do, I feel that I can more than hold my own playing from tee boxes that allow me to hit about the same number of greens in regulation that they do from their farther-back tee markers. They enjoy competing against me since they no longer have to give me any strokes whatsoever. In our system, the golfer who accumulates the most total points from his/her properly designated tee box is declared the winner. There are never any handicaps or slope rating to figure out as our rules are straightforward and cut-and-dried. Since everyone is clear about the rules and all the advantages that GITCA allows, there is never any controversy, and the matches are always hotly contested until the bitter end. Sometimes, we play as teams, and sometimes, we all compete individually against one another. No matter which way we decide upon, a great time is had throughout the round by every combatant. I am so excited for everyone to embrace GITCA GOLF and learn to enjoy this great game as much as my friends and I do every single time we are lucky enough to tee them up.

GITCA GOLF Allows All Recreational Golfers to Have Universal Enjoyment

The main premise of GITCA GOLF is to make golf easier and much faster to play while at the same time keeping it very competitive and infinitely more enjoyable for all its participants. The status quo has been to allow recreational golfers to simply approach the game haphazardly without any clearly defined rules. Now certainly the USGA has clearly defined rules for its tournament golfers to follow to the exact letter of the tee, but everyone else who plays recreational golf kind of designates their own way of playing based on their foursome's normal protocol and etiquette. On any given Saturday, there might be forty different foursomes teeing off, all playing by slightly varying rules and interpretations. For example, most foursomes allow first tee mulligans, while other groups might not allow them under any circumstance. Likewise, many foursomes allow everyone to "roll" their ball but only in the fairway, whereas some play the ball as it lies with no exceptions whatsoever. Other groups may be far more lenient and allow both mulligans and to improve your lie whenever you deem it necessary. Similarly, many groups insist on granting "gimme putts," while other foursomes insist on putting everything out. Many foursomes play with handicaps, while other groups never utilize them. In other words, there is a lot of gray area concerning the varying rules and their interpretations.

The range of variance among all these varying groups often leaves golfers confused as to what the rules of engagement for each given foursome are. As a result of these variances, the pace of play is often inconsistent among the varying groups and often leads to backlogs on the course and much controversy. Often, it is those golfers who insist on following the exact letters of the rule handbook who are the golfers that take forever to finish their round and whom you never want to get stuck behind or forced to try and play with. This can be maddening to everyone who has to follow these slow groups and is often cited as one of the main reasons many golfers end up quitting the game for good. Most golfers simply want to go out and have a great time and play at a brisk pace without having to be bogged down trying to follow the precise letter of the law. Following the GITCA GOLF guidelines allows every golfer to be on the same page and have ample opportunities for a thoroughly enjoyable round. The rules are straightforward and simple for every group to follow without any controversy or gray areas to try and decipher. As a result, no one is ever accused of bending the rules or being labeled a "cheater."

Behold GITCA: A Faster, Easier, and Much More Enjoyable Way to Play

What if I told you that I have invented a way to play golf that simply keeps track of your good holes while quickly turning the page on your bad holes? What if we could hit an 8 iron or less for most of our approach shots? What if we could go out and play at a brisk pace without having to worry about our handicap or trying to follow a rule book that even most of the professionals cannot decipher? What if we could find a way to stay competitive with some of the best golfers we know while also making it fun for some of the less accomplished golfers we know? What if we found a way to greatly increase your odds for having some semblance of success out on the links almost every single time you teed it up? What if we found a way to have the time of your life out on the links no matter what golf track you play?

The way I see it, you have two options every time you decide to tee it up. You can decide to play from tee boxes that stretch your game too far, or you can play from tee markers that give you excellent opportunities to score well. In addition, you can play a course that is so challenging that the world's greatest players would struggle to post good scores, or you can choose to play a much more forgiving course that provides plenty of great scoring chances for you and your playing partners. Choosing the former is almost assuring you and your group of slow play, high scores, and plenty of angst and frustration. While choosing a more manageable course from tee markers that you can handle should speed up your play and increase the scoring opportunities and satisfaction level for everyone in your foursome.

Golf is already hard enough. Don't make it nearly impossible to ever enjoy yourself out on the course. Learn a much more forgiving way to play this grand old game so that you and all your playing partners have a much more enjoyable time each and every time you tee it up. Just imagine if we could make the game much less taxing for everyone in your foursome so that everyone is having many more positive moments. Let's put the odds in our favor to have success out on the links and have as much fun as possible. I believe we have done just that with GITCA GOLF, and I am excited for each and every one of you to try it out and have more fun than you ever thought possible out on the links with your beloved friends.

Remember, the overall goal of any recreational activity is to increase your enjoyment while decreasing your stress level. If your current golf game is greatly increasing your stress level while your enjoyment is continuing to wane out on the course, then in all likelihood, you will be giving up this game way too prematurely. It is my lifelong goal to be golfing well into my nineties with my closest friends and family members and to be enjoying the heck out of this game every single solitary time that I am fortunate enough to hit the links. If golf isn't a blast, then why play it? It is my overall goal to return the exhilaration of this great game to the masses. I want to introduce a less torturous game for players of all abilities so that everyone can enjoy playing golf to the hilt. Time spent out on the links should be glorious and heartwarming, not gut-wrenching and rage inducing.

My main goal for GITCA GOLF is for all recreational golfers to follow the same simple straightforward guidelines that allow for much faster and far more enjoyable playing parameters for all participants. I want everyone to play from tee markers that allow them to have very good odds to reach a majority of the greens in regulation, and I want everyone to score better than they ever thought possible. If you find yourself failing to reach a fair amount of greens in regulation, then in all likelihood, you are playing from tee markers that are above your pay grade, and your likelihood to post a good score and have a great time out on the links is severely diminished. In order for your golf experience to be as positive as possible, you must give yourself ample chances to accumulate a large number of GITCA points. This can only be accomplished by swallowing your pride and moving up to those tee markers that are going to allow you to hit a large number of greens in regulation.

For perhaps the first time in your life, finally admit that you will never be able to hit the ball as far or as straight as the best golfers in the world, and that is okay. 99.99 percent of us cannot hit the ball as far or as straight as the professionals, so no longer dupe yourself into thinking that you can play the golf courses that they play from the tee markers that they do. You and your buddies must accept the fact that you need to move up to tee boxes that allot you realistic chances to reach a majority of the greens in regulation. Continuing to play from tee markers that give you few opportunities to realistically reach the green in regulation is going to leave you frustrated and unfulfilled almost every time you hit the links. At your very best, you are most likely going to be playing bogey golf or worse. It is this sadomasochistic approach that leaves most golfers eternally frustrated and apt to eventually quit this grand old game for good.

Whenever I am fortunate enough to get out and golf, I never ever want my honesty or integrity questioned. I want to follow a relaxed set of rules and play from tee markers that give me ample opportunities for success on a majority of the holes that I am fortunate enough to get to play. I want everyone else to tee off from tee markers that give them just as many opportunities as me to be "successful" in their own right. If we are all playing from our correct tee markers and abiding by the same straightforward and less penal rules, then the competition should be intense right down to the bitter end. Granted that we all have many opportunities to be successful, we all should be having a very enjoyable time out on the links, and the pace of play should be rather brisk. Along with a few other ways to make golf much more positive, this is the premise for the GITCA GOLF system.

GITCA is a way to play golf that gets rid of most of golf's nitpicky rules while encouraging much faster and more enjoyable rounds for all participants. Almost everything involved in GITCA GOLF has been done before with various golfing formats: Stableford, scramble, play it forward, match play, winter rules, etc. We have simply combined what we feel are the best parts of all these methods so that every golfer can maximize their enjoyment every single time they tee it up. For example, the Stableford scoring system has been utilized for over a hundred years. We simply augmented it to make the scoring totals much higher on a regular basis. Every golfer gets to add to their running point total whenever they get a bogey or better on a hole. Points can never be subtracted, so the entire golf outing becomes much more positive than the traditional stroke-play scoring method. With the way that we have exponentially increased the point totals for outstanding holes, there are numerous opportunities to achieve momentous comebacks.

Jack Nicklaus, arguably the greatest golfer who ever lived, has been promoting the "play it forward" initiative for years. Unfortunately, most golfers have been too set in their traditional ways to see the benefits of moving up a tee box or two. The "Golden Bear" obviously sees all the benefits to moving up a tee box as he too has moved up a tee box or two from where he used to play in tournament golf, and it has made all the difference. Now if perhaps the greatest golfer of all time has swallowed his pride and moved up to a tee box where he can consistently score well, then why in the world wouldn't everyone else follow his lead? No longer let your ego get in the way of you thoroughly enjoying playing golf every single time you tee them up.

Tiger Woods just won the 2019 Masters as he hit nothing more than an 8 iron for the majority of his approach shots. The tournament lengthened the par 4 fifth hole this year, and Tiger was forced to hit a 4 iron for his approach shot on this hole every day. Consequently, he bogeyed this hole all four days. In spite of this, Tiger was able to triumph as he had nothing more than a 6 iron for a majority of his second shots on the par 5 holes. What an incredible comeback story for one of the greatest golfers of all time following many back and knee surgeries as well as countless swing changes. For the younger generation to see this great champion rise up once again to the forefront and then passionately hug his beloved children: priceless.

Don't make golf any more challenging than it already is. Hit from tee boxes that allot you to hit an 8 iron or less to the green for most of your approach shots following a decent drive on most par 4s. Play from distances that are well within your capabilities so that you never feel that you have to overswing in a desperate attempt to reach the green. By using a more lofted club and swinging smoother, you are much more apt to hit the sweet spot more often and send the ball effortlessly to your intended target with much greater regularity. Doesn't this sound much more appealing than rearing back and swinging with all your might, only to find your golf ball deviating way off the intended target line? Golf is simply much more fun when playing from distances that allow you to swing within yourself and hit far more greens in regulation.

Our system *mandates* that everyone tee off from their correct tee markers, or the competitive balance between the participants will be skewed. In other words, if you refuse to tee off from what our guidelines suggest for your distance limitations, then you are going to get your doors blown off by your fellow competitors. You will hit very few greens in regulation, and no one is going to want you to be their playing partner. You will be a hindrance to your foursome's pace of play as you will likely spend a lot of time looking for your ball in the woods or other hazards. In other words, swallow your pride and play from your proper tee markers so that you can have abundant scoring opportunities and be competitive with the rest of your foursome. Everyone in your foursome and those foursomes behind you will be greatly indebted that you finally got with the program and played better and faster than you ever have in your life.

Since most average golfers rarely ever get to play in conditions as pristine as the professionals do when they play tournament golf, GITCA GOLF invokes winter rules on a permanent basis for all participants throughout each hole. Our rationale is that we don't want any golfer to ever have to play from an unfair lie due to less-than-perfect course conditions or being stuck in another golfer's divot or unraked bunker. We want every golfer to have the most enjoyable experience that they can every single time they tee it up, knowing full well that course conditions can vary greatly. Provided that not every golf course is as well maintained as Augusta National, we allow every participant the opportunity to lift, clean, and place the ball before every shot they play. Since every golfer is allotted this same opportunity, there should never be any questioning of a golfer's integrity. By allowing each golfer to have a near pristine lie for every shot, the scoring opportunities should abound for everyone. Once again, far more greens should be hit in regulation, and no one will ever have to complain about the course conditions being less than pristine. Remember the first golfer ever to break 60 in an official PGA tournament, Al Geiberger, did so with the aid of lift, clean, and place as the course was not in great shape. So if professional tournaments grant this stipulation when conditions are not ideal, then why not grant all recreational players this same leeway as they often play in less-than-perfect conditions throughout the year?

GITCA GOLF also recognizes that most golfers are apt to screw up at least a tee shot or two during their round. Since most golfers often head to the first tee box without a single practice ball, the GITCA guidelines encourage all participants to take a first tee mulligan if they so desire. In addition, we also grant each golfer one additional roving mulligan to be used on any other tee shot of their choosing during the remainder of the round. Obviously, mulligans are never allowed in tournament golf, but we fully acknowledge that we are not out here trying to make a living. We are trying to have as many good holes as we possibly can so that the experience will be far more positive for every participant. Certainly, having a roving mulligan in your back pocket can ease a golfer's apprehensiveness and oftentimes leads to more fluidity and straighter tee shots. It sure eases a golfer's mind knowing that one no longer has to be perfect on every single tee shot. A relaxed mind often correlates to a relaxed swing and, thus, more well-struck shots. It is one of those catch-22 experiences that GITCA GOLF allows us to work in our favor.

In addition to making it easier to score well, our system also greatly eliminates many of the controversies often associated with the way golf is traditionally played. With our Stableford scoring system set in stone, there is never any controversy over what score a golfer received on a hole. Any score of bogey or better adds to one's point total, while any score worse than a bogey is simply recorded as a zero. Thus, it is no longer necessary to quibble about if a golfer actually got a double bogey or a triple bogey on a hole, which we all would just as soon forget. Once a bogey can no longer be attained, a golfer is encouraged to simply put his/her ball in his/her pocket and to start mentally preparing for the next hole as a simple zero is written down on the scorecard. No questions are ever asked, and no rulings have to be discerned. The golfer simply moves on from that hole with the only damage done being that no points have been accrued on that particular hole. This greatly increases the pace of play, stems off most of the controversies, and one's day is no longer ruined by one or two dreadful holes.

We only have eight simple-to-follow rules, and handicaps are no longer necessary. The handicap system usually leads to great controversy among golfers before, during, and after the round as it is based on a barometer of what a participant has done in the past. GITCA GOLF totally eliminates the need to declare a handicap as our scoring system is only concerned with how a particular golfer scores during the current round. Everyone starts the day on equal footing and with zero points, and the golfer who accrues the most points on that particular day from their properly designated tee box will be declared the champion. No strokes are ever given as the varying distance between the tee markers becomes the great equalizer. Our main goals are to speed up the pace of play, greatly decrease controversy, and give every participant ample opportunities to play better than they ever thought possible. We feel that we have accomplished all three of these goals and are anxious for you and your foursome to experience more enjoyment out on the links than you ever dreamed possible.

Some of the Most Iconic Moments Often Take Place during the Masters Par-3 Contest

The USGA has done a wonderful job of endearing youngsters to the game with their "Drive, Chip, and Putt Championship" that culminates at the Masters. I would love to see them go one step further and have a "National Par 3 Championship" that holds their finals at the beloved Par 3 course at *Augusta National*. This championship could be open to all ages and have city, state, and regional qualifying in order to make it all the way to the finals for a chance to play in the official Masters Par-3 contest with whatever group you choose. What a thrill it would be to tee it up next to the Golden Bear, the Black Knight, and Mr. Tom Watson. What a boon this would be to par 3 golf courses around the world to have golfers of all ages assaulting their courses in hopes of making it all the way to these hallowed grounds. Indoctrinating golfers of all ages to the wonderment of playing par 3 courses would certainly help many of these often overlooked courses to greatly increase their revenue while allowing golfers of all ages and abilities to see firsthand how enjoyable golf can be when attacking the flagstick from distances that are accessible to all of us. Playing nine holes in less than an hour is certainly feasible on these short courses, and everyone quickly learns how much fun it is to have many good looks at birdies and pars. Certainly, playing in the Masters is beyond most of our wildest dreams, but having a realistic chance to compete in a par 3 event is a distinct possibility for those of us who don't possess "tour length."

Anyone who witnessed the 2018 Masters Par-3 Contest will attest to it being one of the finest days in the history of golf. Tom Watson won the event by shooting six under par at the ripe old age of sixty-eight. Jack Nicklaus was no slouch himself as he shot four under par. Not bad for a seventy-eight-year-old. Not too far behind was the miraculous Gary Player shooting two under par at age eighty-two! Jack's grandson, JT, recorded a hole-in-one on his only swing of the day in front of this storied group of golfers. Witnessing this phenomenal feat led Jack Nicklaus to state that this was now his greatest golfing memory of all time! These are just the type of memories that GITCA GOLF hopes to inspire in all of us no matter what age we might be.

Just think how tragic it would have been if Jack, Gary, and/or Tom had decided that they didn't feel up to competing in the par 3 contest or if Jack's grandson GT had chosen not to take a single swing on that magical day. The entire sports world would have missed out on one of the greatest thrills any of us have ever seen. To see some of the most iconic figures in golfing lore shoot lights out and thrill the crowd from start to finish and then have one of their grandsons have his first hole-in-one ever in front of millions of golf fans and these legends: *priceless!*

Unfortunately, there will come a day when we no longer get to witness these moments that stir all our souls, but in the meantime, let's relish these for as long as possible. Eventually, these legends will hang them up for good, but hopefully, this will be many years from now. With all the dramatic moments these golfing greats have provided for many decades, it wouldn't surprise me one bit to see them all repeating these magical moments a decade from now. What great role models for the rest of us to try and emulate. Never give up on yourself and your dreams and keep swinging the club as long as humanly possible, for there are plenty of magical moments out there waiting to happen.

What Sports Can You Really Play and Compete at for Most of Your Life?

Baseball is indisputably America's pastime, but how many Americans play baseball past the age of eighteen? Less than 0.001 percent of the population actually plays the same game that the Major Leaguers abide by past their teen years. Why? Because the game is too damn hard to have sustained success. The game itself is too slow, and thus, most people end up quitting the game altogether. For pitchers, the amount of undue stress on the arm just gets too much for most people to continue having to endure. For hitters, trying to hit a ball that is traveling in varying directions at speeds approaching ninety miles per hour is very difficult for most people to try and achieve on a consistent basis. Since the ball is rarely put in play, most of the fielders grow quite weary of the game very quickly. As a result, most people quit playing baseball altogether and discover that softball gives them far more satisfaction.

Whenever we go to a Major League Baseball game, we all quickly realize that we could never compete against these amazing athletes. But we all still love getting hits, running the bases, and playing stellar defense from time to time. As a result, thirty million Americans love to play slow-pitch softball every chance they get (Sports Destination Management, August 2012). Softball is fast-paced and high scoring, and most participants have at least a moderate amount of successful plays each game. The ball is simply lobbed over the plate so that hitters have a high probability of making consistent contact, and as a result, the defensive players are always kept on their toes. The learning curve for slow-pitch softball is very short, and everyone has a high probability of ascertaining at least a few hits each game. When a game has ample action for all its participants and is relatively easy to excel at, rest assured, most people are going to want to repeat this wonderful experience as often as possible.

If golf is going to survive and, in fact, thrive, then slight rule changes need to be made for those golfers not playing in a sanctioned stroke-play event. No longer must all golfers erroneously believe that they need to play the same game that the professional golfers play in order to have fun. In fact, it is foolhardy to dupe ourselves into believing that we can play the same game that the professionals play. These select few have honed their skills with such precision that they can make the golf ball do things that the rest of us can only dream about. In addition, they are hitting the ball so much farther than we can ever imagine. We must find a way to make golf infinitely easier, faster-paced, and inherently more enjoyable for the masses, or we run the risk of more and more golf courses shutting down their doors permanently.

My solution to this aforementioned problem is to make the game easier so that there is a much higher probability for sustained success out on the links for golfers of all ages and abilities. By adopting the guidelines that I have put forth with GITCA GOLF, golf is made much more enjoyable and infinitely faster for all its participants. GITCA GOLF is to traditional tournament golf what slow-pitch softball is to Major League Baseball. Once golfers learn to incorporate all these guidelines, we should see smiles return to their faces and the level of participation increase dramatically across the board. Once most amateurs finally acknowledge that they can't play golf at the same level as the best players in the world, only then will they be willing to play under the much more user-friendly auspices of GITCA GOLF and consequently have more fun than they ever imagined.

Making Golf Infinitely More Enjoyable

To be certain, GITCA GOLF is infinitely easier than the traditional rules set forth long ago by the ancient ruling bodies, and this is a welcome relief for 99 percent of the golfers who will never compete in sanctioned stroke-play tournaments. No longer will golfers have to face long odds in order to ascertain any level of satisfaction out on the links. Every golfer should have a much greater chance to reach attainable goals and should be doing so at a much faster pace of play. If everyone is scoring better and playing at a much faster pace, then what is wrong with breaking with long-standing traditions? With the world continually evolving, golf must get on board and adapt or risk being left further behind. Playing golf should be a thrill throughout one's lifetime. Following the GITCA format makes the game infinitely more enjoyable for everyone who tees them up.

If golf is going to survive and in fact thrive in the future, then the golfing establishment must make some wholesale changes in the way that recreational golf is played by the majority of its constituents. I just finished watching a professional golf tournament where a world-famous golfer just took ten minutes to finally hit his next shot. He and his playing companions took over six hours to finish their round. There were so many delays due to all the rulings that had to be made by the on-course rule officials that even the most ardent golf fans had to grow weary of this snail's pace of play. For this to be the model for how recreational golf should be played would be obscene. In my opinion, recreational golf should be played at a very brisk pace and with a great amount of leniency given in order to maximize the fun for all participants. In our fast-paced society, everything must be done efficiently and with some reward, or the action is not likely to be repeated with any frequency.

Playing from tee markers that give you few opportunities to reach a majority of the greens that you play in regulation is going to deny you the opportunity to break out your divot repair tool on a regular basis. On the other hand, playing from tee markers that leave you with short irons for most of your approach shots is going to allow you to experience golf blissfulness many times throughout your round. The key question all golfers must ask of themselves is, When do they want their ego satiated? Do they want it gratified as they are choosing their tee boxes at the beginning of the round? Or would golfers rather swallow their pride and play from tee markers that allow them numerous opportunities to score well on almost every hole? Since most golfers have been led to believe that only attaining a par or better on a hole should be cause for celebration, then most of the golfers who choose ego-driven tee markers will find only fleeting moments of happiness during any given round. Trust me, it is much more ego gratifying to continuously post good scores than to satiate your ego at the beginning of the round. I implore you to move up a tee box from where you normally play so that you can experience the ecstasy of hitting a large number of greens in regulation and greatly increase your chances of scoring well. But most golfers are too prideful to move up from where they have played most of their golfing lives. As a result, the scores are often atrocious, the pace of play is horrendous, and there is little satisfaction to be had by most of the participants.

To add to the misery is the fact that almost every golfer is continually scrutinized over the legitimacy of their stated handicap. If every golfer in the foursome doesn't record a score that is congruent with their stated handicap, then rest assured, every golfer will either be dubbed a "liar" or a "cheater" based on the incongruences of the day's proceedings. So not only is your golf game wreaking havoc with your self-esteem, your honesty is also now being continually challenged by everyone else in your foursome. So from start to finish, you are continually disappointed with most of your efforts while your integrity is constantly put under the microscope for the entire five-plus-hour duration. When you finally arrive home, your spouse is wondering where the hell you have been all day as you have missed out on a majority of the rest of the family's activities. So for all your troubles and hard-earned cash, you have experienced masochistic torture from all sides with only fleeting moments of actual pleasure.

Now you don't have to have your PhD in psychology to figure out that this type of behavior is not going to be repeated on a frequent basis by mostly sane individuals. Unfortunately, this is the typical scenario that is being played out again and again on most golf courses around the world. Is it any wonder that the appeal of golf has taken such a drastic downturn?

In order for people to become passionate about golf, their egos must be rewarded from time to time while at the same time satiating their souls. That is why playing shorter courses must become a staple for golfers of all ages and abilities. Following the GITCA guidelines certainly makes playing any course a far more positive experience, but starting out playing par 3 and executive courses can really boost one's ego and overall enjoyment of the game. Once golfers graduate to the longer, more challenging courses, it is imperative that they choose to play from tee boxes that allow them to have short iron approach shots so that they can hit a large percentage of greens in regulation. The ultimate goal is for people to get out as often as they can on the links with their friends and family and have such an enjoyable time that they can hardly wait to repeat this process as often as possible. I guarantee that if a large percentage of greens in regulation are being recorded, a fast and enjoyable round will be experienced by nearly all the participants. I have seen this happen with everyone that I have introduced to GITCA GOLF, and I am excited for the rest of the world to start embracing a passion for golf the likes of which have never been seen before.

Many people have remarked that I can't wave a magic wand and make golfers infinitely better simply by changing a few guidelines. Certainly not, but following the GITCA guidelines certainly promotes a much higher likelihood of every golfer finding the putting surface in fewer shots than they are accustomed. By promoting tee markers that put a shorter scoring iron in the hands of most of the participants for the majority of their approach shots and allowing everyone to improve their lie via "lift, clean, and place," far more greens will be hit in regulation, and the scores and the pace of play should improve dramatically. Ask any archer or marksman if it is easier to hit the bull's-eye from forty yards closer in. Undoubtedly, they all will respond emphatically, "Yes!" Basically, I am promoting moving most amateur golfers thirty to forty yards closer on each hole before the round even starts so that it is much more fathomable to hit more greens in regulation. Hitting an 8 iron instead of a 5 iron allows all golfers to produce more backspin and far less sidespin. As a result, a fairly well-struck 8 iron should fly higher and with much less dispersion than a 5 iron. Hence, more greens are likely to be hit, and everyone is going to score better and have an infinitely more enjoyable time out on the links. So simply by shaving at least thirty to forty yards per hole for each participant, I have greatly increased the probability of everyone enjoying their golf outing a heck of a lot more. By allowing all participants to improve their lie and granting them a few more additional liberties that would never be allowed in a sanctioned stroke-play event, I believe I have made everyone's golfing experience infinitely better.

The pros realize that even with all their great skill and devotion to this wonderful sport, at the end of the day, golf is still an almost impossible sport to try and master. Thus, you will never hear the professionals assess a course as being too short or too easy for them. They enjoy getting to control the ball with their wedges and allotting themselves numerous birdie chances throughout their round. Why in the world does the average golfer feel the need to challenge themselves with harder predicaments than the top players in the world? It is this ego-driven machismo mindset that many golfers embrace that is destroying the enjoyment factor for most golfers across the globe. I implore every golfer out there to take a lesson from the pros and learn to enjoy having a great look at birdie from time to time. The top professionals never feel guilty about shooting great scores: it is high time the average golfer put themselves in position to score well on the majority of holes that they are fortunate enough to play. Phil Mickelson, one of the top 50 golfers of all time, just posted an opening round 60 that included ten birdies and an eagle on a pristine course in the desert air that was playing much shorter than the posted 7,000 yards. Shockingly, I didn't hear Phil say that the course was too easy and that the scoring conditions were too perfect. He was simply smiling from ear to ear with that big lovable grin as we all should be so lucky to ever score so well just once in our lifetime.

Scrambles Give Us a Glimpse into the Pro's Realm

Every once in a while, golfers get to play in a scramble event for charity in which they score better than they ever dreamed possible. Most scramble formats take less than four hours to play, and a boatload of fun is had by almost all the participants as the rules and the mood are often very lax. Every shot is played from a pristine lie, and the team gets multiple chances to produce a great score. In addition to raising a large amount of money for a good cause, a scramble allows golfers of all abilities to come together in a team event to see just how low a score they can post. In most big-time scramble events, a professional is usually paired with the amateurs so that each team is almost assured of posting a score much lower than they ever imagined.

Even though each participant will attempt fifty or more shots, only about one or two of these amateur shots will actually contribute to the team cause, and that is perfectly fine with all the participants. The rest of the shots will simply be discarded as not quite good enough, even if they are horrible. Just as they are feeling pretty good about themselves and their approach shots, the pro will usually step up and hit nothing more than a wedge that leaves the team with a short uphill putt for birdie or eagle. Everyone high-fives the pro as they realize just how much a chasm exists between the top professionals and the rest of us rank amateurs. Similar to playing golf on Xbox, scores of double digit under par are usually the norm as everyone gets to relish going lower than they ever dreamed possible. The team camaraderie enhances the outing even more, and golfers lament the fact that they can't play in a scramble format almost every time they tee them up.

What GITCA GOLF does is take many elements of the scramble format and adapt them to playing your own individual ball. First of all, every golfer is *required* to play from tee markers that give them a realistic chance to hit a large percentage of greens in regulation.

Most golfing foursomes all tee off from the same "ego-driven tee markers," which offer few chances for any of the participants to hit a high percentage of greens in regulation. This is simply setting almost everyone up for disappointment and an overall sense of helplessness out on the links. By forcing everyone to check their ego at the door, GITCA GOLF allows every golfer the opportunity to attack the green with a short scoring iron following a decent drive. Thus, no longer does a golfer have to hit a career drive followed by a perfect fairway metal in a desperate attempt to reach the putting surface in regulation. By reducing the playing distance by at least twenty yards on every hole for almost all the golfers, most of the participants are going to reach more greens in regulation than they ever believed possible. Provided that GITCA GOLF allows all golfers the same ability to lift, clean, and place their ball within a club length of where it landed (no closer to the hole) similar to a scramble format, the scores across the board are going to be infinitely better. Just imagine how much faster your foursome will be playing when almost everyone is on or near the green in regulation on a majority of the holes played. When everyone is scoring better and playing much faster, the mood is likely to be much more jubilant, and everyone will be much more apt to want to play this way forevermore.

 With everyone in your foursome abiding by these uniform rules, the scoring opportunities should be much more plentiful for everyone, and the pace of play should be at least thirty minutes faster than you and your foursome are accustomed. Since everyone is playing by the same less stringent rules and without handicaps, there are few to any controversies, and almost everyone is going to have a wonderful experience. No one is ever going to mistake GITCA GOLF for an ultraserious stroke-play tournament format, and that is our point exactly. There is never any finger-pointing or accusations with GITCA GOLF as everyone simply enjoys hitting their ball well from excellent lies. The scores are usually very good, the camaraderie is high, and everyone can hardly wait to repeat this wonderful time spent out on the links with their beloved friends as soon as humanly possible.

HOLE NUMBER 7

The Eight Simple Rules of GITCA GOLF

GITCA GOLF Rule Number 1: First Tee Mulligan

Rule number 1, which is standard fare among almost every foursome I have ever teed it up with, is a first tee mulligan. Certainly, first tee mulligans are never permitted in tournament golf because the ancient rules of golf would never have allowed it. My rationale for GITCA GOLF is that everyone should have two opportunities to get their round started on a positive note. Most golfers usually head out to the first tee without ever having hit a practice ball, so why not give them two chances to get off to a good start. Nearly all professional golfers would never dream of heading to the first tee without hitting the driving range for at least an hour or two. Oftentimes, your opening tee shot can set the tone for the entire day, so why not give yourself two opportunities to gather some positive momentum? Remember, our mission statement with GITCA GOLF is to maximize the entire golfing experience for every golfer who tees it up. Right away, we are breaking with the traditional bylaws laid down several hundred years ago by the Royal and Ancient Golf Society, and that is okay because we are not playing in an official tournament setting. Our goal is to have as much fun as we can out on the links with our friends in the limited time that we have to tee it up. Our bank accounts are not being augmented one bit by our recreational play, so why not increase our likelihood of having a much more enjoyable time out on the links with our beloved friends?

GITCA GOLF Rule Number 2: Everyone Must Tee Off from Their Proper Tee Box

Rule number 2, and perhaps the most important rule that needs to be strictly enforced in order to maximize everyone in your foursome's golfing experience, is that everyone in your foursome *must* play from the tee box that properly corresponds to their standard carry distances of their driver added to their standard 8 iron length. I realize that this immediately breaks tradition with the way your foursome usually plays as you all usually agree to play from one set of tee boxes, but I am here to emphasize to you that this is where the traditional way of thinking is bogging down the game and making it inherently less enjoyable for everyone in your foursome. If there are any golfers in your foursome who are playing from "way-too-far-back tee boxes," then your entire foursome will be slowed down immensely as these golfers are forced to play from distances that are way beyond their capabilities. When these golfers try in vain to muscle the ball in order to try and keep up, the errant results will put a mental strain on everybody in your foursome as well. In addition, your pace of play will suffer greatly as you all scavenge the woods and weeds in often vain attempts to locate their wayward shots. As a result, all your games will suffer as you lose your rhythm, and the time added to the round will make the game much less enjoyable for your foursome and every foursome that unfortunately has to follow your group's train wreck.

Most golf courses only have four or five varying tee boxes to try and suit their clientele, but it is my contention that each championship-length course should have at least six different tee markers. By having six or seven different tee boxes with combo options in between, every participant will be able to properly find their comfort zone, and the playing field will be much more equalized. I realize that many courses may be limited with their tee box options, but simply throwing down some more tee markers along the fairway can go a long way to evening out the percentages of greens hit in regulation. If everyone is playing within their capabilities, then the scores are going to be much improved as well as the pace of play and overall satisfaction for each foursome. Trying to play from distances that strain your capabilities is likely going to add many strokes and much greater frustration for your entire foursome. No longer accept playing from distances that overwhelm you and cause you to constantly reprimand yourself and ruin your overall experience out on the links. You rarely see the professionals overwhelmed as the majority of them are constantly breaking par and hitting a high percentage of greens in regulation. Most amateurs, on the other hand, are constantly struggling to break 90 and are recording only a sparse amount of greens hit in regulation.

If your combined distance for your average drive plus your average carry distance of your 8 iron is above 450 total yards, then it is highly recommended that you tee it up from the way-back tees, which on most courses are known as the tournament tees. Only the professionals and a very few long-hitting amateurs will ever tee it up from these prodigious distances. These very long hitters should not be overwhelmed teeing it up from the tournament tees if they are truly as long as they claim to be.

Now if your combined distances for your average 8 iron and average drive add up to between 430 and 450 yards, then by all means, have at it teeing it up from the next set of tees, which on most courses are the black tees. Again, most golfers greatly overestimate their abilities, and many people erroneously tee it up from these tee boxes even though they have very little chance to hit most of these greens in regulation from these faraway distances. As a result, entire foursomes are oftentimes guilty of slowing down the entire course due to their egos getting in the way of their actual golfing limitations. Once GITCA GOLF takes hold and becomes the standard practice for all nontournament golf, golf rangers around the world will be trained to identify these bogus groups and will encourage them to promptly move up to their correct tee boxes so that they and the groups behind them can be spared eternal suffering.

The standard tee box on most golf courses for the average golfer has almost universally been designated as the white tee boxes. It is my contention that the white tee markers on most championship courses should be set at approximately 5,800 yards. Although many golfers often scoff at the white tees as not being challenging enough for their standards, I can assure everyone that the statistical data will provide ample proof that 90 percent of all golfers should never tee off any farther back than the white tee boxes. In fact, a high percentage of people who have always chosen to play from these markers should in fact get accustomed to teeing it up from the green tees so that their scores and their spirit will greatly improve. I guarantee that once you make the leap forward, you will have infinitely more fun out on the links with your golfing brethren. If everyone plays from their appropriate tee boxes, then many more greens in regulation will be hit by everyone in your foursome, and the entire golfing experience will be much more efficient and infinitely more enjoyable for all.

Since the average amateur golfer averages less than 210 yards with his driver and just around 100 yards with his/her 8 iron, then the majority of golfers should be teeing off from the green tee markers, which should measure around 5,400 yards. On most courses, the distance between the white and green tees is often around 20 yards per hole. Wouldn't it be nice to immediately add 20 yards to your drives by simply walking up one set of tee boxes? Who wouldn't appreciate an immediate 20-yard boost to their tee shots? Remember, you are not trying to prove your mettle out here. Your main goal is to maximize your enjoyment and make the total experience that much more enjoyable for everyone in your foursome. Following the GITCA guidelines to a tee, I believe that teeing off from the green tees rather than the white tees will be the accepted norm for most golfers. Or perhaps the best solution is to tee off from the white/green combo tees as a wonderful compromise. You tee off on half the holes from the white tees and the other holes from the green tees. Simply alternate tee boxes on each hole in order to essentially split the difference.

If you are having any doubt as to which tee markers you should be playing from, then simply ask yourself which tee boxes are going to allow you to have roughly the same club that the professionals have for their approach shots on most of these holes. Now is not the time to overestimate your abilities. Choose tee markers that are going to allow you an excellent chance to reach most of the greens that you play in regulation. Remember, the pros on tour these days are hitting an 8 iron or less for a majority of their approach shots. If you have chosen to play from tee boxes that force you to hit a 5 iron or more for most of your approach shots, then you are clearly playing from the wrong tee markers. In most cases, the top golfers on the planet are 100 yards longer than you off the tee and at least three clubs longer with their irons. That equates to approximately a 130-yard advantage in length that the pros have over you. In other words, no longer feel sheepish about moving up at least one set of tee markers so that you have a fighting chance to battle the golf course in a similar manner to the best golfers in the world.

To find where you *must* tee off from assuming the golf course superintendents have placed each tee marker approximitely 20–30 yards apart

Add the combined distances of your average drive and your average 8 iron:

Longer than 450 yards = tournament tees (level 12) should measure over 7,000 yards

Between 430–450 yards = black tees (level 11) should measure about 6,600 yards

Between 410–430 yards = black/blue tee combo (level 10) should measure 6,400 yards

Between 390–410 yards = blue tees (level 9) should measure about 6,200 yards

Between 370–390 yards = blue/white tee combo (level 8) should measure 6,000 yards

Between 350–370 yards = white tees (level 7) should measure about 5,800 yards

Between 330–350 yards = white/green tee combo (level 6) should measure 5,600 yards

Between 310–330 yards = green tees (level 5) should measure about 5,400 yards

Between 290–310 yards = green/yellow tee combo (level 4) should measure 5,200 yards

Between 270–290 yards = yellow tees (level 3) should measure around 5,000 yards

Between 250–270 yards = yellow/red tee combo (level 2) should measure 4,800 yards

Less than 250 yards = red tees (level 1) should measure less than 4,600 yards

The parameters that I have set up basically equate to the average par 4 length that you should be facing for your typical round of golf. Thus, if you hit a pretty good drive on most of the par 4s you play, you should be left with nothing more than an 8 iron for most of your approach shots. Certainly, most tour players are left with nothing more than an 8 iron for most of their approach shots on most of the par 4s they play following a decent drive. So why then should recreational golfers be forced to try and hit a longer club in for most of their approach shots? The simple answer is that they shouldn't, and it is high time that the golfing world got on board with making golf infinitely easier for all recreational golfers to score better and play much more efficiently. These tee marker distances are far more forward than they are currently set up on most courses around the world. My number 1 objective is to set everyone up for far more instances of gratification out on the links. Most golf courses must be willing to move most of their tee boxes up and add more tee boxes if they hope to keep their patrons happy and their course afloat.

Failure to adhere to the GITCA tee marker guidelines I have provided is simply setting your foursome up for a long and unsatisfying round. The statistics clearly show that failure to adhere to these guidelines due to one's overinflated ego will clearly lead to far fewer greens hit in regulation and hence much more scant scoring opportunities. Almost every golfer who tees off from markers that are too long for their game will most likely have far fewer scoring opportunities than those who do play from their correct tee boxes. Since there is often a wide variance in golfing abilities in many foursomes, every golfer in your foursome might be teeing off from differing tee boxes. It becomes readily apparent that this is no big deal and in fact speeds up the pace of play greatly as far more greens are likely to be hit in regulation. Remember, our goal with GITCA GOLF is to make the game of golf much more enjoyable, more competitive, and much more expedient for all participants. If everyone properly adheres to the GITCA guidelines I have put forth, then many more greens will be hit in regulation, and the scores should be extremely competitive right down to the final putt on the final hole.

More and more golfing venues are in fact adding more combo tee boxes to further accommodate their clientele and provide them with more options. Every single golf course in the world should be offering combination tee yardages so that everyone can find their proper niche out on the links. The beauty of playing combo tees is that you can alternate between tee boxes so that the course plays differently by varying which tee boxes you choose to play from on that particular day. Combo tees are made by teeing off from one set of tee boxes on the odd holes and the other set of tee boxes on the even holes. If you play the same course on a regular basis, simply alternate the odd holes and even holes each time you play from the combo tees in order to spice things up a little bit.

With the tee marker guidelines I have provided, that gives every golfer twelve different tee box options on every championship course, assuming the golf management team has followed my suggestions. It is my belief that every new golfer should start at the red tee boxes and move up in accordance with their mastery of the game. In other words, once you are consistently accumulating at least twenty-five GITCA points nearly every time out with ease, you should consider moving up one tee box rung. Of course, a pro or your friends should testify to your mastery from your current tee box and verify that you are indeed ready to further test yourself by moving up one level of the twelve varying options. I can hear you all saying right now, "Well, I will never be good enough to ever move up to the next tee marker!" My response is emphatically, "Then don't!" Trying to play the course from lengths that strain your capabilities is only going to add to your frustration level and lead to slow play throughout your round.

Do everyone a favor, especially yourself, and play from the jurisdiction that you can successfully navigate nearly every time out. If you have designated yourself as a green tee player, you can also vary the looks of the course by choosing to play the white/green combo tees on certain occasions as well as the green/yellow combo tees from time to time. The key is for everyone in your foursome to fall in accordance with their proper designation in relation to you. This will keep the competitive balance and will prevent all of you from having to face nearly the exact same challenges every time out. Certainly, playing the course from farther back should decrease your scoring chances, while playing the course from farther up should greatly increase your scoring opportunities. Don't ever be ashamed to admit that Father Time has finally caught up with you and that you need to move forward a tee box or two. Failure to swallow your pride at this point in your career is only going to make golf painful for you and everyone in your foursome. Move up so that you can attack these greens with the same vigor as everyone else in your foursome. I think you might be surprised at how the scoring opportunities will even out throughout the round.

These twelve different tee box options, I feel, should be similar to moving up the rankings in tae kwon do. Only after you have demonstrated consistent mastery of your current level should you ever be allowed to test yourself at the next level up. There are very few true "black belts" in the world. Similarly, the actual number of true "black tee golfers" is minuscule as well. If there is ever a doubt about your true distance capabilities, then by all means go to a swing monitor with a shot tracker and have your distances calibrated. Of course, hitting the ball a prodigious distance does not guarantee great scores. Use your actual distance markers as well as your average GITCA scores to properly determine which of these twelve tee box options you should consistently tee off from. Don't worry about where everyone else in your foursome is teeing off from as you ultimately are battling it out against the course. Contrary to popular belief, playing from your correct tee box is a much better equalizer than the handicap system. The key is to not be embarrassed to tee off from your proper designation. Swallow your pride and learn to love playing golf again. Give yourself a chance to score well on almost every hole that you play. Chances are, if you are teeing off from your correct tee markers and some others in your foursome are letting their inflated egos get the best of them, then you will be scoring much better than them throughout the round. They may make fun of you at the start of the round, but believe me, you will garner the last laugh as you hit far more greens in regulation and record far more GITCA points than your stubborn companions.

The key to playing GITCA GOLF is to follow the aforementioned guidelines so that you have a great chance to compete with every other golfer in your foursome. Simply because they are teeing off from farther back than you does not guarantee them of scoring better than you. It simply means that they are longer throughout the bag than you are. If everyone has correctly identified their proper domain, then the scoring chances should equal out throughout the round. I could care less how much longer my opponent is than me; the bottom line is, Can they outscore me today from our corresponding tee markers?

Since nearly every golfer has overestimated their true capabilities for most of their golfing career, my suggestion is for everyone to start out two rungs lower on the board than you would normally play from and earn your way back up to where you think you really are. For example, if you have always teed off from the white tee markers, my suggestion is for you to tee off from the green tee markers until you are consistently averaging over twenty-five GITCA points per eighteen holes. Naturally, once you are consistently accumulating these points, try your luck from the white/green combo tees, and stay there until you are once again averaging over twenty-five GITCA point per eighteen holes. Now if you are struggling to ever break twenty GITCA points, then once again swallow your pride and move back up to the much more user-friendly green tee markers. It is far better to underestimate your abilities and put yourself in position to have many golden scoring opportunities than it is to overestimate your abilities and once again put yourself in peril for most of the day.

With twelve different jurisdictions, every golfer should eventually find his/her niche and feel comfortable attacking the course from that properly designated length. The golfer that I play against most, Steve, is a level 9 rated golfer who almost always tees off from the blue tees. I, on the other hand, rate myself as a level 7 golfer, and I almost always tee off from the white tees. As you will see in the pages to follow, we almost always have a knockdown drag-out fight that is usually not decided until the final putt on the final hole of the day. It doesn't bother me one bit that he outdrives me on most occasions by over twenty yards and is at least 2–3 irons longer than me because if the golf course superintendents have properly allocated the tee boxes, we should have a great GITCA duel every single time we tee them up. Now if we play a course that doesn't exactly match up to my suggested guidelines or if Steve and I want to simply mix it up or try our hand from varying tee boxes from the last time we challenged that particular course, Steve simply chooses the tee box that he wants to play from, and I will then tee it up two rungs below him accordingly. As long as we keep the two rung buffer between us, our scoring opportunities should be roughly the same, and the GITCA battle will likely ensue right down to the final hole or two. If everyone in your foursome has correctly identified their proper designation, then everyone should know exactly where they should be teeing off from in relation to everyone else. No longer be that group that designates that everyone tee off from the same tee markers. Doing so will throw off the competitive balance and make for a long and frustrating day for a majority of the golfers in your group and for the poor groups that are being delayed by your group's slow play.

When everyone in your group adheres to the proper teeing guidelines, then your golfing group will reach a competitive level that you never dreamed possible. In addition, no one will ever have to experience the often hollow win that comes from a handicap-aided victory over a competitor who clearly outplayed everyone else. The varying tee box yardage distance is the only variance you need to keep things on an even keel, so handicaps are no longer needed to keep things ultracompetitive. Everyone gets a clean slate to start the day, and points can only be added to everyone's total. The worse score you can get on a hole is a zero, so your point total can never be subtracted. Everyone starts with zero points, and every golfer will hopefully add many positive points to their overall tally for the day. The days of sandbagging or having to give or receive strokes are over. If the golf course superintendents and course designers have done their jobs properly, then there should be approximately twenty yards between each successive tee box, and as a result, everyone should have ample opportunities to hit a fair amount of greens in regulation.

On the other hand, if they fail to adhere to the proper GITCA spacing distances between tee boxes and simply put them all about ten yards apart, then the longest-hitting golfer in your group should win a vast majority of the time. If golfer A is thirty yards longer off the tee than golfer B with his driver distance, then in all likelihood, he is at least one to two clubs longer with his irons as well. Thus, golfer A has a built in forty- to fifty-yard advantage over golfer B before any tee shot has been struck. Due to this pertinent fact, it is imperative that the golf course architects construct varying tee boxes that fully acknowledge this distance differentiation, or it is never going to be a fair fight between the golfers.

Once everyone in your foursome sees the logic in playing from these varying tee boxes, the golf will be ultracompetitive, and there will no longer be any whining about handicaps. If the statistical averages play out, then nearly every golfer in your foursome should be hitting at least one-third of the greens in regulation. Pars and bogeys will be commonplace for most of the holes you play, and there might be some realistic opportunities for a birdie or two for every golfer in your foursome. Doesn't this sound much more enjoyable than some golfers being forced to play from tee boxes from which they have little chance to make bogey or better? Of course, since we all are not professionals and we don't have the same opportunities to practice as they do, we still will record our fair share of double bogeys or worse, which won't ruin our round anymore as they are simply recorded as zeroes on the scorecard. Once you can no longer achieve at least a bogey on the hole, you are encouraged to pick up your ball and simply calm your jets before the next hole. A simple zero is recorded on your scorecard, and you can get refocused as the steam rises from your ears as you watch the rest of your foursome joyfully complete the hole as you applaud their efforts on a hole that clearly got the best of you.

Warning: For safety's sake, please stand behind the people in your group teeing off from farther-back tees than you so that someone is not struck by a wayward tee shot.

Once the golfers from the farther-back tees have hit their tee shots, gleefully walk up to your properly designated tee box, which hopefully will be at least a few dozen yards or more in front of your farther-hitting playing companions. Please don't look upon this as a sign of your weakness but rather as a sign of your intelligence. It is okay to admit that you cannot hit the ball as far as your opponent, but that doesn't mean that you can't beat them or at least stay competitive. If everyone is playing from the properly assigned tee boxes, then realistically, everyone should be hitting approximately the same number of greens in regulation because everyone should be hitting roughly the same scoring iron into each green for their approach shot. Not only will hitting more greens in regulation greatly speed up play, just think how much less time everyone will spend searching in the woods for their ball now that they no longer need to swing from their heels in order to try and keep up with their much longer-hitting playing companions.

I envision club championships being contested for every level of play from the twelve different tee markers. You will then have twelve different champions who then can compete against the other eleven champions from their properly designated tee marker, with an eventual GITCA champion being declared for the year based on most points accrued in a tournament setting. Obviously two-, three-, and four-person GITCA competitions can also be contested with every member of the team tallying points for the team from their properly designated tee box. The possibilities are endless and will lead to much more spirited competitions for all participants. You can have local, regional, and national champions declared, with pros certifying which tee markers everyone should be playing from. Each club can also post the top 10 daily, weekly, monthly, and all-time GITCA tallies from each of the twelve different tee markers. Since everyone loves to see their name posted for others to admire, the more press you can doll out, the better. Now everyone can have goals to shoot for and should be content to become one of the best players at the club from their properly designated tee box.

GITCA GOLF Guideline Number 3: Our Supermodified Stableford Scoring System
Double bogey or worse = 0 points
Bogey = 1 point
Par = 2 points

Birdie = 4 points
Eagle = 8 points
Double eagle = 16 points
Hole-in-one = 20 points
Sasquatch = 24 points (A two on a par buster par 5)
Double ace = 40 points (A hole-in-one on a par buster par 3)
Quadruple ace = 80 points (A hole-in-one on a par buster par 4)

Yes, our system is similar to the original Stableford system, but our scoring system is much more exponentially rewarding for excellent play. By rewarding a point for a bogey, we have made it infinitely easier for golfers to add to their scoring totals on most holes. With our extremely generous scoring system, almost everyone is guaranteed to be in positive numbers for the round. Remember, we are trying to create the most positive atmosphere that we can out on the links with the possibility to record some truly epic scoring totals.

GITCA GOLF Rule Number 4: Everything Is Played as a Lateral Hazard

With GITCA GOLF, we eliminate the need for the golf rule book entirely by simply playing everything as a lateral hazard, no questions asked. Thus, if you hit a ball into the woods, a lake, or out of bounds, you simply drop a ball laterally somewhere near the point of entry so that you have a good lie for your next attempt with only a one-stroke penalty and no loss of distance. It is simple to remember in that we tell golfers to imagine that they somehow found their ball deep in the hazard, and they magically punched it out laterally to their now pristine lie from which they are allowed to lift, clean, and place their ball. Now I realize that golf purists are going crazy right now and probably discarding the GITCA GOLF system altogether, but that is okay because my intent is to make golf more streamlined and a much more positive experience for all recreational golfers. After hitting into a hazard and incurring a one-stroke penalty, achieving a par is usually out of the equation, but salvaging a bogey and a point is still very much in play.

Remember, we are not playing for big purses here, and our livelihood hopefully is not dependent on our golf game, so let's loosen the reins a little bit and create an environment that evokes as much positive energy as possible for every golfer who tees it up in a non-tournament setting. Our overall goal is to entice the golfing masses to enjoy themselves so much on the course that they can hardly wait to come back. We don't want golfers to have to try and decipher the two-hundred-year-old golf rules every time a new situation occurs. We would rather all our golfers abide by this one simple rule so that play is expedited and that their golf hole and day are not ruined by differing interpretations. Research has shown us if people feel overwhelmed or experience negative experiences too often, then they are likely to discontinue pursuing that experience entirely. With golf's mass exodus over the last two decades, this is exactly what we are trying to avoid entirely. So let's no longer try and cater to the old-school purists who insist on making the game as penal as possible but rather cater to the rest of the golfing public who simply wants to have as much fun as possible whenever they get the rare opportunity to tee it up.

GITCA GOLF Rule Number 5: Every Shot May Be Lifted, Cleaned, and Placed

Another grand deviation that we have made standard with GITCA GOLF and that is bound to make the golfing purists sick to their stomachs is the implementation of "rolling your golf ball as though you were playing in a scramble format." Now I realize that sticklers for golf's most ancient rule of "play the ball as it lies" are right now throwing up in their mouths, but again, I am not trying to appease these select few but rather the rest of the golfing population. Remember, the reason that everyone loves scrambles is that you always give yourself as pristine a lie as possible for every shot your group takes. It has also been my observation that most golfers in non-tournament play "roll their ball" in order to give themselves the best chance to pull off a decent shot attempt. Again, why make this game already harder than it already is? Why force yourself to hit the ball out of a divot or an unraked bunker because someone was too lazy to replace their divot or rake the bunker? So if you find yourself in an unraked bunker or a bunker that hasn't been raked in weeks, then by all means lift your ball so that you can rake the bunker before placing it so that you have a reasonable chance of playing a proper bunker shot. So our acceptable protocol for how much you can improve your lie is similar to the protocol when playing a scramble. Again, I know that this sounds like blasphemy to many, but please remember that we are making these rules universal for everyone who plays GITCA GOLF. Thus, there is no longer any accusations of cheating or that so-and-so improved his/her lie because we have given the green light for everyone to improve his/her lie and to smile as they are doing so, knowing that they have just greatly improved their chances to increase their overall point total. When golfers are playing Topgolf or hitting off a simulator or driving range mat, they always give themselves pristine lies. So why not grant recreational golfers these same near perfect lies for every shot out on the course?

Since these rules are allowed for everyone who tees it up under the GITCA GUIDELINES, everyone in your golfing group should take full advantage of this leeway so that everyone has the maximum opportunity to add to their point totals and overall enjoyment of their golfing experience. Certainly, improving your lie makes this game infinitely easier, and that is our point exactly. Since our opportunities to actually tee it up have become fewer and fewer in today's fast-paced society, why not make these limited opportunities as enjoyable as humanly possible? Remember, we are trying to make golf more appealing for the masses and make it as enjoyable as possible so people are inspired to repeat this positive experience as often as they can.

GITCA GOLF Rule Number 6: One Additional Roving Mulligan as a Lifeline

In addition to granting every participant a first tee mulligan, each golfer is given a "roving mulligan" that they are allowed to invoke only once on any of their remaining tee shots. Thus, each golfer gets an additional chance to bail himself/herself out on a hole in which the first attempt was rather feeble and left little chance to record positive numbers on this hole. Obviously, it is often wise to save this "lifeline" for when you really need it later in the round on a difficult hole, but sometimes, you have to utilize it earlier than you sometimes would like because you don't want to butcher a hole that usually allows you ample opportunities to post positive numbers on it.

GITCA GOLF Rule Number 7: One Par Buster Lifeline for Each Golfer

The other fun nuance that I have added to the GITCA GOLF guidelines to make everyone's golfing experience infinitely more enjoyable is a "lifeline" that I have dubbed a "par buster." A par buster increases the set par for a hole by one stroke on any hole chosen by the golfer. This is a very strategic part of GITCA GOLF as each golfer must determine which hole out on the course gives him/her the best chance to maximize their scoring potential for the round. Since the par buster increases the "par value" by one stroke on its designated hole, each golfer should determine which hole out on the course gives them the best chance to reach the green in regulation. For many golfers, this is often the shortest par 3 on the course, which now becomes a very score-able par 4, while for others, it might be that short par 5 hole that with the par buster utilized has now become an extremely short par 6 hole. Or it could be that drivable par 4 hole that with the par buster now becomes that extremely enticing drivable par 5 hole. Thus, by reaching any of these shorter holes in regulation or less than regulation, you are now putting for at least an eagle, which can greatly increase your chances for adding to your positive scoring output for the day. Securing an eagle or even rarer double eagle will quickly add eight to sixteen points to your tally, respectively, while a tap in birdie for four points is always going to bring a smile to your face as well. So determining which hole you are going to choose for your par buster is going to go a long way in deciding the overall point leader for the day. If you are able to play your designated par buster hole well, you are likely going to move up the leaderboard very quickly.

As a result of all these benefits, it greatly behooves every golfer to choose their par buster wisely because it can only be utilized once per round. The par buster must be declared prior to teeing off on that particular hole, so you better make sure you hit a good tee shot or that you have saved your "roving mulligan" to be used in conjunction with the extremely valuable par buster. Some golfers like to utilize their par buster on the very first hole, granted that they already have a "first tee mulligan." Others, however, choose to save their par buster for near the end of the round so that they can often leap-frog their combatants at the bitter end. Failure to record any points at all on your par buster hole is often going to leave you behind the eight ball for trying to procure more overall total points than your fellow competitors, so please choose this "lifeline" wisely.

GITCA GOLF Rule Number 8: A Putt May Be Given if Majority of Golfers Agree upon It

Another rule that is a standard for GITCA GOLF and that is already a mainstay in just about every nontournament foursome is the utilization of the "gimme putt." This giving of short putts has been utilized by most golfing groups since the dawn of the sport, but it certainly has no place in tournament golf where the hole is played out until the ball finds its way to the bottom of the cup. With GITCA GOLF, we have determined that a putt is given when a majority of the other golfers in the group determine it to be so. Thus, if you are playing in a typical foursome, two of the other three golfers must call your putt good for it to be given. If only one other golfer declares the putt good, then you must putt it out and hope the golf gods are smiling on you! We have found that using our jury system is quite fair and that what goes around comes around and that karma will usually rear its ugly head at some point later in the round. Another rule that we have is that all putts for birdie or better must be made no matter how short the putt might actually be. Our reasoning is that for a great scoring hole to be authenticated, the often given putts must now be made in order to validate the legitimacy of your awesome hole.

So there you have the simple eight rules of GITCA GOLF:

1. FIRST TEE MULLIGAN
2. MUST TEE OFF FROM YOUR PROPERLY DESIGNATED TEE BOX
3. OUR SUPER MODIFIED STABELFORD SCORING SYSTEM
4. WINTER RULES INVOKED ANYWHERE ON THE COURSE YEAR ROUND (Lift, clean, and place)
5. EVERYTHING played as a lateral hazard
6. ONE ROVING MULLIGAN to be used on any *one* of your remaining *tee shots*
7. ONE PAR BUSTER that must be declared *prior* to teeing off on that particular hole
8. MAJORITY RULES ON GIMME PUTTS

GITCA GOLF Allows Uniformity for Recreational Play

If every recreational golfer would adopt these simple eight rules for a round or two with their usual foursome, then I guarantee that every golfer would soon learn to love all the benefits of adapting to the GITCA GOLF format forevermore. By simply following the aforementioned rules, everyone is going to have a much faster and enjoyable time out on the links. There will no longer be any ambiguity about what is the proper protocol out on the course. It will not take long for everyone to determine their proper tee box as long as everyone is truly honest with themselves about their true average distances. We know that most golfers greatly overestimate their abilities, but after a few rounds of GITCA GOLF, the scoring discrepancies will exemplify which golfers are playing from their correct tee boxes and those who are not. If there is a golfer in your group who is barely hitting any of the greens in regulation, then clearly that golfer needs to move up at least one set of tee boxes, if not two. Likewise, if there is a golfer among your foursome who has so much power that he is a making a mockery of the course with his/her length, then perhaps that golfer should be strongly encouraged to move back at least one tee box. Remember, the idea of GITCA GOLF is for the competition to be as fair as possible for every single person who tees it up in your group. This can only occur if indeed everyone is playing from the appropriate tee boxes for their true golfing ability.

Although the longest hitter in your group may call foul because he/she has to play from farther back than the rest of the group, he/she will readily see that when everyone hits a decent drive, similar scoring irons will be hit for everyone's approach shot. Even though this long knocker doesn't receive any strokes from the other golfers, he/she no longer has to give anyone any strokes, and his/her ego is likely to be stroked from being the longest hitter among the group. If the golf course superintendent has properly spaced the varying tee markers, then everyone in your group should be hitting comparable scoring irons into most greens. As a result, everyone in your group should be hitting approximately the same number of greens in regulation. Some days will be better and worse than others, of course, but we have found that when everyone is playing from their proper tee boxes that on average most golfers in your group will be hitting at least one-third of the greens in regulation.

If everyone in your group is in fact playing from the correct tee boxes and invoking all the GITCA rules and "lifelines," then you all should be playing at a much brisker pace than you are accustomed to, and you all should be having infinitely more fun than you ever thought possible out on the links. Since there are only positive numbers to tally, scoring is simple and infinitely easier for everyone to keep track of. When you are abundantly aware of where each golfer is in the pecking order, it goes a long way in determining who is likely to be given the short putts or not. It also can help you properly determine when best to utilize the all-important lifelines.

Strategy is a huge part of GITCA GOLF as you must surmise when best to utilize your par buster as well as your "roving mulligan." Once golfers get the hang of playing under the GITCA format, they will try and determine early on in the round which is the best hole to properly utilize their par buster. As a result, they will want to try and save their roving mulligan in order to maximize their scoring chances on the hole that they have proclaimed their par buster on. Even if you don't need to pull out your roving mulligan on your declared par buster hole, it is always nice to have that lifeline in your back pocket. Since the par buster has just increased by one the par value on a hole, you should have a relatively good chance to make at least a par or better on this extremely important hole. In other words, you don't want to blow your best scoring opportunity of the day with a horrendous tee shot, so it is always nice to have that roving mulligan to cash in on in the rare instance when you hit a bad tee shot on your par buster hole. I have witnessed many "par buster eagles" and have even witnessed a few "par buster double eagles," so you had better make the most of this golden opportunity since you only get one chance per round to cash in on it.

I have also noticed that once golfers begin to fully embrace the scoring mentality of GITCA GOLF, they seem to become much smarter golfers almost overnight. Instead of shooting at every sucker pin placement, GITCA golfers readily see the beauty of a par and its extremely valuable two points. When golfers do get in big trouble on a hole, they readily see the beauty of making a great bogey save and its subsequent point to add to their overall tally. As a result of this paradigm shift, most GITCA GOLFERS are trying much less brazen shots, and the result is far less double and triple bogeys on the scorecard and far better opportunities to add to their GITCA scoring tallies.

Now I know that there are a lot of you out there (about 20 percent of all golfers) who have been so ingrained to only play with handicaps that you will be unsure of how many strokes to give or receive with GITCA GOLF. The simple answer is *zero*! Playing from your properly designated tee box becomes the great equalizer so that handicaps have now been negated. As long as each person in your foursome tees off from their properly designated tee marker, then there is no longer a need to give or receive any strokes whatsoever. You also no longer need to worry about the legitimacy of anyone's stated handicap because with GITCA GOLF, handicaps never come into play. Every single time you tee it up, you start with zero points, and your score can only improve from there. For every single hole that you manage to score a bogey or better on a hole, your point total is increased, and your point total can never be diminished. Every golfer in your group starts the day with zero points, and each hole then becomes a subsequent challenge for each golfer to pad their overall point total. Even if you struggle with a certain hole and record a double or triple bogey or worse, points can never be subtracted from your overall total.

Doesn't this sound like a heck of a lot more fun than constantly trying to be perfect for all eighteen holes of your round or having to continually defend yourself about accusations about your stated handicap? Golf becomes a much more positive experience for everyone as everyone starts the day with an equal opportunity to accumulate the most points and be declared the champion for the day. You no longer have to worry about playing to your handicap as you simply focus in on accumulating as many points as possible in relation to everyone else in your group. If you are having one of those special days when you are hitting nearly every fairway and green in regulation, then you can simply smile from ear to ear as you go about setting a personal record-breaking GITCA point total that you will be able to cherish forevermore. On the other extreme, if you are having one of those days when you can't seem to do anything right and are struggling mightily on the majority of the holes you play, you can often salvage a little bit of respectability if you properly utilize your par buster and add a bunch of points to your running total. I personally have witnessed several golfers who were struggling mightily vault to the lead with a quick "par buster eagle" and leave the other golfers wondering how they just got lapped by a once struggling golfer. In my own personal best success story, I once managed to make a walk-off hole-in-one to defeat my archrival with my last shot of the day. Of course, this happened on a par 3 course, but that did not dampen my enthusiasm one iota. I jokingly told him of my intentions, as this was the only way that I was going to come out victorious. So when the ball left my club and headed straight for the pin and dropped into the bottom of the cup, it was one of my all-time favorite sporting highlights.

In our fast-paced let's-get-it-done-yesterday culture, fewer and fewer people are willing to give up an entire day to play golf. As a result, more and more golfers are resorting to play a "quick nine" holes so that they can hurry back home or return to the office before too many people miss them. I know that this breaks with the long-standing tradition of playing the customary eighteen holes, but we must break the mold if golf is going to survive and eventually thrive once again. Golfers need to be encouraged to get out for a quick nine holes, and the golf courses need to monitor their pace of play so that golfers can get their nine holes in less than two hours and be back to where they are needed before all hell breaks loose. All golfers should be able to play nine holes in less than two hours, or they should be reprimanded and forced to learn how to play expediently or to let faster golfers play through. There is nothing worse than having to wait behind extremely slow golfers whose pace of play ruins the golfing experience for everyone unfortunate enough to have to follow them.

If my buddies and I go to a course that does not properly enforce the speed of play, then you can rest assured that we will not be returning to that course any time soon. In most instances of slow play, nearly all the golfers in the group are playing from tee boxes that are way too difficult for them, and as a result, they are taking way too long to finish each hole. As a result, not only are they going to suffer, but everyone else in their foursome and everyone else who is forced to play behind them must suffer as well. In addition, they are probably spending way too much time trying to figure out all the intricacies of the handicap system and who gets strokes on each particular hole.

The simple answer to alleviating all the aforementioned heartache is for everyone to simply embrace the simple guidelines set forth by GITCA GOLF. By making GITCA GOLF the universal norm for all recreational golfers, the pace of play at every course in America will be vastly improved. No more heroes trying to prove themselves by teeing off from tee boxes that they don't have the distance capabilities to handle. I feel that by streamlining the recreational rules of golf down to eight easy rules to follow and by allowing a few more liberties, GITCA GOLF allows everyone to feel less intimidated about following all the complex intricacies involved with traditional golf. Not only will the pace of play encourage more golfers to play more often, by allowing a few more liberties, GITCA GOLF allows for a much higher success rate, which also will entice many more golfers to return to the links as often as possible. By making the game infinitely more fun for all their participants, every golf course in America should witness a huge influx in the number of rounds played on an annual basis.

What have been the hidden benefits you have found since switching to this scoring system?

1. Stress has been reduced greatly. I now feel very relaxed out on the golf course.
2. No one has to take out a calculator to tally their and everyone else's scoring totals.
3. Matches are much more competitive and enjoyable from beginning to end.
4. You can still have a bad hole or two and still win the title and have a memorable day.
5. Golfers who are now finally playing from the proper tees are enjoying the game a heck of a lot more and are far exceeding their expectations with their scores.
6. Golfers are spending a lot more time on the putting and chipping green, knowing that getting up and down is tantamount to scoring with this system.
7. Golfers are starting to play a lot smarter and shooting for the middle of the greens and laying up on par 5s and gladly taking their two points for attaining par.
8. Golfers are scoring better because they no longer have to swing out of their shoes in order to reach most greens in regulation now that they are playing from the proper tee boxes.
9. Golfers no longer fear playing certain holes on courses, for they realize that the entire round is not going to be ruined by one or two diabolical holes.
10. End of the rounds are now exhilarating rather than terrifying because one cannot lose points and blow leads, but opponents can catch them with some great golf play.

11. A nine-hole match with this scoring system is just as enjoyable as an eighteen-hole match.
12. Team competitions are a blast, especially when you switch partners every six holes.
13. Players of varying abilities can all compete with one another, assuming everyone is teeing off from their properly designated tee boxes.

How Does GITCA Format Speed Up Play Dramatically?

1. Playing from your correct tee boxes allows you to hit many more greens in regulation and keeps you swinging within yourself.
2. As soon as you have exceeded a bogey on a hole, you are encouraged to pick up.
3. You are prompted to spend no more than *one* minute searching for a lost ball.
4. Everything is played as a lateral hazard with a one-stroke penalty.
5. Having a first tee and an additional roving mulligan allows you two chances at a redo during the round, so the pace of play is expedited due to the elimination of two of your poorer tee shots.
6. Gimmes greatly reduce the time spent agonizing over short putts.
7. No need to dillydally over varying rule interpretations since everything is played as a lateral hazard and the eight simple-to-follow rules eliminate controversy.
8. Allowing golfers to roll the ball eliminates many of the errant shots that would have resulted from having to play the ball from a divot or some other hazardous lie.
9. There are no handicaps to tabulate, so no one has to try and figure out how many strokes to give and receive, and the running GITCA scores are easy to keep track of.

10. Once a golfer is out of the hole, they can remove the flagstick and rake bunkers while other golfers finish the hole expeditiously.

Different Ways to Play GITCA GOLF

PLAYING ALONE: Tally a GITCA score for however many holes you get in that day. Keep track of your eighteen-hole GITCA scores so that you can monitor your progress and record personal bests. If you only have time for nine holes or even six holes, tabulate your score so that you have a tally to try and beat your next time out.

PLAYING GITCA GOLF AS A TWOSOME: You can play an eighteen-hole match with one set of lifelines for the eighteen holes, or you can break the match down into two separate nine-hole matches with a new set of lifelines for each nine-hole contest. Naturally, your scoring totals will likely be increased with new lifelines for each nine-hole match, but the rules are the same for both parties. You can have a front nine winner, a back nine winner, and an overall match winner.

PLAYING GITCA GOLF AS A THREESOME: Every golfer for himself/herself following the same guidelines as a two-person match. You can have a front nine champion, a back nine champion, and an overall GITCA point total champion. It is possible to have three different champions crowned, which makes everyone a winner.

PLAYING GITCA GOLF AS A FOURSOME:

1. You can play as individuals with the top golfer declared the winner for each nine-hole match as well as the golfer who accumulates the most points on the day be declared the gold medal winner.
2. Or you can play two-person teams for each nine-hole match, or you can have three different six-hole matches where everyone gets to take turns playing with each other golfer. In the six-hole matches, every golfer gets an opening tee shot mulligan on the first hole of the day, but no roving mulligans. However, in order to further add to the scoring opportunities for each golfer and each team, a par buster

is granted to each golfer during each six-hole rotation. In each of the team formats, the GITCA point totals for each team are simply added together for each hole. For instance, if both golfers on the first team record pars on the first hole, then their team total for that hole is four points. If both golfers on the second team record bogeys on the first hole, then their team total is two points, and they obviously are trailing by two points through the first hole. The running score is kept for each team until the allotted holes are finished. Matches may end in ties, or extra holes can be played until the tie is broken.

HOLE NUMBER 8

Learn to Become a Master of Your Domain

Based on the GITCA guidelines, find the proper tee box for your game, and try and become the best player that you can be from those tee markers. No longer be bullied into playing from any other tee box. Hold firm in your GITCA convictions and play from those tee markers that allot you to hit a high percentage of greens in regulation. Once you get adjusted to attacking the greens with short irons, it won't be long before you are very competitive with every other golfer in your foursome, assuming they too are strictly adhering to the GITCA guidelines. In my usual foursome, our much longer hitter tees off from the blue tees, while the rest of us play from the white tees, and the matches are always extremely competitive. Even though he is significantly longer than us, if the course management team have properly spaced the distances between the differing tee markers, no one feels as though they are at a disadvantage. No strokes are ever given, and the best golfer on that particular day is crowned champion. If we all tried to play from the same tee markers, the odds would be greatly stacked in his favor, and the competitive balance would be lost.

It is my belief that once everyone gets comfortable playing from their proper GITCA tee markers, the competition should be competitive throughout most of the round no matter the disparity in skill level and carry distance. A golfer who properly finds his tee marker niche should feel quite comfortable being competitive against those golfers who carry the ball much farther than he/she does, assuming everyone is being honest with themselves and their true abilities. Once golfers around the world start properly adhering to the GITCA tee box designations, golfers of all abilities will have competitive matches and are likely to play much faster than they ever dreamed possible. Far more greens will be hit in regulation as everyone will have realistic distances to traverse for their approach shots. By playing from more realistic distances, golfers everywhere should feel far less intimidated about completing the task at hand. With every golfer feeling confident in their capabilities, the competition should be fierce and allow for many excellent scores to be posted. Golfers of all ages and abilities will now have fun no matter whom they get paired up with.

The beauty of GITCA GOLF is that it allows you to acknowledge that you are a far better golfer than you ever gave yourself credit for when you tried to compete from tee markers that were way beyond your capabilities. No longer will you feel as though you must hit career tee and approach shots just to have a slight chance of hitting a few of the greens in regulation. By once and for all admitting your proper skill level, you can then learn to master your God-given abilities so that you can be the best that you can be given your distance limitations. If everyone is on board and adhering to their proper designation, then you all should have the time of your lives every time you hit the links.

Biggest Problem Facing Both Golf and Tennis: Ever-Increasing Aging Population

Being a tennis instructor, at least once a week, someone approaches me and tells me that they are quitting tennis for good. When I ask them, "Why in the world would you quit playing a game you have played for years and that has allowed you to develop many wonderful friendships and overall has brought you so much joy?" Their curse retort is "Because I can't win anymore and the other competitors make it so that it is not any fun anymore." Of course, I know that this is often a gross exaggeration and that they do in fact win some of their matches, but oftentimes not nearly as often as they had in the past and obviously not enough to satisfy their often fragile self-esteem. In addition, I have seen firsthand just how downright awful and ugly the competition can be. There are numerous accusations of cheating and berating going on among opponents and teammates that can turn off anyone who simply wanted to go out and "have fun."

When I commiserate my story with golf instructors, they tell me that many golfers quit the game because they can no longer hit the ball as far or as straight as they once did and that many golfers are constantly bombarded by competitors questioning the validity of their handicap. This is a real problem facing both of these wonderful recreational sports as the baby boomers continue to age and their skill levels begin to diminish from what they once were, and people are getting downright nasty during these recreational activities. As our bodies begin to slow down, we obviously can't compete in these sports as previously accustomed. Over the years, we have obviously accumulated great wisdom on how to be proficient at these endeavors, but unfortunately, Mother Nature will no longer allow us to flourish as we once had. In both of these sports, a lack of power and distance covered prevents us from competing equally with competitors who are in their prime. Obviously, this is a blow to anyone's self-esteem as we are no longer able to perform tasks that once came so easily for us. So not only is this a blow to our self-esteem, we now are having more and more people question our integrity and honesty. These recreational pursuits that used to bring us so much joy are now turning into stress-inducing activities that are becoming less and less appealing to us.

The obvious answer, although no one wants to hear it, is to give yourself more opportunities to succeed with the regularity that you are accustomed to and simply remove yourself from those competitors who are taking the joy out of the game you used to love. In tennis, this often entails moving down a rating level or two or by signing up for a "senior league" so that you no longer have to compete against those much younger players. This seems like a highly logical and natural solution, but unfortunately, our damn egos intervene and oftentimes prevent us from accepting this as a viable option. In golf, we see the same problem every single day taking place on every golf course ever built: golfers refusing to accept the fact that their skills have deteriorated to the point that they can no longer be competitive from the tee boxes that they have played from for the last thirty years. God loves these competitors in both sports as their human spirit will never allow them to give up on themselves and their oftentimes grandiose expectations that they have for themselves.

The problem lies in the fact that it is too often a death blow to their self-esteem and that they would rather quit playing altogether rather than having to move down a level in tennis or up a tee box or two in golf. They feel that it would be an utter embarrassment to admit to their friends and family that their skills have diminished to a level that they can no longer be as competitive as they once were. Quitting altogether or playing up injuries is often much easier for their psyche to handle than admitting that it is time to move down a peg or two on the competitive ladder. Thus, rather than swallowing their pride and allowing themselves opportunities to once again be competitive, people across the board in both sports often relegate themselves to quitting the sport that brought them so much joy for so many years. Golf and tennis will be hard-pressed to stay relevant if we allow this trend to continue. With the baby boomers continuing to get up there in age, we must do everything that we can to make these sports much more enjoyable for participants in every age group and demographic. Both golf and tennis can and should be played with great joy by most participants throughout their entire lives.

I am happy to say that tennis has readily identified this grandiose problem and has offered alternative ways to play the game such as "pop tennis," platform tennis, and pickle ball to keep the passion for their sport alive. What these solutions do is offer ways for our ever-aging population to stay competitive with the younger generations by doing away with the emphasis on the overhand serve. In all these games, a player only gets one serve attempt. As a result, the serve is not nearly the dominant weapon that it is in regular tennis in which you get two service attempts. Subsequently, the competition is kept at a much more even keel, and the points last much longer and are often far more engaging. These alternative ways of playing are growing by leaps and bounds among the tennis community, and many people are rekindling their passion by once again being competitive with their peers. Initially, everyone laughed at these alternative ways of playing as "old people's tennis" or deemed them as only being appropriate for young children. Once initiated, however, people have been drawn in by just how much longer and more competitive the points and the games are for all participants.

I truly believe that regular tennis should take heed of the success of these alternative ways of playing and should think about incorporating some of these methods into their own way of playing so that the sport can continue to grow and thrive for all age groups. One simple solution would be to outlaw second serves in order to make the serve less of a weapon and allow the points to be longer and more engaging. Of course, many traditionalists would initially rebuke this novel idea, but I believe that almost everyone would eventually see the great merit in allowing the game to be played more competitively across the varying age brackets. Another simple solution would be to go back to playing with less dynamic rackets or with rally balls that allow for longer and more strategic point play. Returning to less space-age material gives everyone more time to recover, and the points would naturally be longer and involve more finesse and strategy. Whatever solutions the powers that be come up with, the clientele must be reinvigorated to stay competitive for as long as humanly possible, and everyone should be having the time of their lives. The governing bodies can no longer sit idly by and assume that the status quo will allow the game to grow and flourish. Alternative solutions must be looked into so that tennis players across the board are excited to play for the duration of their lifetime.

The golf governing bodies better wake up as well before they lose entire generations of golfers. Alternative ways of playing the game must be looked into so that we can engage all the younger generations while reengaging the aging part of our population. I truly believe that looking at GITCA GOLF as a viable way to play golf can rekindle that spark that has been lagging among the golf community. It is a far easier way for all golfers to play and have many more opportunities for sustained success. As a result, the embarrassment factor is going to be greatly reduced as everyone is going to tee off from tee markers that allow them great opportunities to achieve contentment with themselves and playing the game of golf. No longer will tee boxes be labeled as "ladies tees" or "kids tees" or "old people's tees." Rather, everyone will move to their correctly designated tee box based solely on statistical analysis. By being forced to play from certain tee boxes based on mathematical probability rather than simply one's age or gender, everyone will soon see the beauty of returning the competitive balance and fairness to the game. By properly implementing the user-friendly GITCA GOLF guidelines, all golfers will find themselves having far more opportunities for success out on the links, and their honesty and integrity will never be questioned again. The competitive balance will be restored, and every golfer should be competitive with everyone else in their foursome. Many more greens in regulation will be recorded, and everyone should thrive under the GITCA GOLF modified Stableford scoring system. No longer will participants have to try and play under conditions that offer them few opportunities for success.

Although many of the golfing traditionalists might initially rebuke many of the liberties granted in GITCA GOLF, once they see the popularity of golf rise due to the GITCA GOLF protocols, I am confident that they will quickly get on board. Both tennis and golf must think outside the box if they hope to see their sports continue to grow and thrive for many years to come.

The Main Goal of GITCA GOLF: For You to Have the Same Scoring Iron in Your Hand for Your Approach Shots as the Pros

Professional golfer Chez Reavie recently recorded a PGA record 3 eagle hole-outs during a single round at the 2019 Sony Open in Hawaii. All these hole-outs came on par 4s in which Mr. Reavie hit nothing longer than a 9 iron for all these slam dunks. The course they were playing only measures just over 7,000 yards, so the majority of the approach shots hit by the professionals for their approach shots were taken with an 8 iron or less. In fact, following their bombing tee shots, most of the approach shots are similar in length to those distances found on your local par 3 course. Certainly, the pro greens have far more treacherous hazards to overcome than your local par 3 course, but I guarantee that their greens roll much truer than your local muni.

Go look at the scorecard of the course that you play most frequently. If the best golfers in the world teed it up from the farthest-back tee boxes at your course, what iron would they have in their hands for a majority of their approach shots? At my preferred golfing venue, *Glenview Golf Course*, which measures just over 7,000 yards from the tips, the longest-hitting pros would hit nothing more than an 8 iron for most of their approach shots. In other words, even from the tips, the best players in the world would make a mockery of your home course as they would be attacking each green with their favorite scoring irons. Now go back to your scorecard and determine which tee boxes you would have to play from that would allot you the same short scoring iron in your hand for a majority of your approach shots. In my case, I would have to move up from my usual white tee markers to the much more distance-friendly gold tee markers. Doing so would knock 600 yards off the distance that I would have to contend with, and as a result, I would have an 8 iron or less for almost all my approach shots. Most golfers would initially struggle playing from these much shorter distances because they are not used to attacking these same familiar greens with much shorter irons. However, once they get acclimated to hitting these much shorter irons, their scores should improve dramatically. Now I am not promising that you are likely to hole out three approach shots over the course of your entire golfing career, but in all likelihood, you will hit far more greens in regulation playing from distances that allow you to attack most greens with short scoring irons.

Provided that I have played a ton of par 3 and executive courses in my golfing career, I am quite accurate in hitting most greens when left with 130 yards or less for my approach shots. Once I got used to playing my familiar digs from these much shorter distances, I would realize that I would no longer have to hit driver on every par 4 and par 5. Similar to the pros, I would be able to attack many of these now much shorter holes with my far-more-accurate hybrids off the tee. Finding more fairways while still leaving myself with shorter irons into all these greens should lead to much better scoring opportunities on nearly every hole. As a result of hitting far more greens in regulation, I will have much more golden scoring opportunities throughout the majority of my round. Naturally, my score will be much improved over my usual tally, and this will allow me to play golf much more efficiently. If everyone in my foursome also moves up from their usual tee box, then we all will be playing much more efficiently and having more fun than we ever thought possible. We may even realize that we are all much better golfers than we ever gave ourselves credit for.

    Now most of you are scoffing at my premise of moving up a tee box from where you normally play, but I can assure you that not a single tour player has ever complained about a course being too short. Many of the top touring professionals are clearly making a mockery out of most of the courses on tour, but I have yet to hear one of them say that the course was too short or simply too easy. Most of them gladly record scores in the sixties and thank their lucky stars that they are fortunate enough to make a living playing a game that they love. The majority of them work on their craft every single day, and they play as often as they can for fear that they someday might lose their amazing length and accuracy. Once the day finally comes when they no longer can compete with the majority of the other touring professionals, a few fortunate pros are old enough and still good enough to compete on the *Champions Tour*. Fortunately for them, this tour plays from what most courses would consider their black tees. Even though many of these top pros can no longer keep up with the length of the young hotshots out on the regular tour, playing on the "older guys tour" allows them to still have nothing more than an 8 iron or less for a majority of their approach shots. Since most of the guys on the "older tour" have played golf for most of their lives, they are going to eat up a majority of these courses with scoring irons in their hands on almost every hole. In fact, with their lifetime accumulation of golfing knowledge, most of these older gentlemen are wizards with short irons in their hands. The winning score for a majority of these tournaments is almost always double digit under par, and these tournaments are usually concluded after three rounds.

The amazing talent out on the LPGA is producing double-digit under par scoring totals for a majority of their three-round tournaments as well, and no one is complaining that most of these tournaments are played from what equates to most golf courses' blue tee markers. The amazing consistency and fluidity of these top women players are incredible to watch, and the talent seems to keep getting better every year. Yet once again, I never hear any of them complain that a course was too short or the setup was too easy. The top players almost always break 70, and they seem to love every single second of it.

So if the top professional golfers in the world aren't complaining about having nothing more than an 8 iron for a majority of their approach shots, why in the world would the "average Joe golfer" ever object to playing golf from distances that leave him/her with an 8 iron or less for most of his/her approach shots? Aside from habit and being told that these are the tee markers that we should be teeing off from, it is our damn egos that prevent us from having the same crack at a good score that the professionals are allotted on nearly every hole. I've got some startling news for you and almost every other golfer out there, "You have been lied to for years by the golfing establishment!" Playing from the tee markers that you currently do is a disservice to you, your golfing foursome, and everyone else out on most golf courses. 99 percent of golfers tee off from at *least* one set of tee markers too far back! As a result, the pace of play is atrocious, and the scores are even more grotesque. Playing from tee markers that have been deemed to be appropriate for our ability, we are often left with a 5 iron or more for a majority of our approach shots. The great dispersion afforded by these longer and less lofted clubs leads to far fewer greens hit in regulation and infinitely higher scores on most holes. In fact, most golfers erroneously play from tee markers that allow them to hit fewer than 20 percent of the greens in regulation. Some golfers play from tee markers in which they would have to hit a career drive and a career approach shot just to get close to the green in regulation. You satiate your ego on the first tee by improperly declaring that you can handle the course from this faraway tee box.

Unfortunately, it does not take long before you figure out that you are in for a long and nonprosperous day. It is this ego-driven line of thinking that is simply setting you and everyone else in your foursome up for an unfulfilling day out on the links.

Why not once and for all swallow your pride and tee off from tee markers that allow you the same juicy scoring opportunities that the professionals afford themselves? Why would it be so horrible to shoot better scores than you ever dreamed possible? Aren't you tired of looking for your ball in the woods or trying to fish it out of yet another pond? How much more enjoyable would golf be if you and your playing companions were playing from the fairway and finding the green in regulation most of the time? How much quicker would you and your foursome be getting around the links if you all were playing much more efficiently? Just think how nice it would be to play golf if everyone else swallowed their pride and was playing much more efficiently as well. If you are ready to play golf much more efficiently and shoot far better scores, then you are ready to get yourself and your foursome on board with the GITCA GOLF guidelines.

It Is a Good Thing That the US Open Is Only Held One Week a Year

At the 2018 US Open at Shinnecock, Jordan Spieth, Tiger Woods, Rory McIlroy, and Jason Day shot a combined 41 over par, and all missed the cut. These are four of the greatest ball-strikers who have ever played, and they were playing on a course that employed over two hundred greens keepers to make certain that the course was in immaculate shape. In spite of all their diligent work to keep these greens pristine, many of the pros complained that the greens were far too bumpy. I invite these unappreciative pros to come play some rounds down at the local muni with me and see how true their ball rolls on these largely unkempt greens. Now certainly wind played a big factor in producing such high scores, and the fact that the course was now stretched out by over five hundred yards since the US Open had last been played there in 2004 certainly hindered the scoring opportunities. But without a doubt, the biggest factor between the

US Open and much of the rest of the PGA Tour schedule is the brutality of the rough. As a result of perhaps all these factors, the cut line was at plus 8 for the championship while it is usually well under par for most of the rest of the golf season. So the scores on average were at least eight strokes worse than usual and led to countless frustration for the majority of the field. The USGA did not see any harm in all this as they proudly proclaimed, "These high scores made it once again feel like a US Open."

I personally love watching the greatest golfers in the world struggle once a year as most of us amateurs do on a regular basis. In order to give the greatest golfers on the planet a taste of what most of us amateurs feel like nearly every time we tee them up, I suggest that the USGA stretch the tee boxes out another seven hundred or eight hundred yards. I wonder just how high the scores would have been had the USGA done that for the US Open. I'm quite certain that the average score would have been at least five strokes higher. Needless to say, the USGA would have received much more criticism from its critics if the average score was in the mid 80s. For golfers who are used to shooting scores around par or better, posting a score in the mid 80s is a hard pill for anyone to swallow. It can wreck your self-esteem while causing many to question their worthiness as a golfing professional.

Certain golfing Hall of Famer Phil Mickelson recently just lambasted the 2018 Ryder Cup venue as being "almost unplayable" with its extremely tight fairways and overgrown rough. Here is how Phil really felt: "The fact is they had brutal rough, almost unplayable. And it's not the way I play. I don't play like that. And I'm 48, I'm not going play tournaments with rough like that anymore, it's a waste of my time. I'm going to play courses that are playable and that I can play aggressive, attacking, making a lot of birdies, style of golf I like to play" (*Golf Digest*, October 2018).

Other than the US Open where high scores are expected, nearly every other course on the PGA schedule is expected to have such pristine and fair conditions that the winning score almost always comes in at least double digit under par for the tournament. Fifty-one weeks of the year is devoted to ensuring that the greens, fairway, and sand traps are in near perfect condition and the height of the rough is kept to a manageable length for the duration of the tournament. The weather forecast is almost always in the mid 70s, and the ball flight conditions are usually optimal. In addition, most of the courses play less than 7,400 yards, which is much more manageable for these professionals to combat than it is us rank amateurs trying to navigate our way around our local courses from distances between 6,000 and 6,800 yards. Given the disparity between just how far the pros hit each club compared to us, the pros should have to contend with courses that measure nearly 8,500 yards on a weekly basis if we truly want to compare apples to apples. Since most courses on tour are stretched out as far as they can possibly go for the most part, the only viable solution is for all of us amateurs to swallow our pride and move up at least one tee box from where we normally do.

If all amateurs agree to move up one tee box and the golf course management team has properly done their homework and spaced twenty to thirty yards between each tee box, then each of us will now face the demons of our course from at least four hundred yards less than we normally would. This should translate into many more good looks at par and the occasional birdie and should greatly increase the pace of play and overall jovialness of most foursomes. Pars and bogeys should now be the norm, rather than the dreadful bogey golf and worse that now make up the majority of the scores posted on each hole by you and your foursome. No longer accept setting yourself up for failure every time you hit the links. Maybe once a year, play from the tee boxes that you currently do, but the rest of the year, move up so that you can experience much better scores and have a hell of a lot better time with those closest to you.

Most Golf Courses Set Their Clientele Up for Failure

Nearly every championship-length golf course sets the majority of their clientele up for failure prior to any shots being taken. Most of these courses are intent on making the design of their course so stifling that even the most ardent amateur golfers would find it difficult to break par a majority of the time. Most clubs take great pride in this fact, and many of them boast that their course is one of the most difficult to score on in the country. Many of them keep their greens cut so low that they are lightning fast and run at least 12 on the stimpmeter. Running the greens this fast is going to make it very difficult to hold the green on most approach shots and is certain to create havoc when putting. Although the greens themselves may run very true, finding the putting surface with one's approach shot is going to be difficult for anyone who cannot produce high spin rate with their approach shots. In addition, many courses have cut down a good percentage of their trees in order that the rough can grow so thick that it is usually impossible to hit the ball cleanly out of. Thus, any wayward shot that finds the rough is almost guaranteeing a bogey or more and will lead to very high scores and slow play for all patrons.

The main mistake the majority of these clubs do to slow down play and ensure high scores for most of their patrons is to promote tee boxes which few golfers have opportunities to score well from. Again this promotes extremely high scores and extremely long days for all but a few of the best golfers. "Oh well," many of the golfers say, "our course is so hard no one except the pros can score well on it. Besides, my handicap will travel well when I go play less severe golfing treks." So I guess misery loves company, and everyone simply throws a handicap on their score, and many of them seem to accept this miserable fate for many years. Eventually, after many frustrating years out on the links, most golfers break down and find other more enjoyable ways to spend their golden years. As a result, most foursomes are disbanded, and seeing their beloved friends regularly becomes almost nonexistent. I blame the egos of most of these course management teams for the ruination of many golfing rounds and ultimately for the decay of most friendships.

The Number 1 Golfer in the World Recently Stated That He Spends 80 Percent of His Practice Time on His Wedge Game

Now you would think that the top-ranked golfer in the world would spend the majority of the time working out the kinks with his driver. But as we all can clearly see, Dustin Johnson might be one of the most consistent long drivers of the golf ball ever. As a result, he spends the majority of his practice time working on the different nuances of his wedge game. DJ knows that if he is going to compete for the title, he better have his "A" wedge game clicking on all cylinders. On most of the par 4s that he plays on tour, DJ is most likely going to be hitting some sort of wedge shot for a majority of his approach shots. If he is able to get most of his wedge shots within a fifteen-foot radius of the hole, then DJ knows that he has a great chance to be near the top of the leaderboard that week.

So clearly, the number 1 golfer on the planet realizes the importance of continually honing his short scoring irons, but how many amateurs really devote any reasonable amount of time at all to their scoring clubs? Certainly, most amateurs devote a majority of their time out on the range working on driving the ball as far as they can muster. Unfortunately, the scoring irons are only used to warm up their swings before they let the big dog out to eat. Provided that most golfers play from distances that allot them few opportunities to reach the putting surface in regulation with their scoring irons, once again, shots from 140 yards and in are rarely taken and honed. My buddies and I have discovered that the best way to practice our shots from 140 yards and in is to play par 3 and executive courses as often as possible. This allows us to play these shots in a competitive environment, and by playing enough of these shots, we have gotten quite proficient at them. This has paid off handsomely as we now normally shoot great scores while playing these shorter courses. In addition, since we follow the GITCA GOLF doctrines to a tee, we are left with approach shots from 140 yards and in on most of the holes we play on regulation courses. Since we have practiced honing these shots so often, we are now hitting a ton of the greens that we play in regulation with our scoring irons. As a result, our GITCA scores are usually excellent no matter what course we decide to play on that particular day. We have all amazed even ourselves by our now stellar play with our scoring irons.

People who play with us for the first time are often dumbfounded by how accurate we often are from 140 yards and in. Their only defense response is that we have made the game too easy by moving up to the proposed GITCA tee markers and that we are hitting short scoring irons for most of our approach shots. Our response is that we are simply trying to emulate the best golfers in the world, who often leave themselves with nothing but very short irons for most of their approach shots. We acknowledge that we certainly don't have the carry distance of the top golfers on the planet but that we now have supreme confidence that we can hit most of the greens that we play in regulation with our scoring irons. Leaving ourselves with numerous birdie opportunities never gets old! I will let you know when it does. But by all means, if you are truly enjoying racking up bogeys and double bogeys all day from your "vanity tee boxes," then don't change a thing about the way you are playing. While you leave the course exasperated almost every time out, my buddies and I are whistling "Dixie" as we contemplate what golf course we are going to enjoy scoring well at next.

HOLE NUMBER 9

Golf Myths That Need to Be Eradicated

1. You must play a championship course that is in pristine shape in order to have a great time: False.

    We have found that as long as you are having fun and are surrounded by great friends and family members, a course of any length and condition will lead to some very memorable rounds as long as the GITCA format is being followed.

2. The more money you pay to play a course, naturally, the more enjoyment you will muster: False.

    Oftentimes, the more expensive the course you play, the more difficult the course will play and hence the more likely you are to experience utter frustration. How many people are going to pay $495 to play TPC Sawgrass and rarely break 100? The average golfer might play this beautiful but fiendish course once or twice, but they aren't likely to continue to spend this type of coin regularly to get their brains beaten in.

3. Everyone has a handicap, and if you don't have one, you are most likely a sandbagger: False.

    Only about 20 percent of all golfers have a registered handicap. Thus, almost 80 percent of golfers do not have a legitimate registered handicap. Fortunately, our system does not utilize handicaps one bit, so for all those golfers who don't have one, you don't need one to play our format.

4. Everyone needs to tee off from the same tee box in order to speed up play: False.

    If you are playing from tee boxes that are way above your pay grade, then in all likelihood, you are going to be taking far more swings each hole than if you had simply teed off from your appropriately designated tee marker. As a result of you and many of your playing companions not being able to record many greens in regulation, the pace of play of your foursome is going to be infinitely slower than had you all simply teed off from the markers that correspond properly to your golfing capabilities.

5. All golfers clearly understand the basic tenets of stroke-play scoring: False.

    Even the professionals are often very unclear as to how to properly decipher the golf rule book. Fortunately, our golf system has only eight simple-to-follow guidelines that make the game infinitely easier to understand and implement and that greatly increase the pace of play.

6. I must shoot close to par if I am going to truly enjoy myself out on the links: False.

    With the GITCA supermodified scoring system, you no longer have to be perfect on every hole in order to have one heck of a good time. Our system acknowledges that we are not as good as the top golfers in the world. Once we fully comprehend this fact, it is not hard to embrace a system that is infinitely more enjoyable for all its participants. Just think of the freedom you will now enjoy swinging the club knowing that you no longer have to be perfect on every swing.

7. I can only play with golfers who are about the same ability as me: False.

    With our system, you can tee it up with the best golfers on the planet as well as some of the most complete novices and have the time of your life. With our system, each golfer is teeing off from the tee markers appropriate for their ability, and each golfer is pitting his/her own battle

against the course on each hole. Good to great golf holes are richly rewarded, while less-than-stellar holes are quickly forgotten. There is little lingering pain following a bad hole, and each golfer is encouraged to simply get revenge on the course on the following hole without much carnage to show for it.
8. Given the amount of time that I have dedicated to golf, I ought to be as good as the pros: False.

    No matter how much time that you may have dedicated to golf, in all likelihood, the top professionals have put in ten times the number of hours dedicated to honing their craft than you have ever dreamed. As a result, the top golfers in the world have distance and accuracy that, in all likelihood, will far surpass your best efforts a majority of the time. Once you realize that you are not counting on golf to pay your bills and that you are pretty decent compared to most, only then will you truly be able to enjoy all the wonder that this game has to offer.

Why GITCA GOLF Is the Solution to All These Aforementioned Dilemmas?

With the parameters clearly laid out for all participants to follow, golfers of any age and every ability level can have a great time out on the links no matter what course they are playing. It can be one of the greatest courses ever built, or it can be a run-down par 3 course, and every golfer who tees it up is going to have the time of their life. Since every golfer is teeing off from the marker that best suits their abilities, numerous chances to record many greens in regulation should be had for every participant. No longer will golfers have to swing outside their comfort zones in order to reach most of the greens in regulation. As a result, tempos on most swings will be unhurried and most likely will lead to far better contact and more favorable results far more often. If all participants are in their comfort zone and attacking most greens with scoring irons, then far more greens should be hit on average, with the pace of play increasing dramatically for everyone on the course. Not only is the pace of the round going to be greatly increased, the enjoyment factor is going to be far greater for everyone as numerous scoring opportunities are likely for all participants. With a point being awarded for a bogey, attaining a bogey on a hole is no longer considered taboo. As long as most of the participants are recording points on most of the holes trekked and the pace of play is brisk, then rest assured, this new way of playing golf will be embraced passionately by golfers across the globe.

Shooting Par or Better Is Routine for the Professionals

Henrik Stenson just won the Wyndham Championship with a winning score of −22, and he attacked this 7,100-yard course without a driver. Using his 2 and 4 iron off the tee on most of the holes, he hit over 87 percent of the greens in regulation. I know that this is hard for the average hack like me to understand, but a course just over 7,000 yards is like a pitch and putt to most of these long-hitting professionals. Obviously, length was never an issue for this major winner as he hit most of these greens with nothing more than a 9 iron on a majority of the holes. Certainly, a course of over 7,000 yards would be an impossibility for most of us rank amateurs, but a course of this length is no problem whatsoever for any of the pros out there. I predict that leaving the driver at home is going to be an ongoing trend for many of these long-hitting superstars. Why risk hitting a driver wayward when a fairway wood or hybrid is going to leave you most often in the middle of the fairway with nothing more than an 8 iron for a majority of your approach shots?

To further prove my point of contention, my buddy Steve recently moved up a tee box on a course he regularly plays just to try and prove or disprove my hypothesis that every 100 yards is equal to about a stroke and a half. The last three times he played *Majestic Springs*, he played from his familiar blue tees, which measure about 6,400 yards, and he shot an 85, a 78, and a 79. Now these are certainly very respectable scores that would please 95 percent of golfers who play this beautiful but challenging track, but Steve was often mad that he wasn't shooting in the low 70s like the pros do. By playing from the white tees and lessening the course by around 500 yards, Steve was able to hit his 4 iron off most of the tee boxes, which allowed him to find the fairway and green on most of the holes he played. He was able to coerce four birdies to offset his four bogeys to go along with his ten pars to end the day at an even par. Naturally, he was ecstatic, and I thanked him for proving my hypothesis correct and that he now had an idea as to what the professionals feel as they play courses that don't overwhelm them lengthwise. In other words, if everyone were to play from distances that they could readily handle, then most scores would improve dramatically, and there wouldn't be such a discrepancy in the scoring average between the professionals and many of the amateurs. Now certainly, the distance discrepancy would remain, but every amateur would feel a whole hell of a lot better about their scores and their overall golfing abilities. Simply moving up several tee boxes is not going to guarantee success, but it is going to lead to a much higher probability for sustained success. Making the parameters much more inviting is going to lead to far more contentment for every golfer. If everyone is playing faster, posting much better scores, and having the time of your life, then the likelihood of everyone getting out and golfing more is going to increase substantially.

Most Golfers Are Stubborn and Don't Take Kindly to Paradigm Shifts

Almost every golfer whom I talk to about GITCA GOLF, all say that it sounds good but that they and their foursome are too stuck in their ways to change their routine. They want to play the same old way that they have always played even if it brings them little to no joy. So year after year passes, and the same old drudgery takes place on the course every time out. Everyone hopes that the latest driver, irons, or putter will certainly bring them closer to golfing excellence. Unfortunately, little changes and everyone scores about the same, and the beat goes on until someone or everyone in your foursome decides to quit and move on to more enjoyable life pursuits.

If only one or more golfers in your group had decided to move up a tee box or two in order to increase the likelihood of hitting more fairways and greens in regulation, then maybe everyone in your group would eventually see the light and finally get a taste of golfing nirvana. But most groups say that they are die-hard blue tee players, even though only a fraction of the greens are ever hit in regulation and scores are often way too high to try and tabulate. Instead of owning up to the reality that the course is too difficult to try and negotiate from these distances, most golfers in the group simply hold out hope that they can somehow string together career shot after career shot in order to finally tame the course from these far-off distances.

The reason these shots are called career shots is that you only hit them a few select times in your career. For you to believe that you are going to pull off these shots repeatedly is simply foolhardy and a certain recipe for sustained misery. Again, I know that we all love to hit the "big dog" whenever we can, but it simply is asking for trouble to try and stripe a career drive right down the middle on every single hole. The pros are well aware that they can't do this darn near every time, and this is their full-time job. Don't put yourself behind the eight ball or a large tree on every hole. Learn to swallow your pride and move up to the tee markers that don't require you to swing out of your shoes on every shot. If you play the course from distances that allow you to have a high probability of reaching most of the greens in regulation, then everyone in your foursome will be playing much faster and having a heck of a lot more fun than you ever thought possible.

Recognizing the Most Significant Moments

Without A doubt, my two favorite movies of all time are *Field of Dreams* and *The Shawshank Redemption*. Both of these movies hold an indelible place in my heart because they both delve into the realm of friendships and making the most of the opportunities we have to spend with our beloved friends and family members.

The ironic part about *The Shawshank Redemption* is that only by being surrounded by prison walls do the main characters allow the walls between them to come down. In the harsh and unfriendly environment of the prison, these characters no longer have to put up any fronts as they share their innermost thoughts and feelings and really open their humanness to one another. With all their facades stripped away, each character is allowed to present his true self with nothing to hide. The two main characters become the best of friends as they really start listening to each other. They find that hope springs eternal and that nothing is more sacred than their eternal friendship.

How often do all of us let life become so hurried that we tend to neglect our most sacred friendships? It is my hope that through embracing GITCA GOLF, everyone will be reminded that it is our friendships and camaraderie that clearly trumps our actual golf scores and that at the end of the day, the bonding is really the only thing that truly matters.

In *Field of Dreams*, the main character never got around to telling his father how much he loved him before his dad suddenly passed away. As a result, his entire life was filled with regret and remorse. Of course, at the end of the movie, his dad miraculously appears in the cornfield, and they are able to make amends for missed opportunities. He quickly introduces his dad to his wife and his granddaughter, and the father immediately asks if this is heaven. When Ray asks his dad if there is a heaven, he emphatically states, "Oh yeah, it's the place where dreams come true." Ray then looks out at the sun setting on his beautiful farmland and baseball field. He then acknowledges his wife and daughter laughing on the front porch and smiles widely with contentment as he thinks to himself that this must be heaven on earth.

This, of course, is very poignant in that we all need to be reminded from time to time that we all have been so blessed in so many ways and that we should never take even one precious moment for granted. Reminding himself that he is not going to let any more precious moments slip away, Ray hurriedly asks his father before he leaves if he would like to have a catch. When his dad turns around and his face lights up, tears abound as they both realize the significance of this simple little act of a father and son bonding. Now throwing a rawhide ball and catching it with leather mitts in and of itself is not a life-changing moment, but rekindling the unspoken love between a parent and a child is one of those precious moments that we far too often take for granted. When those days are no longer possible, there is literally nothing we wouldn't do to have just one of those moments back.

How many of us would love to be able to bring back a close friend or family member from heaven to tee it up with just one more time? Of course, no one would really care about the actual score as the special bonding would be the only thing that really mattered. Truly embracing these rare and wonderful moments whenever we can is the premise of GITCA GOLF. We need to remember what is truly important in our lives and not some stinking golf score. We must make the most of the limited time that we have with our dear friends and loved ones and that, at the end of the day, no one really gives a crap about one's handicap or what the final tally is on the scorecard. We must truly embrace each special moment out on the links as though it were our last time to play with these special people in our lives because you just never know when it might be. We all should be laughing heartily and embracing one another's kinship as though there is no tomorrow. When everyone in your foursome acknowledges the wonderment of each outing, then you all will appreciate golf and one another like you never have before.

As a society, we almost always seem to take things for granted. As improbable as it sounds, those closest to us are the ones whom we take the most often for granted. We always believe that there will be plenty of other opportunities to tell those closest to us how we really feel about them. But alas, the moment rarely presents itself as we are all too busy trying to keep up with the neighbors. As a result, we often delay acknowledging all the wonderful friendships and loved ones that have been bestowed upon us. By the time we get around to mustering up the courage to truly acknowledge those near and dear to our hearts, unfortunately, it is often way too late. This is one of life's great tragedies, not missing some obscure eagle putt on the final hole. Certainly, sinking that eagle putt would have no doubt made your round that much more memorable, but reaching out and truly acknowledging your special friendships would have made a moment that would definitely last a lifetime. Providing golfers around the world with a much more enjoyable way to play golf is one of my goals, but my ultimate goal is to inspire everyone to finally break down those barriers and pay tribute to those special people in your life every chance you get.

The Ego Is a Peculiar Thing

In many ways, our egos are designed to save us from embarrassing and oftentimes humiliating situations. In golf, our ego can cause us to overestimate our abilities. We erroneously believe that if we hit one drive over 270 yards, certainly, we have the capability of repeating that performance on a consistent basis. Likewise, just because we pured our irons a few times, we feel that we can find that sweet spot again and again no matter how little time we actually had to practice. Our ego causes us to scoff at the suggestion that we may want to consider moving up a tee box or two from others in our group. Certainly, our pride would not be able to handle such a transgression, and we would rather face the inevitable humiliation later than the certain humiliation of admitting to our lack of actual ability prior to the first tee ball being struck. So we play this game with our mind and our opponents where we simply tell them that we are having a horrific day, and we have no idea what happened to our usual superb game. Excuse after excuse piles up as we continually search for answers as to why our game is currently unable to handle the challenges placed before us. All is forgiven and made right with the world as the golfing world simply places a "handicap" on us, and this is the scarlet number that we must carry around with us forevermore.

Rather than simply admitting that we can't play the golf course adequately from these far-off distances, a computer generates a number to rate our level of inadequacy in relation to other golfers who are suffering a fate sometimes even worse than our own. We use this handicap to somewhat curtail our anguish, but inevitably, we use it to constantly compare ourselves to every other golfer out there. Our ego rises and falls with this computer-generated assessment of our golf worthiness, and everyone else is quick to question the legitimacy of this assigned number. If we happen to play way worse than what is expected for a player who has attained this lofty number, then we once again resort to our bevy of excuses as to why we are not playing to the level that has been predetermined for us. On the other hand, if we begin to play to a level that far exceeds what is expected of us based on this number, then rest assured, we will often be confronted as a liar and a fraud. Perhaps consciously or unconsciously, our games will begin to unravel to avoid this harsh label. Once again, our ego is looking out for our survival, and our brain will often interfere so that we don't cross into the threshold that would warrant us banishment from our peer group.

Thus, golf presents our egos with many quandaries. We can't tee off from the forward tees because then we would be admitting that we are not worthy. Forcing ourselves to play from tee markers that are above our capabilities often leads to humiliation even with the aid of the handicap to try and ease our pain. No matter how many strokes your playing partners have to give you, no one feels very good about being the worst golfer out there. This constant embarrassment is very hard for our ego to handle. If we repeat this scenario often enough, our ego will implore us to explore other options besides golf. Since most golfers are drawn into this "no-win situation" almost every time they tee it up, is it any wonder that more and more golfers are leaving the game in order to find much more rewarding ways to spend their lives?

Certainly, these and many other excuses are often cited by most golfers as to why they would rather spend their valuable time doing something else. What my method does is turn the ego upside down by filling it with so many positive moments that it can't help being genuinely excited about teeing it up again and again from your properly designated tee markers. By finally learning to accept your true golfing abilities, you will be hitting more fairways and greens than you ever thought possible. Your ego will be constantly stroked as you are now recording scores that would make even the pros happy on most of the holes you play. When you do have an occasional hiccup, your one or two bad holes will no longer jeopardize your entire round or self-worth, and once again, your ego will be sparred. If your ego and your soul are constantly being satiated, then rest assured your entire entity will actually crave these natural golfing endorphins.

Whereas once you feared teeing off for all the usual despair it would bring, you now cannot wait to get out and cherish every second that you have out on the links with your beloved friends and family. In order to get to this happy place out on the course, you simply must swallow your pride and move up to your appropriate tee box. Even though your ego may struggle to handle this initially, when your ego sees all the positive vibes emanating from making this adjustment, it will eventually relent so that you can bask in all this newfound glory. Doesn't this sound like a lot more fun than continually beating yourself up? When everyone else learns to buy into GITCA GOLF and all the ways that it makes golf far more enjoyable, then everyone in your foursome will be excited to try and become the top golfer for the day from their properly designated tee marker. Unlike in the past when most golfers in your group experienced "learned helplessness" throughout the round, playing from comfortable distances will allow everyone to have supreme confidence in their ability to post some darn good scores on a regular basis.

Three of the Game's Greatest Legends Teeing It Up and Having the Time of Their Lives

Flipped on the television to witness the best golf moment of the year: Jack Nicklaus (seventy-seven years young), Gary Player (eighty years young), and Lee Trevino (seventy-eight years young) playing together and winning the Legends of Golf Scramble at *the Woodlands*. The Big Three started off with eight birdies in the first eight holes before finally winning it on yet another clutch putt by Jack on the eighteenth hole. What a sight to watch these legends successfully and expertly negotiate their way around the golf course to notch yet another victory for all of them. Even if they hadn't won, golf would have still been the big winner, getting to watch these legends have the time of their lives out on the links together. Of course, these three golfing marvels can't hit the ball as they did in their heyday, but teeing off from the white tees allotted all these men to put themselves in excellent position to score well as a scramble team. If one of them hit a poor shot, they knew that one of the other two would come through with a clutch shot like they have for most of their careers. It is rare to see Jack Nicklaus dump one in the water and laugh about it, but that is the beauty of the scramble format. Gary Player was able to get the ball close, and Jack sealed the deal with a downhill fifteen-footer to secure the team victory.

Playing from distances from which they all could be successful and getting to lift, clean, and place all their shots led to all the senior teams having the time of their lives out on the links with their peers. The shotmaking was outstanding, and the laughter and camaraderie are what golfers everywhere should take notice of. Certainly, all these lifelong competitors wanted to win just as much as the next guy, but it was the overall jovial spirit of the event that allowed golfers everywhere to recognize what is truly important out on the links. To be able to play in a scramble format with your lifelong competitors and friends and still hit amazing shots and contribute to the team effort, it really doesn't get much better than that.

This event symbolizes perfectly everything that I want nearly all golfers to experience every single time they are fortunate enough to play golf. GITCA GOLF lends itself to providing many more opportunities for positive moments out on the links. In a scramble format, the idea is for the team to have many excellent chances to post the best score possible. GITCA GOLF also offers many opportunities for success and provides many more positive moments out on the links for every golfing participant. Our format offers abundant scoring opportunities while quickly discarding the blow-up holes, which ruin your entire day under the stroke-play scoring method. By offering non-tournament golfers a much easier and far more enjoyable way to play, GITCA GOLF opens the door for golfers around the world to finally start enjoying themselves on the golf course on a consistent basis.

Now what would happen if these three legends were forced to play in a stroke-play tournament from the black tees, which measure over 7,300 yards, against the current number 1 player in the world,

Dustin Johnson? Now certainly, in their heyday and with today's modern equipment, these three legends would be able to bust their drives out near Dustin Johnson's best efforts. But since Father Time has finally caught up to these three ultimate competitors as to how long they can currently carry a golf ball, then the current number 1 is going to have a much easier time contending on a golf course with this vast amount of length. In fact, the tour's top driver of the ball is probably going to have nothing more than a 9 iron or wedge for most of his approach shots. Our slightly past-their-prime-time legends are going to be hard-pressed to reach any of the greens in regulation playing from the way-back tee markers. For most of their approach shots, our legends will be forced to use hybrids or fairway woods and hope they nut them in order to have a chance to reach the green in regulation. While Dustin will be waltzing around the course like it is a walk in the park, our legends are going to be hard-pressed to record scores that don't besmirch their legendary status. Having a short scoring iron in his hand for nearly all his approach shots, Dustin Johnson is most likely going to shoot in the mid 60s. Even with all their excellent touch and feel, our legends are all going to have a difficult time breaking 80. Even if DJ is nice enough to allow all these legends to play off their handicap, none of these prideful champions is going to feel good about their round at the end of the day no matter how many strokes they have been given in order to try and stay competitive.

Rather than tarnishing the reputation of three of the greatest golfers who ever lived, why not simply allow all of them to tee off from tee markers that are congruent with the distance their ball carries? I guarantee that if you allow these three great ball-strikers to tee off from the white tee markers on this course, not only would they all be competitive, but I would bet that at least one of them could best DJ's tally. No strokes would have to be given, and these three champions would be able to show the world that although they cannot hit the ball nearly as far as the world's number 1 player, they still know how to negotiate the golf course from distances they can handle and that they still can be quite competitive.

Forcing these three legends to try and play from distances that they can no longer handle is simply going to create great suffering and agony for some of the best players to ever lace them up. If they were forced to try and repeat this scenario on a regular basis, then rest assured, even some of the finest ball-strikers the world has ever known would find better things to do in their twilight years.

So if this scenario is frightening for some of the best golfers to have ever played this game, what must this scenario be like for the average amateur who is lucky to tee it up only a few times a year? Unfortunately, this exact scenario is played out again and again on golf courses all across the world, and as a result, the future for golf looks very bleak indeed. We must nip this problem in the bud immediately, or we risk losing the game for generations to come. The best way to do this is to finally think outside the box and make the game infinitely more appealing for the masses. We must reserve the extremely challenging aspects of traditional stroke play for only the best of the best tournament-level players who are still in their prime. These players devote their entire lives trying to master something that is almost impossible to ever truly perfect. For most of the rest of us schleps, we are simply trying to get out whenever we can and have an enjoyable time on the links with our buddies. Let's harness a way to make the game infinitely more positive and much faster-paced. I truly believe that if GITCA GOLF becomes the accepted norm for nontournament play, golf will see a revival that few saw coming. Everyone I have shown GITCA GOLF to has gotten on board, and we are anxious for the rest of the golfing world to catch on so that everyone can play faster and have a lot more positive results.

The Inherent Problem with Having a Handicap

The inherent problem with keeping a handicap is that less than 25 percent of all golfers actually have a registered handicap index. As a result, when you go to the first tee, there is a strong possibility that at least one member of your foursome does not have a set handicap to declare. In most cases, golfers will often say that they are pretty much a bogey golfer, so put them down for an 18 handicap. Everyone agrees that this is acceptable until this golfer either shoots lights out or they are in fact "god-awful." In either of the aforementioned scenarios, eyes are certain to roll as well as heads as this golfer is going to be chastised for their "unbelievably awesome day" or shamed for their overall lack of execution as they record a score well north of 100. This golfer is going to feel so thoroughly embarrassed by his play that he will be in no hurry to ever join this group of golfers ever again. Likewise, if this "18 handicapper" shoots a 74 and is literally playing out of his mind, he will once again face scorn from the others, and they might never want to play with him ever again.

Thus, playing way better or way worse than your stated handicap is going to ruffle many feathers, so the only way everyone can enjoy themselves as a foursome is if, in fact, everyone plays darn near what they have declared for their handicap index. Any great deviation from what this piece of plastic says is only going to lead to great duress for any and all golfers who record extremely high or extremely low scores. One is likely to be threatened by accusations of "sandbagger" or "cheat," and most likely, this golfer will no longer be invited to join this golfing foursome anytime soon. This is ridiculous, my friends, and is once again causing so much distaste that golfers are leaving the game in record numbers. Even though the late great Tony Gwynn was a 0.333 hitter a majority of his career, he did not go 1 for 3 or 2 for 6 every single game. In fact, he often would go 3 for 5 many nights, which would make him a 0.600 batter for that game. Obviously way better than his baseball card states he is! Likewise, he might go 0 for 4 many nights, which would make him a 0.000 hitter and once again be far from what the back of his baseball card states that he is. In the first scenario, he obviously had a great night, while in the latter, he had a horrible night. I know many golfers who on a certain day can shoot a 79 and the very next day shoot a 105. Say this golfer's recorded handicap index states that they are in fact a 15 handicap. Does that make them a sandbagger on those great days when everything is going right and likewise a golfer with an overinflated ego during those horrible rounds? I say that it is simply the law of averages playing out, and this golfer should not feel like a louse when they are playing exceptionally well or exceptionally horrible.

Unfortunately, most people who only get to see them play on this certain day are not likely to believe them and are invariably going to make them feel undeservedly ashamed.

So for all those golfing "purists" who feel that everyone should have a clearly stated handicap index, I implore you to reconsider as golf is losing golfers by the millions, and declaring a handicap is only exacerbating this problem. Let's find a better way to make this game more equitable for all so that it is much more user-friendly and a much better experience for everyone who tees it up. I believe by incorporating the bylaws that I have laid out in GITCA GOLF, everyone who tees it up will feel much less threatened and much less embarrassed and will once again learn to play golf with unbridled passion. Every person starts every round with no preconceived notions about what they are or aren't going to shoot, and may the best golfer that day win from their properly designated set of tee markers. Each day that you tee it up is a new opportunity to shoot the round of your life or to not have your best day while still enjoying the heck out of the people you have the fortune of playing with for that particular round. No accusations will ever be made about sandbagging or overinflated egos. Just play from your right set of tee markers and let the chips fall where they may.

THE BACK NINE

How the Idea for GITCA Was Hatched and Developed

The whole idea for finding a better way to play this most wonderful of games began nine years ago while I was on a golf trip to the illustrious *Bandon Dunes Golf Resort*. The trip was planned by my stepfather just prior to his unexpected passing. We were going to cancel the trip, but we all decided that he would have wanted us to go. Thus, the trip became a tribute to everyone's beloved friend, Jay Rhoads. Jay was a truly special man who lived life to its fullest. His true passion was tennis, and he was many times a club champion and a player whom everyone wanted as their partner. He also had a passion for golf, although like the rest of us, he often struggled to break 90. He was a man of great pride, and he was used to achieving a high degree of success in every other aspect of his life, so he had a relentless pursuit to get better at this game that he loved playing with his family and friends.

This trip was comprised of Jay's brother- and sister-in-law and their two sons, Jay's own son, his three son-in-laws, and his three stepsons. The trip was amazing as I got to spend so many great moments with these special people on four of the most amazing courses in the world. We, of course, reminisced and toasted our beloved friend and wished that he could still be with us. We even stopped our round in the middle so that we could honor our beloved friend with a twenty-one-ball salute as we all hit one or two balls into the ocean from the eleventh tee on Bandon Dunes's breathtaking course. After a few prayers and a tearful salute to our sorely missed friend, we proceeded with our round as we were all certain that we could feel Jay's presence among us. As his only son, John, stepped to the tee, we could all feel something magical was about to happen. John was struggling mightily with his round just like the rest of us, so when his 6 iron from 168 yards made a beeline for the pin, we were certain that Jay was looking down upon us. Alas, the ball ended up a few millimeters from going in the hole for what would have been John's first ever hole-in-one. Teary-eyed, John was a little upset that the magical moment had come up a few inches short of perfection. He quickly gathered himself as he tapped in his only birdie of the round and stated that it would have been bittersweet to have a hole-in-one, because his dad wasn't there to witness it. We all assured him that he was in fact there, and we saluted the sky once again for this wonderful man who had given us so many fond memories and life lessons.

So this trip was indeed an amazing week for all of us who had the privilege to be there, but the golf itself could have been much more enjoyable if everyone was not so caught up with the handicap system. There are many inherent flaws with the handicap system in my opinion, the first of which is that not everyone is playing the same golf course all the time. Jay's brother and son-in-laws are all members of *Merion Golf Course*, one of the most prestigious and hardest golf courses in the world. My brother and I play mostly public courses, few of which are even remotely as difficult as *Merion*. Thus, their 12 to 14 handicaps are much more impressive than my brother's thirteen and my 18 handicaps at our varying courses. After watching the pros struggle to break par at *Merion* at the 2013 US Open, I am quite certain that my brother and I would be lucky to ever break 100 at this prestigious course. I realize that slope rating can help equalize the handicaps, but nonetheless, I knew full well that these guys were going to blow our doors off playing from the blue tees.

So as the first round began, I found myself in quite unfamiliar territory. I was playing a brutally hard course from the blue tees with golfers whom I had never played with but whom I knew were much better than me. I was used to playing rinky-dink courses from the white tees with my buddies who all refused to give one another any strokes whatsoever. We simply gripped and ripped it, and whoever was the hottest golfer that day would get the bragging rights and would be bought a milkshake by the rest of us. Adding another wrinkle to the Bandon experience was the use of caddies, which I hadn't had to assist me since I was a teenager. All the caddies at Bandon are top-notch, of course, so now I felt added pressure to not embarrass myself. All the caddies got a good laugh at my mishmash of varying clubs and my long putter, and I could feel the tension mount as I stepped to the first tee, hoping not to swing and miss. Fortunately, I hit a decent drive on the first hole and then stuck a great iron right in the middle of the green. Of course, the catcalls immediately arose that, for certain, I was way better than my stated 18 handicap. As I nearly tapped in my par, I assured them all that that was indeed a fluke that they might not see for the rest of the trip. I had played one phenomenal hole, and already I was being accused of being a sandbagger! The next hole was a relatively short par 3, and I usually excel from this range. Feeling all the doubting eyes on me, I proceeded to pull hook my tee shot twenty yards into the deep woods. Rather than being upset, I was somewhat relieved to prove to these guys that I really am a high-handicap player! After all these guys had proceeded to get on the green in regulation and all make par, I proceeded to struggle and ended up giving myself a 6 on the easiest hole on the course. In truth, I probably should have gone back to the tee and hit my third shot, but I didn't want to hold up the rest of the golfers on the course. The rest of the round went accordingly as I would have several decent holes followed by an occasional snowman or worse. Nonetheless, I was having the time of my life playing on one of the greatest courses I would ever have the privilege to play. My playing companions were indeed much longer and significantly better than me, but everyone had an occasional blow-up hole that really put a damper on their overall score and, hence, enjoyment of the round. At the end of the round, my three playing companions all played to about their handicaps as they all shot in the mid to high eighties. I was quite pleased that I had barely managed to break 100 as I shot a cool 97! In reality, if I was truly keeping scores like the pros, I would have added several more strokes to this score. Fortunately, my playing companions noted that there was a limit to how many strokes I could take on a hole. Thank God, for I might still be out there on some of those holes! I think we have all had that humiliating experience one time or another out on the course and are just praying that it would all be over soon! Nonetheless, I was feeling pretty good about myself that I had somehow managed to break the century mark on this incredibly difficult course.

As the other golfers rolled in, however, my complacency was soon replaced with incredible angst. Jay's brother, an excellent golfer, quickly wanted to see our scorecards. He quickly surmised that everyone was pretty much spot-on with their scores in relation to their handicaps but that I had done significantly worse. My round, which had started out on such an incredible high with me being accused of being a "sandbagger," had now completely reversed, and now I was being called a liar and accused of having a glorified handicap. *Well, okay*, I thought, *I can't win either way here*. So I vowed that I wasn't going to let my score affect my golfing enjoyment for the rest of the trip. When my brother came in next and posted his career round of 79 for a net 66, he was quickly accosted as lying about his handicap. In truth, I knew full well that my brother was far better than me, but I also knew that he was easily capable of shooting a 110 the very next day. He hits the ball a long way, but he can get a case of the quick hooks worse than anyone that I have ever seen for a golfer whose swing reminds everyone of Ernie Els's majestic swing. I shook my brother's hand in earnest and congratulated him on his breakthrough round. Unfortunately, his joy was short-lived as nearly everyone else accused him of being a sandbagger. I quickly came to his defense and made it quite clear that this was an aberration and that, unfortunately, it would not last. So rather than being able to cherish this unbelievable moment, my brother had to spend the rest of the night defending himself. How absurd is this! Suddenly, the wine and fine food did not taste as sweet to my brother as all that was discussed at dinner was the validity of everyone's stated handicap.

Fortunately, for his sake, I guess, my brother proceeded to shoot 105 the next day on a course, which he quickly stated that he "couldn't stand." I had seen my brother completely lose it on the course before, as we all have, but I didn't know that he would shoot twenty-six strokes worse than he had the previous day. My brother had experienced the entire highs and lows of golf in successive days, and both turned out to be horrible experiences for him. I posted a 99, so once again, I was looked upon as being a glorified golfer. I knew full well that I was not capable of reaching most of these par 4s in regulation from the blue tees, not to mention all the hazards that were everywhere on these courses. So midway through the trip, both my brother and I were feeling the full scrutiny of trying to live up to our "true handicaps." Fortunately, after the round, we would go to the driving range and play nine holes on the executive course. As I looked around the range, I was aghast at how bad most of the golfers were. I was infinitely better than most of them, so I was pretty sure that most of these golfers would not come close to breaking 120 on any of these amazing courses. When I beat my brother and brother-in-law on the executive course, I regained some semblance of pride. At dinner that night, I told everyone that I don't care what I shoot for the final two days. I just want to enjoy this once-in-a-lifetime experience. You could tell that they all agreed but quietly were hoping that I would not be paired with them and ruin their chances of winning the trophy.

The next day, we played another one of the amazing Bandon courses, and I had many great holes and a few horrible holes and managed to shoot a 92. This was seven shots better than the previous day, and I won several skins. Although I had several blow-up holes, I was pleased with my overall play for the most part. When my brother came in with a 77, the tension really started to tighten. One day, after having the worst round of his life, he was now twenty-eight strokes better than the previous day, and he was now facing a firing squad of skeptics. I could sense his disbelief, so I quickly went into the pro shop to buy him a souvenir shirt with the course logo on it and told him to always remember this day and not care what the others are saying about his legitimacy.

After this amazing round, my brother was in the lead and had a good shot at winning the trophy. Unfortunately, he was paired with me tomorrow as his partner, and I hadn't legitimized my handicap all week. There was undue tension in the room all night and the next morning. I was hoping that I would play well enough to not blow it for my brother. I started out really well on the first couple of holes, and I was having a great round going. Unfortunately, the pressure was getting to my brother, and the quick hooks had returned: Not what you want when playing one of the hardest courses in the world, *Pacific Dunes*, on an extremely windy day. At the turn, I had an amazing, for me, 41, while my brother was struggling with a 49. I told him to relax and don't worry about some stupid trophy and to simply enjoy playing golf on one of the most spectacular golf courses in the world. Alas, his game turned around, and he fired a 42 on the back nine. Unfortunately, I had a few snowmen, including one on 18, and all hope was lost for him winning the championship. *Oh well, who gives a crap?* I thought as the real beauty of golf should be in playing on these wonderful courses with all these great friends and family members as we reminisce about our fallen beloved leader, Jay. Playing the incredible courses at *Bandon Dunes* should have been one of the greatest experiences of our lives, but unfortunately, this epic trip was marred by all the handicap hoopla. It was following this trip that I vowed to find a better and much more enjoyable way to play golf.

The Search for a Better Way to Play

The next time I got to play an unbelievable course was in Montana at my brother's wedding at the *Yellowstone Club*. This is a very exclusive club, so if you are ever lucky enough to get an invite, please do so as the entire course and amenities are amazing. Again, I was playing one of the most difficult courses in the country for the first time, from the blue tees. Yes, the ball does carry farther in the mountains, but still I had no business playing from there. My brother hits it about 300 yards, as did his buddy, so I vowed to play my own game and to simply enjoy this once-in-a-lifetime experience. I watched Todd and his buddy blast away in awe as I was content to hit my 240-yard drives and simply enjoy all this breathtaking beauty that Mother Nature and the golf designers had placed before me.

After an opening par followed by three successive doubles or worse, I simply told my brother to not even bother with my score but to simply record the number of pars or better that I would get during the round. With no longer having to worry about how embarrassingly high my score was going to be, I started to swing freely and confidently through the ball with not a care in the world. Well, not that anyone should care, but I did manage to record six pars and a birdie. I had a few more doubles or worse in there, but I felt a liberation that I had never felt before on the golf course. I was no longer worried about posting a score as I was simply playing golf for the sheer exhilaration of it. In addition, I was having a ball watching my much more accomplished brother have an amazing round with his equally great playing partner. Even though they both shot at least twenty shots better than me, I dare say that I enjoyed the round much more than either one of them. They were too busy being caught up in besting each other that I feel they really failed to acknowledge the incredible splendor put before us. Since the slope rating on this course was way over 140, both of them had several holes where they simply picked up after exceeding a double bogey. I reminded them to not let it ruin their otherwise wonderful rounds and to immediately get back to enjoying this most wonderful of days. They both ended up in the low 80s, and they were disappointed that they hadn't done better. If only they hadn't had those three blow-up holes each, they both definitely would have ended up in the mid 70s. *So what?* I thought to myself. Does anyone really care if these guys came in with 75s instead of 82s? I certainly didn't. Even though I struggled mightily on many holes out on this daunting course, it was a cathartic round I would remember all my life.

Pioneer Days for GITCA GOLF

When I got back to Cincinnati, I could barely contain my enthusiasm as I related the aforementioned story to my golfing buddies. They agreed wholeheartedly that I had no business playing the blue tees and that only keeping track of my par scores or better was a great idea. The very next round, my buddy Steve and I played a nine-hole par 3 course late in the day on Labor Day. A mighty thunderstorm had just gone through, so we had the course entirely to ourselves. We decided that we would play as many holes as we could, until there was no more daylight. We also decided that we would score a point for every bogey, two points for every par, and four points for every birdie we got. We also jokingly said that twenty points would be awarded for a hole-in-one. What transpired over the next two hours was as much fun as one could have on a golf course.

    The course is relatively short with the shortest hole being 85 yards and the longest 155 yards. Since both Steve and I are pretty good from this range, it was a shoot-out and a dogfight, to say the least. We both took dead aim on every pin and managed to get many tap in birdies to go along with our boatload of pars each. On one hole, I got a little too aggressive and overshot the green and ended up under a tree. With nothing to lose, I promptly hit it under the tree branch and bounced it off the cart path, and it ended up three feet from the pin. When I made the putt for par, I said that even Tiger Woods would have been impressed by that shot. I was leading Steve by one entering the final hole, which was an 85-yard gap wedge for me and three-quarter lob wedge for Steve. When he promptly stepped up and put one eight feet away, I knew I also had to go for it as Steve is one of the most clutch putters I have ever seen. When I nearly tore down the flagstick and left my shot three feet away, I was smiling from ear to ear. I knew that Steve would naturally make his, so when I managed to eke mine in, it made it that much more satisfying. But even greater than the feeling I got from finally beating Steve for the first time in my life was the complete and utter satisfaction that we both got from playing golf with our newfangled scoring system. Since that fateful day, that is the only way that I play golf. If others wish to play golf with their antiquated scoring system also, so be it. But for me, my golf rounds are way too limited to waste them being frustrated or getting down on myself. I simply want to enjoy myself and my friends and the limited times that we have together out on the links.

My Last Hurrah with Stroke-Play Scoring Was Terribly Disappointing

Now the last time I went out to play with my younger brother Todd down at his home course in Florida, I was feeling very confident about my game and was eager to show him just how much better I had gotten and to show him my new scoring system. My joy was immediately tarnished when all the other guys in the foursome were adamant that we all play from the blue tees. Now I know that my brother is significantly longer than me, with his 290-yard drives greatly outdistancing my 230-yard drives, but I knew that my short game was a little better than his. Also, since I was his guest, I knew that I would simply go along with the rest of them and try not to slow them down. I figured his friends would be every bit as good as him, if not better. Boy, was I wrong! The first guy managed to hit his first drive and his mulligan a combined 100 yards straight into the woods. The other gentleman didn't do much better, so I immediately felt at ease. When I stepped up and hit a very good drive for me, I was feeling really good about myself and my chances to compete with my brother. Boy, was I wrong, again! My brother calmly strode up to his ball and majestically launched a high 290-plus-yard drive straight down the middle of the pipe. As the other two guys hacked it up toward the green on their ways to double and quadruple bogeys, I still found myself 60 yards behind my brother's tee shot and 180 yards away from the pin. This is too long for any of my irons, so I hacked away with my five-wood and sprayed it way to the right. I somehow managed to record a bogey, but my brother's beast of a drive left him only 120 yards out, which is an easy sand wedge for him. When he knocked it stiff, I knew that I was in for a long day. But not nearly as long as the other two chaps playing with us. Throughout the round, I found myself hitting drives as well as I can hit them and still being too far back to ever threaten getting on the green in regulation. I think I had four pars on the day as a result of fortunately knocking in several very long putts. I managed to record several bogeys to go along with many doubles and triples.

Clearly, I had no business playing the blue tees on this extremely challenging golf course. The other two guys combined for like three pars and a boatload of doubles or worse. Obviously, none of us had any business playing from the blue tees. In fact, the one gentleman clearly should have been teeing off from the forward tees. My brother, meanwhile, never ever had any problem reaching any of these greens in regulation. In fact, he could have easily reached most of these greens from the black tees. The round was a lot of fun on this breathtaking course, and playing with my brother and his two buddies was a wonderful treat for me. But we all would have been much better suited if we had played from our proper sets of tees and utilized the GITCA scoring system. The next time I have the privilege to tee it up with these wee lads, I will insist that my brother play from the black tees, his one buddy and I the white tees, and the other buddy the green tees and that we immediately pick up once bogeys have failed to be attained. I guarantee we will finish in about an hour less time, and that the entire experience will be much better off for all of us, especially our forecaddie.

March 17, 2013: Premiere Family GITCA GOLF Outing

After my last foray into golf with very disappointing returns, I decided that I was no longer going to play by golf's traditional and, I feel, antiquated scoring methods. I needed to get that bitter taste out of my mouth as quickly as possible and forevermore. I eagerly told my brother-in-law Jamie and my stepfather Don all about the wonderment of GITCA GOLF and asked them if they would participate in being the first family members to try it out with me. They both quickly agreed, but Jamie wanted to know how many strokes he was going to have to give Don and me. When I flat out told him none, he was perplexed and flabbergasted. "But we will kill Don," he stated emphatically.

"Oh ye of little faith." Don smirked back.

"Playing from our correct tee boxes should even things out, and besides, this is Don's home course, so he does have a home field advantage," I reminded them both.

"So essentially, Kelley, you are saying that playing the different set of tees will totally negate the difference in handicaps?" Jaime shot back.

"Yes, I am," I replied with total confidence and glee. "No more freaking handicaps to figure out. May the golfer who accumulates the most GITCA points from their proper tee markers be declared the winner of the day."

Well, it didn't take long for Jaime to eat his words as Don parred the very first hole while Jamie and I both recorded bogeys. In fact, Don parred almost every other hole on the front nine, while Jaime and I each struggled to get a single par each. So at the turn, Don had fifteen points while Jaime and I sat humbly with a mere nine points each. Don was having the time of his life playing his home course from the yellow tees, and he was acting as though he had just discovered the fountain of youth.

"Don't you all play from the yellow tees in your foursome all the time?" I asked incredulously.

"No, we all have way too much pride!" he lamented.

"How many greens in regulation do you all average from the white tees?" I wanted to know.

"Not nearly enough," he retorted quickly, "it sure is a lot more fun playing the yellow tee markers."

"Wouldn't everyone in your group like having infinitely more pars and birdie chances?" I chimed back.

"Of course," he said, "but you know what they say about old dogs and new tricks."

Nonetheless, I was so excited to see Don thrilled with GITCA GOLF that I didn't care that I was literally tearing up the course and losing an extraordinary amount of balls. I could sense Jaime's frustration as well, so I reminded him that we can only go up from here with our scoring and that we all still had yet to utilize our par busters or our roving mulligans. When Don easily parred the first two holes on the back while Jaime and I both recorded matching bogeys, I knew that times were desperate and that I needed to pull out my "par buster" in order to try and jump-start my game and try and get off this embarrassment train. Fortunately for me, the next hole was a short par 3 hole that was playing 140 yards downwind. Seeing that this hole had relatively few obstacles, I promptly declared that I would be invoking my par buster right now. I reminded them both that by declaring this hole as my par buster, I had essentially made this short par 3 a very short par 4 hole. Not wanting to further embarrass myself, and also to show them the simple beauty of the par buster, I took dead aim at the center of the green and promptly hit it right where I envisioned. After watching the ease with which I pulled this off, I think Jaime was tempted to follow suit right there, but he had determined that he was going to save his for the very short par 4 coming up on the next hole. I could see the regret set in right away, however, as Jaime hit a beautiful 8 iron to within four feet of the cup. Had he called up his par buster prior to teeing off, he would have been staring down the barrel of a four-foot eagle putt. Don also thought about utilizing his par buster here also, but he too decided that he would pull it out on the next hole as well. He too promptly hit his ball right next to mine in the center of the green. When we all managed to come away with threes on the hole, I had secured a quick and easy four points while they each had added two point to their totals. Don now had accumulated a cool twenty-one points, while I had vaulted to second with fifteen points, thanks to my well-timed par buster. Jaime brought up the rear with thirteen points but was eager to invoke his par buster so that he could potentially vault right back over me.

When we got to the short par 4 that only measures 285 yards from the white tees, I could see Jaime's heart literally sink as the entire right side of the hole was one big water hazard.

Don could also see Jaime's total shock and awe, and he chided, "Do you still want to bring out that par buster now?"

"I don't know," Jaime quipped back. "Oh, what the hell, why not?"

"You still have your roving mulligan," I aptly reminded him, "just in case you do deposit your first drive into the water."

Having honors and feeling saucy now that I had just secured an easy four points, I let loose with a drive that found the center of the fairway and left me with but a short pitch to the green. Sensing the moment and perhaps trying a bit too hard, Jaime promptly hit a long high drive that unfortunately landed right smack dab in the middle of the water hazard. Being the extremely smart player that he is, Jaime used a 4 iron with his roving mulligan and landed safely in the middle of the fairway. He now had only an easy pitching wedge left for his approach shot.

Knowing how to play this hole like the back of his hand, Don slashed his usual center cut drive two hundred yards right to the end of the fairway. He now only had a gap wedge left for his approach, and he had a perfect angle to attack the pin with plenty of green to work with. Jaime went first and hit his wedge a little thin and flew it just over the back of the green. He was clearly disappointed, but I aptly reminded him that this hole was a par 5 for him so that he was still sitting pretty. Don then coyly stepped up and hit a beautiful knockdown half wedge that nearly knocked down the flagstick. He now only had two feet left for a three and a "par buster eagle." "Wow," I said, "can you hit my pitch shot for me?" I knew that the smart play here was a bump-and-run, but I was feeling confident with my lob wedge. Unfortunately for me, I got anxious as my clubhead approached the ball, and I dug underneath the ball, and it came up woefully short of the green. Anxious to redeem myself, I hurriedly struck my next shot with such force that it flew the green and nestled next to Jaime's ball. I was so distraught with my play that I hurriedly hit the next shot, and it flew over the other side of the green, and I had another GITCA! I was so angry that I had butchered this seemingly benign hole after hitting such a prodigious drive. Oh well, I was going to enjoy watching these two add to their point totals as I quickly tended to the flag. Jaime hit a decent chip shot, but he was unable to make his first putt and settled for a 5 and, thanks to utilizing the par buster, an additional two points to his tally. Jaime said that we ought to concede Don's "eagle putt" to him, and I was all in, but Don insisted that he should have to make the putt for an eagle and its subsequent eight points. He confidently strode to his ball and gave it a firm whack into the back of the cup for the first "eagle" he had ever recorded at *Hawk's Nest*.

"I will take it, but it's not really an eagle though." He sheepishly grinned.

"Bullcrap it isn't!" I quickly interjected. "Under the guidelines of GITCA GOLF, it most certainly is. You correctly strategized which hole would give you the greatest opportunity to receive the greatest number of points for your par buster, and you nailed it. So apologize for nothing and cherish the fact that you are the grand champion for today."

Don was all smiles from ear to ear for the rest of the round. Unfortunately, both Don and I bogeyed in the last five holes, but Don was still easily the grand champion as he finished the round with an incredible thirty-four-point GITCA total. Jaime finished the last two holes with pars to beat me by two points and secure the silver medal as his GITCA total was a very respectable twenty-two points. Although I finished with twenty points and the bronze medal, I also was all smiles as I enjoyed watching my family members embrace the wonderment of GITCA GOLF. We had a beautiful lunch on the course's spectacular patio as we rehashed the ups and downs of the rounds over a couple of wonderful craft beers. We even saw a hawk or two fly over as we lamented about our few bad holes, but we all will forever remember Don's first eagle and the grand introduction of GITCA GOLF to the family. So Jaime's prediction of us having a big advantage over Don was quickly laid to waste, and I was relieved that the shortest hitter with the highest handicap actually thrived and, in fact, kicked our butts! Don triumphantly stated, "I really think you are on to something here, and I think that once my golfing buddies try it out, they are also going to fully embrace it."

Don no doubt was going to be framing this scorecard for many reasons. Number 1, it was the first official round of GITCA GOLF he had ever played. Number 2, he had recorded his very first eagle on his home course. And perhaps most importantly, he had won a tremendous victory for the older generation who don't always hit it as long as many in the younger generation but who can still carve up a course when placed in the right scenario.

The Circle of Life

I recently had the privilege of going down to Palm Beach to visit my brother Todd and play a few rounds of golf with him and, more importantly, to fully indoctrinate him into the GITCA GOLF scoring system. He suggested that we start out with the Palm Beach Par 3 Course. This course was designed by Raymond Floyd, and it is one of the most spectacular par 3 courses that I have ever played. The course runs right along the ocean for many of its holes and its clubhouse, and the adjoining restaurant offers magnificent views and excellent food. It is like your own little par 3 country club, and the course was packed to the gills with eager golfers of all ages and differing abilities. It did my heart good to see so many golfers out on the course based on all the information that we have been bombarded with about how golf is losing millions of participants each year. Seeing all these people out here simply reaffirmed my assertion that the golfing bug is alive and well at courses where you can play fast and that are not so difficult that they discourage their clientele.

I told my brother the basic tenets of GITCA GOLF, and he immediately stated that we would both be playing from the tips since it was simply a par 3 course. I reminded him that under GITCA guidelines, I must tee off from the white tees in order to make the scoring realistically competitive. Now normally I would like my chances to compete with Todd on a par 3 course as I am usually an excellent par 3 player as my two holes-in-one last year would validate, but I was struggling mightily with my irons, and Todd was purring ever iron in his bag. Whereas my ball lacked power and direction, Todd was hitting every ball high and true, and the ball was pin hunting with every swing of his club. While I was extremely fortunate to have two pars through the first six holes, Todd made five effortless pars and one unfortunate bogey. He was hoping for a perfect score, so he took his mulligan on his one wayward drive but, alas, failed to get up and down and suffered his first bogey of the day on hole number 5. Even though I was getting soundly trounced at this point, 11 to 8, I knew that if Todd had made any of his birdie putts, this match would already have been decided. This was becoming a bludgeoning, so I decided that I would invoke my par buster on the shortest hole on the course. I knew that I had to make a par, net birdie at least, in order to get back into this match and put a little pressure on my brother. Alas, I got overly excited and flew the green with my sand wedge. I did manage to make a great 4 to garner two points, but when Todd made another par 3, he was leading the match 13 to 10, and I had used up my most precious lifeline. We both parred hole number 8, with Todd once again narrowly missing his birdie putt, while I was fortunate enough to sneak in a terrifying downhill twenty-footer. When he promptly stepped up and stuck his tee shot into the heart of the ninth green and I subsequently shanked mine, I knew that I had to use up my last lifeline and declare my roving mulligan as an act of complete desperation. Fortunately, I hit a nice one, and we both made our pars to finish the front 9 with him holding a decisive 17-to-14 lead, but I knew full well it could have been a much greater deficit. Although I was only a few points behind, Todd had just missed about five makeable birdie putts, and he still hadn't utilized his par buster yet. I, on the other hand, was lucky to record five pars, and my lifelines had all been obliterated.

Todd picked up right where he had left off on the front nine, and he easily parred the next two holes, while I unfortunately went bogey, bogey. His lead was now a commanding 21-to-16 lead through eleven holes, and I kept waiting for him to utilize the par buster and officially seal my doom. He stated that he was going to save it until hole 18 just in case I had somehow caught up to him or that at that point he could further distance himself from me and thus add salt to my wounds. Todd then pulled his next two tee shots just a little to the right, and he could not manage to get up and down for his pars. I made the score a little more interesting as I was able to par one of the holes to make the score 23 to 19 Todd through thirteen holes. Apparently sensing my little inkling of momentum, he promptly declared that hole 14 would be his par buster hole. When he calmly stepped up and struck his tee shot to within fifteen feet of the cup, I knew that I was in big trouble. My only chance now was to go on a birdie barrage or to somehow make a hole-in-one. Since I recorded two in the last six months, I knew that anything was indeed possible.

I took dead aim at the flagstick and visualized the ball dropping right into the hole. It looked awesome off the clubface, and it was heading right at the flag. Nearly a swish, it landed twenty inches to the left of the pin and unfortunately trickled way down to the back of the green. Luckily, I was able to make two good putts to secure my par, but Todd was now putting for a "net eagle." He nearly made it but nonetheless settled for a 3 and added four points to his almost insurmountable lead over me. With the score now 27 to 21, I knew that I had to birdie out or record another miracle hole-in-one over the final few holes. Unfortunately, my birdie streak never materialized, and I entered hole 18 down by the score of 33 to 27. Todd promptly hit another high arcing tee shot to within twelve feet, and I knew that he had secured at least another par and another two points. Watching his picture-perfect swing and the ball traveling high and true with the ocean crashing down to our left and a beautiful sun setting over the waves was truly a postcard setting. *This is what golf is all about*, I thought to myself.

There was only one thing left for me to do to make this moment even more glorious; a walk-off hole-in-one would definitely make this the most memorable round of golf ever. I told him to stand behind me and to record this moment on video so that we could forever preserve this moment on celluloid. Again, I took dead aim and visualized the exact ball flight that would take the ball into the cup. I knew that even if Todd were to manage to make his very makeable birdie putt, he still would only be left with a grand total of thirty-seven points. I really didn't care if he did beat me as he is a much better golfer, and he had clearly outplayed me all day. But nonetheless, an ace would make for a serious Kodak moment that would forever be etched in our hearts and minds for the rest of our lives. So with the film crew rolling behind me, I confidently strode to my ball, ready to make history. To the best of my knowledge, my earlier walk-off hole-in-one against Steve is the only one that I had ever heard about, so I was quite certain that making another walk-off ace would definitely put me in the record books. The ball left my clubface with an effortless whack and was heading straight for the cup! Had I once again pulled off the totally improbable? Was history about to repeat itself for all to witness on YouTube? Alas, a gust of wind came up strongly off the ocean, and the ball fell a faint four feet short of the cup. *Such is the fate of the golfing gods*, I thought to myself. I had hit the shot exactly as I had planned, and I had nearly pulled off another miracle. In a scene reminiscent of when Jack said to Tiger, "Let's finish this the right way," as Jack birdied and Tiger eagled at Jack's final PGA championship at Valhalla 2000, Todd said the same to me. When we both did in fact make our birdie putts, we had both put icing onto this wonderful golfing expedition. The final score of 37 to 31 was totally irrelevant as the golfing and camaraderie was how I was forever going to remember this moment. Or so I thought. We topped off this exquisite round with a couple of ice-cold beers as we watched the sun set on this picture-perfect horizon. We toasted each other and our special brotherly bond as we thought aloud, "Neither golf nor life can get much better than this!"

"Well, actually it can," he paused, "I just found out that Francis is pregnant and that I am going to be a father!" Tears of joy overcame us as I knew right then that I would indeed remember this moment forevermore.

As we soaked in this moment for as long as we could, I could hardly wait to give Francis a hug and congratulate her as well. When we met her for dinner, she could see the look in my eyes that Todd had in fact welcomed me with the wonderful news. She politely asked, "How was golf?"

"Never better," I blurted out as I gave her a big hearty congratulatory hug. "A magical day indeed!"

Returning to the Scene of the Crime, This Time Utilizing GITCA GOLF Guidelines

Following a wonderful dinner with the "three of them," Todd let me in on another surprise. Not only was I going to get a return visit the magnificent *Dye Preserve*, I was also going to be playing it with one of my boyhood idols, the incomparable tennis legend John Lloyd. I was so excited to get to play this course under official GITCA GOLF rules with my brother and one of my idols and introduce him to GITCA GOLF as well. As we sat down to lunch, Todd's other golfing buddy asked if he could join us for the round. "Absolutely," we all said. He joined us for a quick bite before our tee time, and I explained to them all about GITCA GOLF and asked if they would be willing to try it out as guinea pigs, so to speak, for my research and my book. When I found out that our fourth, Trey, was the club champion at the prestigious *Everglades Country Club*, my excitement rose even more as I was anxious to see how a scratch golfer would take to the GITCA format. When I explained the format for the proper designated tee boxes, it was all agreed that John Lloyd and I would be playing from the white tee boxes while Trey and Todd would naturally be teeing off from the black championship tees. By the way, the *Dye Preserve* does have even farther-back tees for the PGA golfers to try their hand at, but we all decided that the black tees would be a fair enough test.

Since we had the opportunity to hit the range first, we all nailed our first drives, and no one even thought about hitting a mulligan. Even though they hit monster drives of over three hundred yards, both Todd and Trey were still farther away from the green than John and I, given that we teed off almost eighty yards in front of them, with no remorse, I might add. They both nearly made the green with their second shots on this straightaway par 5, and they easily recorded greens in regulation and took their pars and two points each. John also hit the green in regulation and recorded a par, while I unfortunately took a bogey and found myself in last place with a single point. I didn't care, however, as I was getting to spend a spectacular day on this amazing course with my beloved brother, one of my childhood idols, and a reigning club champion. I knew that I was probably going to finish in last place, but I was going to enjoy the heck out of this golfing experience.

This par theme for them and bogeys for me continued as the round progressed, and after four holes, Trey had 8 points, Todd 7, John 6, and me a respectable 4 points. I had hit several of the greens in regulation, but the greens were running about 14 on the stimpmeter, and I was blowing all my first putts way past the hole. I wasn't at the local muni anymore! Surprisingly, at the fifth hole, they all declared that this would be their "par buster" hole. I found this odd since this is the number 1 handicap hole on the course with trouble everywhere. When all three of them hit their drives off-line, I reminded them that they still each had their roving mulligan left. They thought about it, but they didn't want to use up all their lifelines on one hole. We all ended up getting double bogeys or worse on this diabolical hole, and thus, no points were awarded, and they had all used up their par busters. They were pissed, but they were all way ahead of me. The next hole is a drivable par 4, and I decided I had nothing to lose and that this would be as good a hole as any for me to utilize my par buster. When I pulled my first drive into the lake that guards the right side, I immediately invoked my roving mulligan and subsequent last lifeline. They all looked at me with surprise until I bombed my best drive of the day and ended up just short of the putting surface. When I hit the green in regulation and two-putted for a 4, I had secured a "par buster birdie," and I was now creeping up the leaderboard. Everyone else also managed to par this hole, so now Trey had 10 points, Todd 9, and John and I were both tied with 8 points each. Even though I was clearly out of my league with this awesome foursome, I was now making a game of it, and we all were having a blast.

Just as I was having a faint glimpse that I could stay with these guys, all three of them took it to another level. Trey went birdie, par, birdie. Todd went par, birdie, par. John parred out, and I went bogey, bogey, bogey. So at the turn, Trey had 20 points, Todd had 17 points, John had 14 points, and I was bringing up the rear with 11 points. We all got a quick drink at the turn and realized that we had played that nine in about an hour and a half. Everyone was having a ball, and they all were clearly enjoying the GITCA format. I was getting my butt kicked, but I was certain that I would always remember this golf outing no matter how the back nine turned out.

The Gatorade must have rejuvenated me as I parred the next four holes to find myself with a very respectable 19 points. Trey parred three of these holes, Todd two, and John one. So after thirteen holes, Trey had 27 points, Todd 23 points, and John and I were tied at 19. I was all smiles as I had gained a little acknowledgment from my forecaddie that I was doing pretty well. Unfortunately, the best I could do from here on out was to bogey out and finish in last place with a very well-earned 24 points. John also struggled coming down the stretch, but he did manage to post two more pars and finished with a very respectable 26 points. Todd managed to birdie hole 17, but he failed to post any other pars and finished with an awesome 31 points. Trey parred holes 17 and 18 and finished as the "grand GITCA champion" with a robust 34 points. Even though John finished in third place, he seemed genuinely excited about the GITCA format. In fact, they all embraced the fact that a bad hole or two doesn't ruin the rest of one's round and the fact that it was so easy to tabulate everyone's score. They also agreed that playing from the proper set of tee boxes really gives everyone a fair chance to hit greens in regulation and score well. I was so excited that they all loved it, and I reminded them that this round would definitely be in the book and that I was clearly in awe of all of them.

What a difference this golfing experience was in deference to the previous round I had played on this amazing course with golf's traditional scoring system and all of us hacking away from the blue tees. Only Todd had a good time that day, while the other three of us were wondering why we even bothered with this "dreaded" game. Today was a far cry from that gut-wrenching experience as we all ended our rounds excited about spreading the word about GITCA GOLF. Even though I finished in last place, I still had nothing but positive experiences out on the links with my brother and my newfound golfing buddies.

Observing the Folly of Golfers Refusing to Move up to Their Proper Tee Boxes

June 23, 2014. I arrived at the golf course an hour early in order to try and hone my short game. As I was hitting delicate lob wedges and holing putt after putt, I made careful note of the groups of men who were teeing off just to my left. Being a Monday morning, it was mostly senior citizens who were enjoying the golden years of their retirement. But the question I asked of myself was, Were they really enjoying themselves out on the golf course? I was delighted to see that all seven groups that I observed teed off from the white tees. *Thank goodness*, I thought. *Maybe they are listening to Jack Nicklaus and are now playing from the proper set of tee markers for their abilities.* My hopes were quickly dashed, however, as most of these groups had no business playing from the white tees. Except for a few individuals in the last group to tee off, not one of these other men hit their drives farther than 180 yards. Not only were these drives not hit a sufficient distance to justify playing from the white tees, nearly all of them were off the fairway. I am talking way off the fairway. There is no way that these gentlemen were going to enjoy their rounds of golf playing from these extreme yardages. I watched intently all the groups follow up shots to the green, and there were many, and it was readily apparent that none of the twenty-eight men had hit the green in regulation. In fact, the majority of them ended up with a double bogey or more, and they were extremely slow as it took a long time to find their wayward drives and follow-up hacks. The bad news for them and the golfers who had to follow them is that hole number 1 is one of the shortest holes on the golf course. I am quite certain that none of these gentlemen were going to come close to breaking 100 legitimately.

Fortunately for my buddies and me, these golfers had made it to hole number 6 by the time we teed off. When I caught up to these groups at the nineteenth hole, it looked as though they had been in a war. There were not many smiles, and I asked them if they had had a good time. "It beats working, but that is about it." I was curious as to what they had all shot, but I was in fact more curious to see how many greens in regulation were recorded by the twenty-eight golfers as a whole. I am betting less than fifty, and that translates into high scores and very long days out on the course. If I was more brazen, I would have told them about GITCA GOLF and how they all should be playing from the yellow tees if they truly wanted to enjoy themselves out on the course and to make themselves competitive against the golf course. I am quite certain that the group would have doubled and perhaps even tripled their greens in regulation. How much more fun would these hardworking retirees enjoy themselves if they were recording a lot more pars or tap in bogeys? I am guessing a lot more, not to mention the fact that they would greatly increase their pace of play as well as everyone else's. After watching these senior golfers, it dawned on me that if you are not getting on the green or at least pin high at least a third of the time, then you are playing from sets of tees that are way above your pay grade. To me, the number of greens hit in regulation is the most pertinent statistic there is relative to one's enjoyment on the course. Certainly, your score can fluctuate due to your short-game success or lack thereof. But if you are not hitting at least a third of the greens or at least coming close to the green, then you need to move up and allow yourself and everyone around you to play much more efficiently and with a lot more gusto.

Why do people quit playing golf or greatly reduce their number of rounds?

1. Rounds take too long for our busy lifestyles.
2. Most of the courses are not user-friendly.
3. Too expensive to justify overall enjoyment.
4. Playing courses that are too hard and from distances that make for long days.
5. Embarrassment—worried that you will humiliate yourself in front of peers.
6. Guilt from spending quality time away from family.
7. Too many arguments breaking out due to handicap validity.
8. Playing with golfers who are way better than us.
9. Playing with golfers who are horrible.
10. Playing with golfers who take forever to play.
11. Playing with golfers who are too much sticklers for rule interpretations.
12. Being forced to play from tee boxes that overwhelm you.
13. Paralysis due to overanalysis.
14. Having your day ruined far too often by one or two horrible holes.
15. Too many scoring disagreements.
16. Having day ruined by people who take themselves and the game too seriously.

17. Lack of overall joy out on the links.
18. The realization that you have spent too much money and that you still stink.
19. The realization that there are far more important things in life than golf.
20. Self-esteem rising and falling with one's score and handicap.
21. Trying to attain perfection at a sport where perfection is unattainable.
22. Reaching a certain level of excellence and then losing it forevermore.
23. Fear of failure or of totally embarrassing oneself.
24. No longer being able to compete with your playing companions.
25. Being accosted for shooting way better or way worse than stated handicap

I must admit that many of the aforementioned reasons almost caused me to give up the game a time or two. I can only thank my lucky stars for allowing me to persevere even when my game had gone way south. It is frightening to think how many wonderful memories I would have missed out on over the last several years had I let my emotions get the better of me and actually given up the game for good. Although golf has continued to cause me much anguish from time to time, the wonderful moments with my friends and family out on the links have more than made up for my momentary moments of despair. Since embracing GITCA GOLF, almost all my golf outings are memorable and competitive right to the end.

HOLE NUMBER 11

Why Do We Really Even Bother with This Game Anyway?

Had to go back to work this week, but I did manage to get in a quick 9 at the local par 3 course. I was playing by myself, so I took the extra moments that I had to look around and study the other golfers out on the course. The majority of them were kids and senior citizens who were just happy to be hacking it around the course twenty to forty yards at a time. Most of the kids were not very good, but they were slapping the ball around with great glee, while the majority of the very senior citizens were simply grateful to be on this side of the soil. In fact, the elderly couple in front of me who were in their late eighties was downright giddy as they hacked away and occasionally missed the ball. And this got me thinking, *This is what golf is all about: making the most of each moment that you have been given on this earth to truly and thoroughly enjoy oneself on and off the golf course.* The average age that a person lives is around seventy-five years old or roughly twenty-seven thousand days. So why not make the most of each and every one of them? All of us are guilty of ruining so many precious moments on the golf course by being overly concerned with our score or our handicap. Where in reality, no one really gives a crap if you shot 74 or 104 or if you are a 5 or a 25 handicap. So we should quit concerning ourselves so much with our score as though it is a badge of honor or a scarlet letter. Nobody gives a rat's ass about your score; all they really care about is, Are you making their own golf experience more enjoyable?

Personally, I would much rather play with a hack who doesn't take himself or the game too seriously than a near-scratch golfer who is going to get pissed off every time he misses the ball one groove down. I want to surround myself with golfers who play quickly, laugh often, and make my day so much fun it will last in my memory bank forevermore. When we are out on the links for the camaraderie and the quality time with our friends and family members, then these are the moments that we are going to carry in our hearts for the rest of our lives. In fact, when our overall joy is no longer predicated by the number of strokes that we take, then an unnecessary burden has been lifted, and only then will we be able to fully enjoy ourselves. Consequently, our results are usually much better when we relax and don't take ourselves too seriously.

Don't be that guy who is so concerned about his handicap that he fails to appreciate what is truly important in life or out on the golf course. Don't be that guy who is such a jerk or who gets so mad at himself that no one ever wants to tee it up with you. Don't arrive on your deathbed lamenting all the things you never got around to doing. Don't do this to yourself. Start making your friends and family your top priority. Don't get so caught up in the rat race that you fail to really make the most of your limited opportunities. Begin today to start making more of these precious moments in your life. Call a friend and tell them how much they mean to you and that you all need to start prioritizing times to get together more often. What better place to do this than on the links? Quit trying to be so brazen on the course, and learn to really listen to and cherish all your wonderful friends and family. Take every opportunity to compliment them and thank them for always being there for you. Let your kindred spirit flow as well as your golf swing. When your time comes to meet your maker, these are the things that you will be remembered for, not what your blessed handicap was or was not.

So pick up that phone right now and book a tee time for this weekend in the late afternoon so that your round will be ending when the sun is setting. Then call your best friends and cajole them to join you for a quick nine or eighteen. Chances are, you most likely will have the course all to yourselves. Win, lose, or draw, you will have a ball playing a quick round of GITCA GOLF with them. No matter what the scorecard reads at the end of the day, you all will have a special bonding time and a chance to unwind from your hectic workweek and home life. We all know that, of course, the competitive juices are going to be flowing, and you all will want to win badly, but at the end of the day, you all will be so glad that you came out and had the time of your life bonding with your closest friends. Undoubtedly, you will all probably end the round with a few cold beverages as you relish this special kinship, and you want it to continue just a little bit longer before you must return to the real world. Remind everyone just how awesome this was to recharge all your batteries and that you all need to make a pact to do this much more often. When you think about it, these special bonding moments with your buddies have become too sparse due to everyone's busy lives. Make a commitment, and in fact, book a tee time at the same course for two weeks from now so that everyone has something to look forward to with great optimism.

HOLE NUMBER 12

Introducing the Most Ardent Golfer in the Family to GITCA GOLF

Fortunately for me, I was able to go back up to our Michigan cottage in early August this time to overlap with my older sister Betsy and her family. I was very excited but, I must admit, a little apprehensive to tell my brother-in-law Jim all about GITCA GOLF. Now Jim is one of the very best golfers whom I know, and he is a member of some of the finest country clubs in the United States. I knew full well that he was a stickler for handicaps, and I knew that I would have my work cut out for me getting him to change his golfing ways.

As soon as Jim arrived, he immediately hopped in a car with his oldest son Jack and headed two hours away to the beautiful *Crystal Downs Golf Club*. He, of course, invited me to go with them, but I knew that going with them would be an all-day affair, and I, of course, wanted to spend time on the water with my family. Before they had arrived, I had scheduled a nine-hole tee time for later that same day on the brand new *Northport Creek Golf Course*. When Jim and his son returned after their ten-hour expedition clearly exhausted, I assured him that we would simply reschedule our tee time for tomorrow. "Absolutely not," Jim insisted, "I am anxious to try out this GITCA GOLF!"

"How was Crystal Downs?" I asked.

"The course is absolutely gorgeous but way too difficult for me, and Jack is now ready to quit the game entirely. He is so frustrated," he quickly retorted.

"Are you saying that the course is too difficult for a 2 handicapper?" I inquired.

"There is trouble everywhere, and the greens were running a 14 on the stimpmeter, and of course, we played from the tips!" he responded in a clearly exasperated tone.

"That definitely wouldn't be any fun for me," I assured him. "That is why I came up with GITCA GOLF!"

"I am excited to try it out," he responded. "Let's go have some fun!"

"Indeed we will, as GITCA GOLF only accentuates the positives in golf!" I beamed.

I quickly explained the rules to him, and we both agreed that he would definitely be playing the blue tees, while I would be playing the white tees and that no strokes whatsoever would be given. Jim loved the sound of that, as being a 2 handicap, he almost always had to give his fellow competitors a bunch of strokes. I was excited too as this was my first time playing this brand-new nine-hole course. In fact, as it turns out, this was the only new golf course opening in the state of Michigan in 2014, while over forty courses were shutting down their doors for good. This is depressing, but it was exciting to know that they had built this beautiful course five minutes from our cabin.

I told him that we were afforded mulligans on the first tee, but since we both crushed our drives long and far, we did not need them. Perhaps too fired up to get his first GITCA birdie, Jim airmailed the green and wound up taking a bogey as he recorded his very first GITCA point. I managed to safely put it on the green and two-putted for a par to take the lead by one point. We were off, and I had a lead that I knew would be fleeting, but I was going to savor it as long as I could.

The second hole is the easiest hole on the course, and we both easily hit the green in regulation, and both had tap-in pars. I now had four points and kept my precarious lead by one.

The third hole is a short dogleg right, but I hit my drive too far left into the tree line and took a bogey 5. Jim played a perfect hole and easily got on the green in regulation and promptly made his par to tie me for the lead with five points. Game on! Through three holes, I had not been given a single stroke, and yet I was tied with a golfer who is way better than me. I knew that it was only a matter of time before he blew right past me, but I was going to learn by watching his tempo and his decision-making.

The fourth hole is a long par 3 to a very small green, and Jim hit a beautiful 5 iron pin high, while I yanked my utility club into the trap on the left of the green. I failed to get up and down, while Jim calmly two-putted for par and a one-point lead.

"Pars are never a bad thing, are they?" he quipped.

"No they are not," I reiterated, "especially in GITCA GOLF."

The fifth hole proved to be a waterloo for both of us as we both tried to cut off too much of the dogleg left and hit it way into the woods on the left. I reminded him that everything in GITCA is played as a lateral hazard, so there would be no loss of distance, simply a one-stroke penalty. He asked if he could utilize his roving mulligan at this point. "Absolutely," I insisted. And the champion golfer that he is, he promptly striped one way down the middle and just missed getting a birdie on the hole. Again, I reminded him that a par is always a good score and that he had made a great utilization of his one roving mulligan. I, unfortunately, hacked my way down the fairway and eventually put my ball in my pocket for the day's first official GITCA. Jim was now starting to pull away from me with a 9-to-6 lead, and the next hole was a relatively short par 5.

When I reminded him that we both still had our par busters and that this might be a good hole to utilize it on, his ears perked up, and he looked at the hole on the card. Since no one was in front of us or behind us and since we were the last tee time of this glorious day, we decided to drive out in the fairway and survey the hole. Since it had a very narrow landing, I decided to not invoke my par buster on this hole. Jim saw that it was relatively short and that this might be a good opportunity to make a low score, and thus, he decided to declare that this hole would be his "par buster hole." Jim promptly took out his 3 wood since he had already used up his mulligan and proceeded to stripe one about 230 straight-down the middle. I hit my best drive of the day, but unfortunately, it got caught up in the fairway bunker lip, and it would take me two shots to get out. My hole was essentially over, and I was now glad that I hadn't declared this hole for my par buster. Jim, meanwhile, took out a 7 iron and laid up beautifully right at the 100-yard marker. Of course, this is perfect distance for his sand wedge, which he covered the flagstick with on his approach. Although he just missed making a 4, his tap in 5 gave him a par buster birdie and added four more points to his tally. Jim had played such a smart and calculated hole that all I could do was admire the ease with which he had pulled this off. I didn't mind that he was now blowing my doors off by a count of 13 to 6 as we both were having a wonderful time out on the links. I was so excited that he was really enjoying GITCA GOLF. To have a golfer with his pedigree and love of the game be genuinely excited with my system was making me giddy.

    The next hole is another short par 4, but the landing area for a drive is extremely narrow. Jim, unfortunately, pushed his drive into the woods on the right, and when his next shot went awry, Jim officially put his ball in his pocket for his first official GITCA walk of shame. "Keep your head up, laddie," I reminded him. "Those two errant shots and that one bad hole doesn't tarnish your round at all. You still have your thirteen points, and those can never be taken from you!"

    I, too, pushed my drive into the woods on the right, but Jim quickly reminded me that I had yet to invoke my roving mulligan. Desperate to try and regain some semblance of dignity, I quickly reached in my pocket and proceeded to almost drive the green. I hit a poor chip shot but was still able to manage a par, and now I only trailed 13 to 8 with two holes left.

    The next hole is a very short par 3 to an elevated green guarded by all sorts of bunkers and waste area. Jim, of course, being a master iron player, promptly put one right in the middle of the green and, of course, made another par to now give him a grand total of fifteen points. Knowing that the last hole is a very long uphill par 4 to a small and narrow green, I decided to invoke my last lifeline, my par buster. I hit a decent tee shot, but it came up just short of the green. When I just missed getting up and down for my 3, my par buster 4 was good for two points, and now Jim had a 15-to-10 lead heading into the final hole.

We both hit great drives on this wonderful finishing hole, but I failed to reach the green in regulation, while Jim calmly knocked a 6 iron to about eight feet away. Keeping with the trend of the day, I once again failed to get up and down and finished with a very respectable eleven points. I hadn't embarrassed myself in front of Jim, and I was learning so much just by watching him in action. Perhaps the only thing left would be for Jim to knock in his short birdie putt to seal this wonderful round as the sun was setting. Alas, the putt just rimmed out, and he had to settle for his par and a grand total of seventeen points in nine holes on a course he had never seen before! It was clearly an impressive feat, and we both were smiling from ear to ear as we gave each other a hearty handshake on a round neither of us would soon likely forget. Clearly, Jim's spirits had made a dramatic turnaround from his golfing adventure earlier in the day. Earlier, his ego had been battered and bruised, but now he once again was full of confidence and loving golf perhaps more than he ever had. I was just so thrilled that I got to witness this landmark event in person and, more importantly, that he had fully embraced the GITCA GOLF concept.

As we got back to the cabin, everyone had just come in from the beach and was starving. Jim went right to work, feverishly making his "world-famous fettucine alfredo" while I got busy preparing the steaks for everyone. It was nearly 9:30 p.m., but it was still a little light out as the sun was slowly slipping below the horizon. We had a wonderful feast as everyone remarked that these steaks were as good as any steakhouse, while the pasta clearly lived up to its billing. The wine and beer flowed freely, and we recounted our round to our families and friends and told them all about the positive aspects of GITCA GOLF. Jim's son Jack was eager to try it out since his golfing experience earlier that day had left him psychologically scarred. Jim's good friend was also eager to get in on the fun, so the three of them made a tee time for the same time the next night. I was considering joining them, but I realized that I needed and wanted to spend quality time with my family at the cabin. So I clearly outlined the eight simple rules for them, and when I asked them what their distances were, they all surmised that they were all about the same distance. "Perfect," I said, "you all will be teeing it up from the blues."

"Yes, Kelley," Jim chimed in. "But even though Jack is actually a little longer than me, he doesn't stand a realistic chance."

"GITCA has a way of evening things out," I quickly responded. "You never know what is going to happen. Just go have fun and let the chips fall where they may."

For the next two hours, I had an awesome time tossing the football and swimming with my son in the water, but I was very eager to see how the threesome was getting along. I got in my car to head up to the course to see them finish, but as I was pulling out, they were pulling in. The three of them had finished their round in less than ninety minutes. "How was it?" I was dying to know.

"It was spectacular!" they all shouted out in unison. "We had the best time ever, and Jack was the big winner!"

Indeed, it came down to the very last hole, and Jack won it with a par on the brutal finishing hole to nip his dad and his lacrosse coach by a point each. Final tally, Jack 16 points, while both Jim and Ron recorded 15 points each. In fact, entering hole number 8, Jack was in last place, but he had strategically saved his par buster for this hole since it is the shortest on the course and netted a 3 on it for a par buster birdie to put the match in a three-way deadlock. When he knocked in his twelve-foot par putt to beat his father for the first time ever in golf, his shouts of joy could be heard for miles around. Perhaps a father has never been more proud than Jim now was of Jack. Remember just twenty-four hours earlier, Jack was totally intent on quitting golf forever. He now, however, had rekindled the passion that both his father and he had for this wonderful game. He hopped out of the car and gave me a big hug and said, "Uncle Kelley, I love GITCA GOLF!" *Mission accomplished*, I thought to myself. If GITCA GOLF can reignite this type of passion for everyone, then I will feel vindicated in my pursuit of finding a more enjoyable way of playing this awesome game for the masses.

HOLE NUMBER 13

The Passing of a Dear Golfing Buddy and a Lifelong Mentor

Unfortunately, I lost another one of my great role models and dear friends this past year with the untimely passing of the legendary Saul Kaufman. "Papa Saul" or "Papi" as he was affectionately known to everyone was one of those hearty souls who truly lived life to its fullest. Every day that he was on this side of the soil was a blessing for him and for all those who were fortunate enough to get to spend quality time with this kindred spirit. He was by no means a great golfer, although I did witness his only hole-in-one, which brought immediate tears of joy to everyone who witnessed this miracle. But what Saul lacked in golfing prowess, he made up for in spades with his enthusiasm for the game and for life. Watching his passion for this game and for all his friends and family members brought out the best in everyone who was lucky enough to join him on the links. He loved being around the game so much that eventually he became a golf ranger. Everyone whom he greeted on the course soon came to love this man as well, and he quickly garnered the nickname of "the Lone Ranger." Golfers would return to Glenview golf course as much to see their new beloved friend as they would to play golf on this wonderful course.

There are few people whom one encounters in their lives who are beloved by everyone. Saul was definitely one of those kindred souls. If you were ever down when you arrived at the course, you weren't when you left due to Saul's jovial spirit. He often beamed to me, "Kelley, I am the luckiest SOB that ever lived! I have my health [even though he had four bypass surgeries], I have a roof over my head [a double wide], and the greatest friends and family in the world!"

"Indeed you do," I was quick to note as I was heeding my role model. "Plus you get to play golf with me, your main man!" Boy, did we have fun hacking it around the course without a care in the world as to how high or low we were shooting. We were simply enjoying the wonderful camaraderie, the occasional spectacular shot, and a lifetime of fond memories.

Although we miss our dear friend immensely, we are all quick to realize that he never got cheated, and neither did we. We loved this man with all our heart, and he knew it full well. The best way to describe him was that he was like a great big puppy dog that was so excited to see you that he would always shower you with hugs and compliments. What a great role model for all of us to strive to emulate. Saul was always a happy camper, but he was most content out on the links with his loved ones. We miss our dear friend, but his spirit lives on in all of us, especially when all his loved ones are teeing it up together. Rarely a round goes by that we don't quote him or acknowledge his passion for living life to its fullest. If everyone who teed it up could learn to love and appreciate golf as Saul did, then every golf course in the world would be continually packed. Hell, if everyone could learn to appreciate all that we have been so blessed with as Saul constantly did, then in fact the world would be that much better of a place. Hopefully my story of Saul has inspired you and will continue to inspire future generations of golfers who learn to emulate Saul's passion for golf and every blessed day that we have on this planet.

HOLE NUMBER 14

Inherent Problem with Traditional Golf Scoring System

When you are playing the traditional stroke-play scoring system, even a great round of 78 is six shots to the negative. One continually laments about what could have been. With the GITCA scoring system, there are never any negatives. The worst score you can get on a round is zero, and this is not likely to happen that often if you are playing from the correct set of tees. Thus, the GITCA scoring system only allows for mostly positive experiences on the golf course. What a difference in mindset to know that only positive results are recorded. Certainly, you still may hit many poor golf shots, but at least your psyche won't be destroyed. Even if you play a horrible round, you are much likely to say, "Oh well, I will get them next time." With the traditional scoring system, a round north of 100 might tempt you to say, "I will never play this frustrating game again." With GITCA scoring, you may post a very low number such as 3 or 4, but that is all in the positive, and you dwell on the positives rather than the negatives. You say to yourself, "Well, now I have a goal for next time," and you are much more likely to notice where your weaknesses are that are preventing you from attaining more positive numbers. With traditional golf, you are much more likely to simply say, "I suck, and I quit!" Playing from the correct set of tee markers, you are much more likely to have scoring irons in your hand for your approach shots and thus are much more likely to hit far more greens in regulation or at least be green high. Then it is simply a matter of shoring up your short game by spending much more time around the practice green rather than simply heading to the range and mashing your driver as far as you can. With the GITCA scoring system, it is also much easier to put your bad holes and your bad shots in the rearview mirror rather than belaboring them and letting them gnaw at your self-esteem. With the traditional golf scoring system, starting out with a couple of doubles and a triple assures you of having a day you would rather forget. GITCA GOLF allows you to simply shake off your slow start and gear yourself up for the next hole and hence your next opportunity to put some points up on the board.

More Examples of the Beauty of Teeing Off from the Correct Tee Markers

One of the top local female golfers recently finished seventh in the state championships. When asked why her scores had improved from the mid 80s to the mid 70s, she replied matter-of-factly, "When playing with the boys' team, I had to tee off from the white tees, and I didn't hit that many greens in regulation. Now that I am playing with the girls, we get to tee off from the yellow/red tees, and I have a pitching wedge or less in my hand for nearly every approach shot on the par 4s. Naturally, I am hitting a lot more greens in regulation, and thus my scoring average is ten shots better." This is exactly our point with GITCA GOLF and the need for everyone to play from the appropriate tee boxes so that they have ample scoring opportunities. Again, everyone needs to put their ego aside and learn to hit from the tee boxes that are going to allow them to utilize their scoring irons after they have hit decent drives based on their ability. Obviously, this girl could compete and beat the majority of the boys that she squared off against from the white tees, but she could score infinitely better when she was allowed to move up to the tee boxes designated for her during the state championship. I am going out on a limb here, but I don't think this obviously awesome golfer was going to finish seventh competing with the other contestants from the white tees. Again, GITCA guidelines are not gender based at all. If this young lady can consistently hit her drives plus her 8 iron a combined distance of 330–360 yards, then according to our guidelines, she should be teeing it up from the white tees. On the other hand, if her combined distances are significantly more or significantly less, then she should definitely be teeing it up from the tee boxes that fit her averages. She would know her combined distances better than anyone, so when she plays GITCA GOLF, she will know exactly where she should be teeing off from in order to be competitive with the rest of the golfers in her group.

GITCA Scoring Will Be Skewed if Golfers Refuse to Play from Proper Tee Boxes

Case in point happened the very next day as my two most frequent golfing buddies—Steve and Bob—and I decided to go out for a quick nine holes right before dusk. At the last moment, Steve's brother Dave decided to join us and immerse himself in GITCA GOLF for the first time in his life. Being a college golfer at a division III school, Dave was obviously a very good golfer, but we all knew that he was not nearly as long off the tee as his younger brother Steve. When we got to the first tee, I clearly stated the GITCA golfing guidelines and suggested that Dave join Bob and I and tee it up from the white tees, while Steve of course would tee it up from the blue tees as customary. Dave scoffed at this notion and stated emphatically that he had way too much pride to saunter up to the white tees at this point in his golfing career. I warned him that I was quite familiar with his driving and 8 iron distances (220-yard drives and 140-yard 8 irons) and that he clearly belonged at the white tees.

"I can hang with my brother," he insisted.

"I am certain that you can," I assured him, "but you are most likely going to get your doors blown off with the GITCA scoring format."

"I will take my chances," he retorted in an extremely confident tone.

As the match wore on, Bob and Steve were parring darn near every hole on the course while I was getting my fair share. Dave, on the other hand, was struggling to find a par anywhere. He kept asking Bob and me if we were feeling guilty at all for teeing it up at the white tees, while he and his brother were swinging mightily from the blue tees. "Not at all," Bob and I both retorted in unison. "We enjoy hitting almost every green in regulation and putting for birdies and pars. Struggling to make bogeys isn't much fun, is it?"

"No, I guess not!" he spouted back. "But how is playing GITCA GOLF going to get you all ready for playing tournament golf?"

"Are you serious?" I quipped back. "When was the last time any of us played in an actual golf tournament?"

"I don't know, about twenty years ago?" he admitted sheepishly, acknowledging his own fodder.

"The only actual tournaments we all ever play in are charity scrambles in which we play the ball up and only have to take the best shot out of four!" I reminded him. "Scrambles are far more lenient with the golfing rules than GITCA GOLF," I assured him.

"There are just so many rules that I didn't know about coming into GITCA GOLF," he stammered.

"There are really only eight rules that you need to abide by in GITCA GOLF," I assured him.

The final tally for our nine holes: Steve 22 points, Bob 20 points, me with 18 points, and Dave with a measly 10 points. Not bad for his first time playing GITCA GOLF, but I am quite certain that he would have been at least up there with me in the scoring department if he had heeded my advice and teed off from the white tees. Next time, I am going to insist that he move up with Bob and me and play the white tees and possibly surpass his younger brother and get top honors for the day.

Return Trip to Florida with GITCA Guidelines Firmly in Place
March 5, 2015: Par 3 Golf with My Younger Brother and Dad

I jumped off the plane, grabbed my clubs, and made a dash for the beloved Raymond Floyd Palm Beach Par 3 course to join up with my dad and brother before the rains came. It was spitting rain, but it looked like we might be able to get the round in before the big storms hit. I erroneously thought that the rain would scare most of the golfers off, but the course was packed with golfers of all ages and abilities. This was awesome to see and proved my premonition that par 3 and executive courses are the wave of the future in our ever-fast-paced society. Golfers of every handicap level cannot get enough of this truly scenic seaside course.

We finally got on the course behind a foursome in a cart on this very short and relatively flat course. We knew right away it was going to be slow, and it was going to be interesting to see how long my dad would be able to go at this snail's pace before blowing a gasket. I reminded everyone that I was here all week and that if it was too slow, we would just play nine and pick up again tomorrow. We all agreed, and we all hit the green with our opening tee shots. Long-knocker Todd was playing from the tips, while my dad and I hit from the white tees. I once again encouraged Dad to move up to the yellow tees, but he was having no part of it as he felt like it was a total affront to his manhood. Todd and I were really on with our games, but Dad was having trouble reaching most of the greens with his tee shots. His short game, which is usually pretty decent, was a mess today, and he was dejectedly picking up on about half the holes in disgust, saying, "That is enough." I reassured him that picking up is fine and, in fact, is encouraged with GITCA GOLF. Todd and I, on the other hand, were practically knocking down every pin we saw and were having quite an epic battle once again from our respective tee boxes.

Even though it is just a par 3 course, on many of the holes, there is a large discrepancy between the differing tee boxes. On the fourth hole, it is a 210-yard carry-over water from the black tees, while it is only a mere 155 yards from the white tees. This long-forced carry proved to be no match for Todd as he promptly took out his brand-new shiny 2 hybrid and proceeded to hit a laser beam that soared high and straight before landing like a feather four feet from the cup. My dad and I watched with envy and awe as we both knew that neither one of us had that shot in our repertoire. We could stand there with a huge bucket of balls and not come close to replicating anything like that. "See, Dad," I exclaimed, "that is why we don't play from the same set of tees as Todd. He is younger, stronger, and a hell of a lot better golfer than us, which is fine. We can compete with him if we all play from our correct tee boxes."

"Well, I am getting my doors blown off by both of you!" Dad stammered.

"Well, that's because you aren't playing from the right set of tees for your ability. You are seventy-three! I am forty-eight, and Todd is thirty-eight! It's okay to admit that you are older and that you can't hit the ball as far as you once did, and that is okay. It doesn't make you any less of a man, for crying out loud!" I retorted. "Now move up to the yellow tees so that you can enjoy this wonderful golfing mecca with your sons!"

I quickly moved up to my friendly white tee box and proceeded to hit a beautiful 5 iron that landed ten feet below the cup. With both my and Todd's prodding, Dad finally relented and moved up to the yellow tee boxes and hit a beautiful 7 iron from 115 yards that nearly took the flag out of the hole. I couldn't resist, "See, Dad, isn't this a lot more fun to pull off shots that are well within our capabilities?" Dad never liked to admit that he was ever wrong, but I could see a huge grin appear as he was beaming from ear to ear on his near hole in one effort. Both Dad and Todd made their short birdie putts, while mine just lipped out. I could care less as we all were now having the time of our lives, and I knew that we would never forget this landmark moment.

We all played the remaining five holes right around par, and we all were having a blast. Unfortunately, not everyone on the course was adhering to the GITCA GOLF guidelines, and the pace had gotten absurdly slow. We all decided that nine holes was plenty and that we had better get home and cleaned up before Todd's boss (his beautiful wife) got upset with all of us for being late for our dinner reservation. The final tally on the scoreboard was Todd with 20 points, me with a robust 15 points, and Dad with a very respectable 12 points. The scores were totally irrelevant, however, as getting Dad on board with GITCA GOLF was the most triumphant moment of the round. I can't ever remember Dad being so giddy out on the links as he is quite proficient with a 7 iron or less in his hands. I told him that he needs to start embracing executive and par 3 courses as they play right into his forte. Both Todd and I had seen firsthand how exasperating it can be for Dad to try and continue to play regulation courses from the white tees. Hopefully, this quick little outing will encourage him to once and for all move up to the yellow tees with no shame and no remorse so that he can have far more uplifting moments out on the links with those closest to him.

HOLE NUMBER 15

A Boyhood Dream of Mine Comes to Fruition Getting to Meet Jack Nicklaus

Thanks to my new best friend, John Lloyd, I got the opportunity to go play tennis with the greatest golfer the world has ever known. At first, I was under the impression that I was going to be giving Jack a tennis lesson, and being a tennis-teaching professional for the last thirty years, I was extremely confident that I was going to be able to help Jack out with any perceived deficiencies in his game. However, on the way over, Mr. Lloyd informed me that we would be playing with ten or more other guys and that I shouldn't go all out since I was a guest. Naturally I agreed, but since I rarely get the opportunity to play much competitive tennis, I was now worried about embarrassing myself in front of John Lloyd and Jack Nicklaus. To add to the pressure, we would also be playing on grass courts that I had only played on once when I was twelve. When we arrived at Jack's amazing house, I saw that there were at least ten other guys playing, and they were all very good and very competitive. In addition to Jack's stable of good lifelong friends were a few fellow tennis-teaching professionals, so I was made quickly aware that I would have to play very well so as not to embarrass myself in front of two of my childhood heroes. Luckily for me, the first round pairings had already been determined on the front two courts, so myself and two other late arriving compadres headed across the street to warm up on Jack's third grass court. This proved to be a lifesaver for me as I was able to get accustomed to the feel of the grass courts and the pace of a live ball prior to demonstrating my game to Jack and John.

After about a half hour of properly finding our groove, we headed back over to the main courts just off Jack's back porch and waited for our turn to join this lively tennis combativeness. Fortunately for me, I was paired with John for the first set, and I quickly felt right at ease as John's world-class talent seemed to rub off on me just a little bit, and we quickly stormed out to a four-to-love lead within a few minutes. John didn't hit the ball any harder than most of the rest of the guys. He just never missed, and he knew exactly where to put each ball to give us a slight advantage and increase our probability of winning each point. Since touch and feel are the strengths of my tennis game as well, John and I meshed perfectly together, and we were steamrolling are slightly less talented opponents. John turned to me and reminded me that we should let them win a game or two since we were crashing their party, and I agreed wholeheartedly. I started just missing a shot here and a shot there, but John remained rock steady, and we continued to win game after game. I finally turned to him and said, "I thought we were going to let them win a game?"

"I changed my mind, mate," John quickly retorted. "The competitive juices are flowing, and we are in perfect synchronization with each other's game." I quickly realized that I would never ever receive a better compliment for the rest of my tennis career.

The other two combatants finally called "no joy" and forced John and I to split up. John became paired up with Jack on the other court, while I stayed on the same court and battled it out with three other great players. We played numerous sets, and unfortunately, I never got to be paired up with Jack. Nor did I ever get to play against him, but it was readily apparent to me that Jack was an excellent player and that he certainly didn't need any tips from me. I glanced over occasionally at Jack and John and was continually amazed at how intelligent they both played as well as how well they both moved for a seventy-five-year-old and sixty-year-old, respectively. They dominated their opponents, and I could tell that Jack enjoyed playing with John as his partner as much as I had.

This highly competitive competition continued for well over three hours, and I was getting quite winded. When I remarked to Jack that it is quite warm out here, he quickly shot me down by saying, "It feels great!" So there you have it, an out-of-shape tennis pro quickly being put in his place by a seventy-five-year-old man who also happens to be the greatest golfer of all time! I found out later that Jack was also one heck of a baseball catcher and that he started in high school over a player who would later become an all-star catcher in the major leagues. So Jack's stardom and legend grew tenfold in my mind as I became totally enthralled with his competitive spirit as well as his remarkable athleticism.

What I took away from this once-in-a-lifetime experience with these legends is that the competitive spirit never dies and that playing intelligently readily crosses over from one sport to the next. Every player who participated in this wonderful tennis outing was extremely competitive, but more importantly, a great time was had by all. There was a commissioner there who kept a running tally of how everyone was doing, but in reality, no one really paid much attention to who was winning. The real reason that everyone loved being there was for the thrill of the competition as well as the wonderful camaraderie. It was readily apparent that these same guys got together on most weekends to blow off some steam, to have a great competitive environment, and most importantly, to garner some much-needed male bonding and kinship.

When we finished up playing, I told them with all sincerity that playing with them was about as much fun as I have ever had on the tennis court. They all stroked my ego by remarking that I was a very good player and that I moved very well for a forty-seven-year-old. I thanked them all for their kind remarks, and I reminded everyone that I am a full year older than Jack when he was considered ancient upon winning the Masters at the ripe old age of forty-six! Jack got a big smirk out of this, so I felt it fitting to compliment him on how well he moved now at the young age of seventy-five. He said that I was being too kind, but we all knew that what I said was spot-on. When I remarked how intelligent he was as a player, he, of course, deferred to the tennis-teaching professionals who had helped him along the way, two of whom were playing against us and who I concurred with are some of the most intelligent players I have ever gone toe to toe with.

I could tell that Jack was having the time of his life out on the tennis courts with his lifelong friends. I thought to myself, *This is exactly the essence of GITCA GOLF that I hope everyone who tries it out experiences for themselves.* Nobody at the end of the day really cares who shot the best score; it is the camaraderie that really matters and will last a lifetime. My ultimate goal with GITCA GOLF is for everyone to have as much fun with their weekly golf games as Jack and his friends have out on the tennis courts each week.

Getting to Spend a Few Days with My Real Idols: My Parents

I left Jack's place and headed up the coast to Vero Beach to spend a few days with my beloved mother and my beloved stepfather, Don. I was on a high from getting to meet my idol and to not have embarrassed myself in front of him that I was anxious to tell them all about our chance encounter. I immediately told them that Jack was an outstanding athlete and tennis player who possesses unbelievable hand-eye coordination, but what really stood out to me was just how special a group Jack had assembled for his weekly tennis outings. I pointed out that all these men were extremely good tennis players and highly competitive but that their endearing friendship was the thing that really stood out to me. They were anxious to know what Jack thought of my GITCA GOLF concept, but I told them that I didn't want to overstay my welcome by bringing it up on our first acquaintance. I assured them that once the book is finished, I will rush a copy to Jack in order to get his opinion or, better yet, take him and his boys' golfing so that we can all experience the wonders of GITCA together.

We had a wonderful three days together as I got to stay at their amazing dream home that they had purchased together and whose view out to the waterfront is truly breathtaking. We were able to get out and golf each day, with each successive outing topping the previous one by a substantial margin. This was quite easy for me to accomplish as I was truly horrendous for my first eighteen holes of golf. Fortunately, we were playing full GITCA rules, so I was able to pick up once I reached double bogey or worse, which seemed to occur on the majority of the holes we played. Don, per usual, played nearly flawless golf each time out, and he was grinning from ear to ear throughout each round at just how remarkably well he was playing. He was convinced that my positive energy rubbed off on him and was the reason for his wonderful play, but I assured him that he was indeed the poster child for all the wonderment of GITCA GOLF. Unlike when he is forced to play on a regular basis from the white tees, I insist that he play from the yellow tees and that he show no signs of remorse for playing from his properly designated tees. When I inquired as to why many in his group insist on still playing from the white tees a majority of the time, he stated emphatically that it was due to tradition and their selfish pride. When I asked if anyone in his group could reach the green in regulation from the white tee distances on a regular basis, he stated emphatically that it was a very rare occurrence and that he was usually the longest and straightest hitter of his group. "Then it is downright silly," I stated, "that you all continue to deceive yourselves into thinking that you are going to enjoy yourselves from tee boxes that are way above your capabilities." Of course, he concurred with me immediately, but he and I both knew that old habits die hard.

So after the first day out on the links, I was seriously contemplating why I even kid myself into thinking that I am any kind of golfer whatsoever. It got me thinking that this is exactly what a majority of golfers must ask themselves after almost every round, especially if they are playing from tee boxes that allow them little chance of producing many positive results whatsoever. It became clear as day to me why golfers all over the world are leaving this game in droves, and that it is imperative for me to get the message out about GITCA GOLF so that golfers everywhere can learn to enjoy themselves more than they ever have out on the golf course.

Before the second round, Don and I headed to the range, and I was able to find my swing a little bit, and I drove the ball beautifully. I set myself up with very short irons on a majority of the holes, but my iron game was still not clicking, and Don once again lapped me with a score of 31 to 23. Mom was able to join us for the back nine, and she recorded a very respectable eleven GITCA points as we finished the back nine with the sun setting over the water for what was a truly remarkable sight. Over a magnificent steak dinner with yellow rice, we laughed about the ups and downs of our rounds as we rehashed how Mom had uttered an expletive on her way to an eight and a GITCA on the par 5 as she began to seriously question why she ever wastes her time with this stupid game. Alas, the golf gods must have been watching her folly as she came within inches of recording a hole-in-one on the very next hole, which left her with tears of joy. A funny and humbling game golf is indeed, we all agreed, and is one of the reasons why I am so intent about getting GITCA GOLF out to the masses. Special moments like this would be missed altogether if any of us had gone through with our intent about giving up this game for good.

The final day, we only had time for nine holes before I had to head out to the airport, but it was one of my most memorable rounds ever. Again we had time to hit the range prior to our tee time, and I finally found my iron game to go along with my impeccable driving, and I was fortunate enough to par the first seven holes. Don seemed to be matching me shot for shot, and we were both beside ourselves at how well we both were playing. We both managed to bogey the eighth hole after excellent drives, and so we were all tied up heading to the short par 4 ninth. When we both hit excellent drives and approach shots, we each let out whoops of joy and laughter at just how well we had struck the ball all day. Perhaps too giddy with excitement, I somehow managed to three-putt from twenty feet, while Don two-putted for his par and seventeen points total and yet another GITCA victory over me. Mom played fairly well as she ended up parring the last four holes to finish with a very respectable eleven point total for her nine holes. We all hugged one another as the last putts poured into the cup, realizing that no one was likely going to remember the scores but that this moment would be etched in our souls forevermore.

June 20, 2015: A Somber Day as a Legend Was Buried

Tom Beiting may not have been a household name, but for everyone who knew my beloved father-in-law, he was a true hero in every sense of the word. He was just eighteen when he volunteered for the Army, and soon he was shipped off to Europe to bravely fight in the Battle of the Bulge as a proud member of the famous First Infantry Battalion, the Big Red One. Tom was seriously injured in the battle and barely made it out alive. Fortunately, Tom never gave up, and he returned to the United States and settled down and raised a wonderful family of five children with his beautiful bride. I had the great fortune to marry one of his beautiful daughters and have been blessed enough to raise two wonderful children with Tom's youngest daughter, Laura. When I reflect upon all the brave and patriotic things that Tom did with his life, I feel that my life accomplishments to this point have been rather trivial. As the American flag was draped over his coffin and then neatly folded by some brave young soldiers, I gave thanks to Tom and all the men and women who have so bravely fought to uphold the freedom that we often take for granted. We live in the greatest country the world has ever known, and yet we take so many things for granted. We have been given so many freedoms to do with our lives what we choose, and yet we often squander so many of these wonderful opportunities due to self-pity or despair over such trivial pursuits. We must wake up each day eternally grateful for all that has been bestowed upon us, and we must make it incumbent upon ourselves to make the most of each and every day that we have been given to make the world a better place for everyone we know. If we can inspire all the important people in our lives to pursue life with passion and love, then everyone's world is certainly going to be a better place. So get off the couch and start pursuing the life you have always envisioned for yourself and others. No longer accept mediocrity. Life is too short to be anything but the best you that you can be. Start today to reach out to your dear friends and family, and let them know just how much they mean to you. Don't fear failure; fear regret. A life well lived is one that has few regrets!

KELLEY PETER

Tom Watson's Swan Song at Saint Andrews

As Tom Watson headed over the Swilcan Bridge one final time, there was nary a dry eye in the house as he strolled across it arm and arm with his beloved son, who was caddying for him. I thought immediately to myself that this is what makes golf so sacred: these special bonding moments that no other venue in the world can grab hold of your soul as the essence of golf and all its grand traditions can. And it doesn't need to take place at the home of golf, although that does make it extra special. It can occur at some "Podunk" municipal par 3 course with your buddies. The key is to have the special people in your life share these quality moments with you, for they don't occur often, and we too often take them for granted, believing that there will be other days. All too often, these moments come and go without our truly embracing them, and they are gone before we know it. Far too often, a dear friend or family member drifts out of our life for good, or someone becomes too frail to fully embrace the game as they once had. How tragic that we squander far too many of these special moments by becoming too absorbed in our golf score or how it is affecting our handicap or quickly moving on to the next item on our never-ending "to do list" that we never stop long enough to truly embrace the magic moments that have just occurred right under our noses. It is forever trying to keep up with the rat race that prevents us from truly enjoying the splendor laid out before us on a daily basis. If we don't stop and truly cherish all the wonderful opportunities and significant people in our lives, then our lives will be nothing but a dim memory of what could have been. No longer shortchange yourself: get busy truly living your life with passion every single day. If you have a twinkle in your eye and passion in your heart, you will live a rich life far beyond those who failed to fully embrace all of life's wonders. In addition, everyone else around you will become enthralled with your unbridled passion and will long to join you in your blissfulness. Stop shortchanging yourself and all that you have been blessed with. Begin today to really embrace all the wonderful aspects of your life, especially your beloved friends and family members.

July 31, 2015: Green Tee Roberto Joins the Fray

My regular golfing buddy, Bob, and I were paired up with another golfer whose given name was Roberto. As we were shooting the shit stretching before teeing off, I quickly pointed out to our new friend that Bob and I would be playing the white tees but that he could tee off from whatever tee boxes he wanted to play from. Since I could readily assess that he was retired and had to be pushing seventy, I thought he might want to play from the forward yellow tees, which I would be all for based on my GITCA research. When he initially stated that he likes to play from "back here," I thought he was pointing to the blue tees, but no, he was pointing to the way-back tees, which, on this course, happened to be green instead of the customary black tees that most courses designate as their championship tees. I thought, *Shame on me for judging a book by its cover,* as both Bob and I were prepared to see championship golf played from a guy pushing seventy.

After about ten minutes of stretching, he finally proceeded to tee one up, and Bob and I were ready to see this guy really crank one out there. We both watched intently in hopes of garnering knowledge as to how a guy who was way our senior was able to hit his drives so much longer than the two of us. As he reared back and launched it, it was like our own personal "crying game" as the ball soared feebly about 170 yards out and into the rough on the right. I quickly told him that we encourage mulligans on the first tee and that to go ahead and reload. He quickly dismissed me that he was fine and that he would still be able to par from there. I said okay then and looked forward to his approach shot from 230 yards away with great anticipation. Bob and I then gladly moved up to the white tees and promptly bombed 230-yard drives right down the middle. When our new buddy, Roberto, took out his four-wood and proceeded to come up well short of the green, I knew that he was going to be in for a long day on this difficult course playing from the green tees. Bob and I then easily hit our approach shots from 120 yards smack-dab into the center of the green. We both made simple two-putt pars while Roberto scuffled his way to a double bogey. When this same scenario played out over the next few holes, I mentioned to my buddy Bob that I was going to keep a close tab on the number of greens-in-regulation that Roberto recorded and compare them to the number of greens-in-regulation that Bob and I recorded. As I made note to Bob, GITCA GOLF and playing the correct set of tees for your ability should translate into at least one-third of the greens being struck in regulation; otherwise, you are playing too hard of a course for your abilities, or you are simply playing from tee boxes that you have no business teeing off from.

Bob played exceedingly well for the rest of the front nine while I was struggling somewhat with my irons even though I was putting myself in ideal position off the tee. Roberto continued to struggle on every hole, and his score was well into the fifties if he was truly counting every stroke and penalty assessment. It was readily apparent to all of us that he had not recorded a single par and that he had hit exactly zero greens in regulation. Bob, meanwhile, fired a very respectable 38 with a GITCA score of sixteen points, which far bettered my 43 with a GITCA count of eleven. Roberto did not want to participate in our GITCA format, and that is probably best as he would have been lucky to register five points for the front nine. As we got some quick drinks at the turn, I so wanted to convince Roberto to join us way up at the white tees so that we all could play much quicker and have a far better time than continually trying to look for one of his wayward shots from the green tees. But Bob convinced me that he was probably too prideful to do so and that we should just let sleeping dogs lie.

The Gatorade at the turn must have reinvigorated my game because I was on fire for most of the back nine. My drives were exceedingly long for me, and I had very short irons into most of the greens. Seeing that I was coming out like gangbusters must have inspired Bob to pick up his play another level as he was matching me drive for drive and shot for shot. We started a new GITCA game for the back nine, and I led him by a single point entering the final diabolical hole that I can't ever remember parring. I told him that I would be fine with a bogey on this hole and that I fully expected him to par it and tie me for the nine. However, when we both hit career drives on this hole and were left with a mere 120 yards for our approach shots, suddenly, par seemed like a very attainable score for both of us. Knowing that simply hitting my approach shot to the center of the green would likely lead to victory for me, I naturally pulled my 8 iron left into the greenside bunker, which led to an unfortunate double bogey for me and zero GITCA points. When Bob hit his ball on the green, I was certain that victory was once again going to be his. Unfortunately for him, he three-putted, which left us in a tie with fifteen GITCA points apiece for this wonderful nine holes of exceptional golf played by the two of us. The same cannot be said for our dear buddy Roberto as he once again failed to record a single green hit in regulation, and his score was once again well above 50 for the nine holes. Even with our hiccups on the last hole, both Bob and I came in with forties, and we both had a very enjoyable time. Roberto did not have much fun at all on either nine, and he deemed it as "just one of those days, I guess."

I was again ready to lecture Roberto that he better get used to struggling if he continues to dupe himself into thinking that he is truly a championship tee box player. I am certain that he validated the discrepancies in our scores due to the fact that he was playing from tee boxes way farther back than ours, in fact 1000-yard difference, and that he could easily have shot as well as we did had he lowered his standards and joined us up at the white tees. He was a very good golfer, and he knew how to play the game well enough. The distance that he chose to play from was simply too much for him to handle. If he would only swallow his pride and join us up at the white tees, he no doubt would have shot in the 80s, and we all would have had a much more enjoyable and quicker round. Roberto will no doubt continue to kid himself into thinking that he can, in fact, handle any course from the championship tees, and undoubtedly, he will rarely break 100. My hope is that once my book comes out and GITCA GOLF is fully embraced by the public, everyone will soon learn the folly of trying to tee it up from tee boxes which leads to very few greens hit in regulation. Once everyone learns to play from the correct tee markers, everyone will have so much more fun, and the pace of golf rounds will be way under four hours at every course. It took the three of us exactly four hours to finish our round, which is not bad but much longer than Bob and I are accustomed to playing. Bob and I both took great glee in knowing that we had played awesome golf from the white tees, and we saw the disdain that so often occurs when someone's ego prevents them from playing from their proper tee markers. We hope to play again with Roberto after GITCA GOLF comes out, only this time we hope that he will be brazen enough to join us from tee markers that makes the round faster, more competitive, and immensely more enjoyable for everyone.

HOLE NUMBER 16

Focusing on Family and Friends

August 10–16, 2015: Vacation with My Children

As I look out at the lake on another beautiful morning in Northport, Michigan, I am reminded of all the beautiful wonderment life has to offer: the fresh air, sun shining down on the water, and a gentle breeze, making for a truly spectacular setting for all of us to soak in and enjoy. Northport is a truly enchanting place for boating, swimming, fishing, hiking, golfing, and playing tennis. Although I have brought buddies up here to golf on all these amazing courses up here, this trip was all about reconnecting with my children. It seems like yesterday that they were toddlers wading in the sandy shores, and now here they are as young adults looking to carve out their own niche in the world. The only advice I really ever give them is to live with passion and a purpose. Don't sit idly by and watch your precious life pass before you. Be active in your community and with your friends and family. I constantly remind them that life is not a spectator sport and that they must grab life by the horns and live every day to its fullest. Be optimistic and cheerful as everyone tends to gravitate toward happy and engaging individuals. I remind them that no one of significance really cares about the type of car they drive or how big their house is or isn't and that all anyone really cares about is one's content of character. So I constantly remind them to make that extra effort to be that type of person whom everyone enjoys being around. I make it clear to them to be constantly engaged in what they are doing so that their time is always well spent and significant. I also encourage them to be bold and leave their comfort zone from time to time and to not ever be afraid of rejection or failure. Certainly, you might experience setbacks from time to time, but you will have always gained knowledge about how to better approach things next time. I am vigilant about impressing upon them that the only person whom they ever need to impress is themselves. If they can look themselves in the mirror and be satisfied, then nothing else in the world really matters. The only way that you can ever come close to fulfilling any of your dreams is to dare to take some chances and to risk being in an uncomfortable place from time to time. I am quick to remind them that it is okay to aim higher than they ever imagined because, inevitably, they will end up much higher than those who set the bar too low. I encourage them to get as specific as possible about what their ultimate dreams really are and then to work backward on how they are going to ultimately get close to achieving this dream in a step-by-step manner. One of my favorite quotes is, "Inch by inch, life's a cinch. Yard by yard, life is hard." This encourages them to break down their grandiose dreams into small, manageable steps that don't seem too overwhelming. Remember, if you build tiny steps of success, the momentum will often carry you through the setbacks that would often derail less committed individuals. I encourage them to think positive and keep plugging away, and before they know it, they will be well on their way to achieving what they had once deemed impossible.

I am constantly encouraging my kids to make every day count and to truly cherish all the special moments and people that they encounter on a daily basis. One of my favorite sayings to them is "to be so positive in everything that you do that everyone else around you has a better day because of you and your positive energy."

Describing the qualities that I hope that my children will always try and emulate is exactly the type of people that I like to surround myself with out on the golf course: positive people giving off positive vibes so that all our time spent on the course will be truly memorable. In fact, these are exactly the characteristic traits of those people whom I do play golf with the majority of the time. There is a high probability that if you are not cordial and optimistic and you are constantly complaining out on the course, you most likely will not get a return invite to play golf with me very often. On the other hand, if you are a real go-getter and someone whom everyone loves to be around, you will probably be asked to join our group on a regular basis no matter how good or bad you are at this grand old game. We don't care if you aren't as good as we are at golf. We only ask that you play at a brisk pace and that you insist on having the time of your life. Now don't get me wrong. We are competitive, but we have a healthy sense of competition. Certainly, we all want to do our best and come out on top a good deal of the time, but it is the camaraderie that we hold sacred above all else. If you are one of those endearing golfers who is a joy to be around and who is continually soaking up all the wonderment of our golf outings, then most likely, we will extend the olive branch to you as often as possible. Our main goal whenever we golf is to make the experience as wonderful as possible for everyone because we now realize how fleeting some of these opportunities have become in our ever-hurried lives.

August 2015: Golfing in Utopia

I got the rare opportunity to spend time with two of my all-time favorite people—my beloved mom and my stepfather—at their wonderful farmhouse in Vermont. The weather for the trip could not have been more perfect with temperatures in the seventies and almost no humidity. There was barely a cloud in the sky, so the mountain backdrop was spectacular throughout the entire trip. I arrived in the late afternoon, and we had time for a quick nine holes at the magnificent *Dorset Field Club*, which I quickly learned is the oldest continuous golf course in the United States. We were in a hurry to finish before the sun set gloriously down behind the mountains, so we neglected to keep score as we were too busy soaking in all the spectacular scenery and Kodak moments amid our family. We returned to the farmhouse to enjoy some amazing wine and various cheeses out on their deck, which offered impeccable views of the mountain splendor. The wonderful conversation continued to flow throughout our amazing steak dinner, as did the wine, and we were quick to toast one another and thank God for blessing us all with so much to be eternally grateful for.

I could barely sleep that night as I reveled in all the previous night's wonderment, and I eagerly awaited the next morning and the full eighteen holes of golf that was to be played under the auspices of the GITCA GOLF guidelines. Stir-crazy, I awoke at 6:00 a.m., just in time to view the most spectacular sunrise that I could ever recall. I tiptoed out the door and embarked on a magnificent five-mile walk around the quaint and quintessential colonial town that is Dorset, Vermont. It seems that every house has been beautifully restored to its original form, and there were ample horses and livestock in most of the fenced-in pastures. My only regret was that I did not have my camera or phone with me to catch all these breathtaking views, but I made a note to remind myself to definitely bring my camera to the links.

We arrived at the field club thirty minutes ahead of our tee time, so we quickly headed to the driving range in a desperate hope to find our golf swing. After a few awful swings, both Don and I began striking the ball beautifully. By the time the starter called us over for our 10:30 tee time, we both were brimming with confidence and eager to get the round started. All the morning dew had evaporated, and there literally was not a cloud in the sky. We were both giddy as we could sense a magical round just waiting to unfold. Don was well versed on all the GITCA GOLF rules by now, but we both hit such perfect opening drives that we knew better than to anger the golf gods by taking mulligans. When we both almost knocked down the flag with our approach shots, we both let out shouts of glee at the wonderment of our assault on this now defenseless flagstick. I told Don to take a picture of our approach shots that both were inside of five feet of the hole as we may never open a round of golf with shots this good ever again. Don then stepped up and calmly knocked his putt in for an opening birdie and four quick points, while I just missed my birdie and had to settle for a ho-hum two-point par. When he emphatically stated that he loves GITCA GOLF, I put my arm around his shoulder as we strode to the next tee box.

Since it was just the two of us, I decided that we should make each nine holes a separate GITCA format with a winner declared for each of the nine holes played. I informed him that this is what my buddies and I do when we are going head-to-head in order to give each golfer a fresh start in case someone is getting blown out after the front nine. He agreed and was excited to get a first tee mulligan for each nine as well as having a roving mulligan and a par buster for both the front and back nine. We both knew that this would greatly increase our overall point total opportunities for each nine and would simply add to our overall enjoyment of the day's festivities. Remember, the more points everyone is scoring, the higher likelihood that everyone is having a much more enjoyable time out on the links.

Provided that hole number 2 is the shortest and easiest hole on the course, both Don and I decided to declare it our "par buster" for the front nine. When we both hit perfect irons to the green, we knew that today was indeed a special one and that going to the driving range had definitely improved our ball-striking as well as greatly increased our confidence. We both easily two-putted for our par buster birdies, so after two holes, Don had a whopping eight points, and I had a not-too-shabby six points.

We both hiccupped on the next hole, with Don and I receiving double bogeys on this rather benign straightforward hole. After marking zeroes on our scorecards, we quickly moved on to the very difficult fourth hole that has water guarding the entire left side of the fairway. When we both striped our drives long and far down the middle of the fairway, we both had only nine irons left for our approach shots, which both found the center of the green. We both safely two-putted and left the green full of satisfaction for having bounced back on this treacherous hole. So through four holes, Don had now accrued ten points, and I was right on his heels with eight points and loving this golf course and life. Not only was I excited about how well I was playing, it perhaps gave me even more satisfaction to see Don playing the round of his life on his home course.

The next hole is a very long and difficult par 5 with an elevated green that is guarded on all sides with water and cavernous bunkers. We both managed excellent tee shots and second shots, but we both had very difficult tee shots to this well-guarded green. When my approach shot ended up in the back fringe, I was somewhat elated that I had stayed clear of all the hazards, but I now faced one of the fastest and biggest bending putts of my life to try and circumnavigate. Don hit a beautiful approach shot that he masterfully kept below the hole, leaving him with a straightforward and slightly uphill ten-foot putt. Since this is Don's home course, I asked him to pick out a proper line for me, which he did with the warning that I needed to die the ball at the crest of the hill, or it would end up off the green. I followed his advice to a tee, and the ball did just as Don had advised and made a slow beeline for the cup. We both thought it was going to stop on the edge, but alas, gravity won out, and the ball trundled into the cup for a miraculous birdie. We both let out screams of euphoria that most of the other golfers on the course must have been startled by, but we didn't care as we knew that a small miracle had just occurred right before our eyes. Don must have been so inspired by the aura flowing among us that he easily followed suit and knocked his own putt into the back of the cup for his own wonderful birdie. So through the first five holes, Don had already made three birdies and a par and accrued fourteen points, while I was still nipping at his heels with twelve points of my own.

The sixth hole is an extremely long par 3 that plays close to two hundred yards. I was tempted to pull out my driver, but I decided to play it safe with my three-wood, which turned out to be a mistake. I pushed it way to the right of the green and ended up taking a double on the hole to add another zero to my scorecard. Don took out his five-wood and was able to salvage a bogey, which is a decent score for this hole by anyone's standards.

The next hole is a rather short and straightforward par 5, but somehow, I managed to muff my third shot and had to settle for a bogey. Don playing with more confidence than I can ever remember played three magnificent shots that allowed him to two-putt for yet another par and add to his ever-increasing lead over me. Don now led me by four points with just two holes left to play in our front nine match. When I put my tee shot down into the gorse on this uphill par 3, hope was all but lost for me as Don hit a perfect tee shot that found the back of the green. Sensing that Don had all but assured himself of yet another par, I decided to place all caution to the wind as I hit a perfect lob wedge out of the gorse that landed a mere three feet from the cup. When Don uncharacteristically three-putted while I calmly knocked in my par putt, I now only trailed him by three points with a drivable par 4 remaining.

Trailing by three points, I realized that I needed to birdie this hole to have any chance of catching up to Don's remarkable point accumulation on this front nine. Normally, Don would suggest that I simply lay up on this hole, but he was well aware of the GITCA point total, so he encouraged me to go for it, and he aptly reminded me that I still had my roving mulligan in my back pocket if things went awry with my first drive. Although I crushed my first attempt, it landed in the green side bunker, and since I stink at getting out of bunkers, I reloaded, and my second attempt came up just short of the green in the fairway. From there, Don and I both realized that I might get a chance to birdie, so Don took out his driver, and he came up well short of my drive but was in the fairway nonetheless. When Don's approach shot overshot the green, I knew that he was probably going to make a bogey or worse, so a birdie by me and a double by him would allow me to beat him by a single point. I took dead aim at the flag, and my shot came out perfectly. But when the ball hit the green, it ended up at least twenty feet away from the hole. Don hit a nice recovery shot but, alas, ended up with a bogey for a tidy nineteen points for his front nine tally. Now all that was left to do was for me to sink this treacherous putt to salvage a remarkable tie of Don's most impressive score. The putt was tracking the hole all the way but unfortunately scooted over the left edge, and I had to settle for a par to leave me with an also very impressive seventeen points for the front nine.

Don and I were both beside ourselves at the turn as we looked back on the amazing golf we had both just displayed. I know that I have never played a better or more enjoyable nine holes of golf, and yet Don had bested me once again. Any thoughts of envy I had quickly dissipated as I saw the joyous grin on Don's face as he stood in awe of what he had just accomplished. "Is that the best nine holes of golf you have ever played?" I asked him.

"Absolutely!" he stated emphatically. "I have never had more fun either, but don't tell your mom."

I knew right then that I really didn't care how the back nine turned out because I knew that golf didn't get any better than this. The beauty of playing two different nine-hole GITCA matches is that we both would start the next match deadlocked at zero, and no matter how poorly we shot, the glory of the front nine match could no longer be tarnished.

After a quick iced tea at the turn, we headed to hole number 10 where we both gladly utilized our first tee mulligans to leave us each with short irons to the green for our approach shots. Again, we both almost knocked the pin out of the hole with our deft approach shots, and we both settled for our pars after just missing our short birdie attempts. A good start was needed for both of us as the next hole is one of the most unfair holes on the course in my humble estimation. The hole plays over 400 yards for me from the white tees, while it is a long 375-yard hole for Don from the yellow tees. Even if Don and I were to hit career drives, we still would probably be forced to lay up because there is a shallow creek that traverses right in front of the green. In my opinion, this then becomes a three-shot hole for each of us to reach the green and therefore should be labeled as a par 5. Now on the scorecard, I noted that there is a 4/5 under the hole, which Don quickly explained that this hole is a par 4 for the men and a par 5 for the ladies. From my standpoint, not only is this par rating wrong but is also sexist! There are plenty of women who can outdrive me by a country mile, and the majority of these long-driving women are also way longer than me with their irons. In my humble opinion, this hole and the eighteenth hole, which has the same 4/5 designation for men and women, should be a par 5 for everyone who is not playing from the tips. If you are long enough to legitimately play from the tips, then you hit your average drive over three hundred yards and will be left with a 9 iron or less on both of these holes, and it will play as an outstanding par 4. For the rest of us mere mortals, however, both of these holes should clearly be denoted as par 5 holes and should be relatively easy pars if we play the hole wisely. So I boldly announced to Don that both hole 11 as well as 18 would now be playing as par 5s for our GITCA scoring guidelines. This seemed to relax both of us as we hit fairly decent drives and second shots, leaving ourselves with pitching wedges for our short approach shots. I hit my approach shot to within ten feet of the cup, while Don uncharacteristically skulled his wedge over the green and ended up making a six on the hole for one point. I was able to two-putt for my par, and for the first time all day, I held a lead over Don four points to three. We both concurred that making this hole a par 5 was indeed the fair thing to do, and courses around the country should follow suit to appease the majority of their golfers. Remember, we want every golfer out there to have as much fun as possible out on the golf course, and where I come from, pars are always more fun than bogeys and doubles.

Hole number 12 is a short par 3 that is fortressed all around by deep bunkers and requires a very precise tee shot to hit and hold the green. Unfortunately, neither Don nor I was able to properly complete this task, and both of us had to settle for bogeys. Hole number 13 is the number 1 rated handicapped hole on the course, and my white tee boxes placed me a cool seventy yards behind Don's much more user-friendly yellow tee markers. We both hit excellent drives, but my approach shot came up short while Don almost knocked the pin out with his short-iron approach shot. I could only muster a bogey, while Don gently two-putted for a par and had now tied me for the lead on this nine. Unfortunately for me, this was the last time the two of us were tied as Don parred the next three holes as well, while the best I could manage was a par and two bogeys. He had now forged ahead of me by two points with just two holes remaining.

We now only had the very short downhill par 3 seventeenth hole left as well as the now very short, newly designated par 5 eighteenth hole, so choosing when to invoke our par busters was going to be essential as well as determining when we were going to invoke our roving mulligans. Don declared that he was going to utilize his par buster on this short par 3 because the eighteenth hole had always given him fits. I reminded him that it was now a very short par 5, and he might want to reconsider, but his mind was already made up. I decided that there was too much trouble surrounding this par

3 green, and thus, I was going to save my par buster for hole 18. When I hit my 9 iron just over the pin, I was quickly lamenting my decision to save my par buster for the next hole. Properly following my lead, Don hit his 8 iron almost on top of my ball, and he now was faced with almost the exact same putt as me. The only difference was that I would be putting for a birdie, while Don would be putting for an eagle and its subsequent eight points. We both just missed our attempts, so Don quickly added four points to his total while I was left to add a mere two points to my tally. So entering the final hole of the day, I now trailed Don by a robust four points, and my only hope was to somehow eagle this final hole and snatch victory from the jaws of defeat.

Granted that I had saved my all-important par buster for this final hole, I only needed to record a four to secure my "net eagle" and most likely come out as the overall winner for this nine-hole match. I also had prudently saved my roving mulligan, so if my first drive went awry, I had another in reserve. I hit a decent first drive, but I knew that I needed to do much better with my mulligan if I had any hopes of netting an eagle. So with nothing to lose, I reared back and let out a mighty grunt as my clubface tore through the ball and sent it soaring long and straight down the center of the fairway. I now had a chance to maybe reach this green in two, but it would take a herculean effort on my next shot as well. Don, meanwhile, hit a decent drive and second shot, which left him about seventy-five yards out for his approach shot. Seeing Don's cool demeanor, I knew that I had to go for it with my never-trusty five-wood and pray for the best. Alas, I hit a worm burner about up to Don's ball and, with it, had blown any realistic chance at securing a net eagle. Don went first and properly showed me the way by placing his approach shot dead square in the middle of the green. "I really like this hole better as a par 5 because it sucks as a par 4!" Don exclaimed emphatically. I followed his lead and was fortunate enough to also find the middle of the green. I was slightly away, so I lined up my putt on all sides before giving it a firm wrap that just missed, forcing me to settle for a five and a net birdie. Don then followed suit and easily tapped in for his par 5, which added two points to his grand total for this nine and which left him with a very robust eighteen points. My par buster birdie had allowed me to finish with a very respectable sixteen points and another silver medal playing against the immortal Don. I immediately declared that pound for pound, Don might be the finest GITCA player on the planet, and his two nine-hole point totals added together for an outstanding thirty-seven points, which left little doubt that I was playing alongside one of GITCA GOLF's defining pioneers.

Mom had just finished her tennis match and joined us on the porch for a magnificent lunch and some more beer at this truly majestic club. She could tell by Don and my giddiness that we both had played extremely well, and she was sorry that she had missed out on our historic round. Mom didn't fully understand the scoring system, so she didn't fully comprehend just how remarkable a round Don had just shot. I then made it clear to her when I emphatically stated that Don only had one double bogey on the round and had made numerous pars and birdies. If Don wasn't completely sold on GITCA before, he certainly was now as he was all smiles from ear to ear. Seeing him so happy with my system brought me equal joy, and to see him and Mom so happy in their life together here in utopia is something that I will treasure forevermore.

Fortunately, Mom was able to join us the next day for our next eighteen-hole GITCA GOLF escapade on this marvelous course. Clearly learning from our time spent at the range on the previous day, we all headed over to the driving range to once again try and rekindle the magic we somehow bottled up just twenty-four hours earlier. Now as we all know, golf is a funny game in which one can totally lose it in a twenty-four-hour span, but fortunately, spirits were high as we once again were all striking the golf ball beautifully. We were all feeling pretty good about ourselves and our games until we watched the young pro hit a few balls. It was an incredible display of power and accuracy beyond anything we could ever hope to reproduce in our own golf games. I laughed it off and lightened the mood by emphatically stating that, "Clearly he would be playing from the way-back tees if he were ever to join us for GITCA!" Now of course a player of his incredible caliber would clearly score infinitely higher than us under the auspices of GITCA, but I think he would enjoy watching all of us attack the course from our proper tee boxes given our limitations. I am certain that having him play with us would give us tremendous insight into what a true championship golfer is assessing as he plays a round of golf, and this no doubt would help all our games immensely. Provided that we all played from the proper tee boxes, I think this young pro would be impressed with the number of greens in regulation that we all would most likely hit.

Don and I again started out on fire by easily parring the first hole while Mom had a nice up and down for her bogey. When we got to hole number 2, we encouraged Mom to join us in declaring her par buster for this nine on this relatively short and easy hole. Playing from the white tees, I hit a 130-yard 8 iron that traversed right over the flagstick before coming to rest ten feet from the pin. Don and Mom both hit onto the fringe, and when both made incredible ups and downs, we all settled for well-earned par buster birdies, and we were all smiles as we quickly added four points to our tallies. We took pictures of all of us together against this magnificent backdrop as we asked ourselves, "Does it get any better than this?"

Mom and I both doubled the next hole, while Don kept up his hot start with another par to lead the pack with an impressive eight points through three holes. I managed to cut Don's lead to one as I parred the fourth hole while he and Mom had to settle for bogeys. Don bounced back quickly by easily parring the brutal par 5 fifth hole, while Mom and I both struggled mightily before both putting our balls in our pocket and embracing the true meaning of GITCA!

Clearly inspired by Don's awesome golf, I decided to get my head out of my butt and try and match his golfing prowess. I started hitting every drive beautifully and was pinpointing my irons so well that I hit every green in regulation on these final four holes. I managed to par out and finish with a robust fifteen points to edge out Don by a single point as he had a string of bogeys coming in. Mom capped off her nine with a par to finish with a very respectable ten points. I was very excited about how I had finished off this nine, and I was quick to note that this was the first and perhaps last time that I had ever beaten Don at GITCA. He scoffed at the validity of that statement, but I knew that I had never come close to beating him until yesterday. I reminded him that the back nine starts with a clean slate for all of us and that I clearly expected him to get his revenge.

Revenge indeed is what Don got as he made a mockery of me by besting me with a score of 15 to 9 on the back nine. He only had one hiccup as he recorded four pars, three bogeys, and a birdie to go along with his one double bogey. I, meanwhile, struggled mightily as I recorded but two measly pars, five bogeys, and two GITCAs! Mom struggled early but managed to salvage her round with two great pars coming in to finish with a tidy eight points. Our overall GITCA scores for the combined nines was Don securing the gold medal with a total of 29 points, I got the silver medal with a combined score of 24 points, while Mom secured the bronze medal with a tally of 18 points. Don was a model of consistency throughout the thirty-six holes that we played together. He hit almost every fairway, and he must have hit at least 60 percent of the greens in regulation. All I know is that it was impressive to watch and that we all had the time of our lives. I asked him if he had ever had more fun out on the links. "Absolutely not," he responded. "I love GITCA GOLF since it masks my bad holes and greatly pumps up my self-esteem whenever I have a decent or great hole. It also helps that you are so enthusiastic and that you continually encourage me to forget about my poor shots and to prepare myself for the greatness that lies ahead. To get to play golf with my beautiful bride and wonderful son-in-law on this magnificent course on this most perfect of days, I don't know how life could get any better!" My sentiments exactly, as we once again headed to the bar to toast our great fortune.

A New Inductee into the World of GITCA GOLF

I was scheduled to meet Bob for a quick nine holes before the sun set on this perfect afternoon in the late fall at the magnificent *Circling Hills Golf Course*. I had worked all day, so I was very excited to be getting in as much golf as we could in the last remnants of sunlight knowing that winter would soon be upon us in the next several weeks. Initially, I was miffed that Bob had invited his brother-in-law to join us because, first, having another golfer would limit the amount of golf that we could squeeze in, and second, he probably had no interest in playing under the auspices of GITCA GOLF. Boy, was I wrong on both accounts, and this turned out to be one of the most enjoyable rounds ever recorded in the infancy of GITCA GOLF.

Bob's brother-in-law, Jim, greeted me warmly and said that he had heard so much about GITCA GOLF from Bob and that he was all in to experience it firsthand. I was now extremely delighted to show him just how simple and how wonderful GITCA GOLF can be when everyone is fully bought in to following its eight simple rules. Naturally, the first thing I asked him was how far he hit his average drive and how far he normally carried his 8 iron. He stated with all-knowing confidence that his average drive was around 220 yards and his 8 iron carried about 130 yards. "Perfect!" I shouted out, "Then you will be joining Bob and I in playing from the white tees." I quickly explained my guidelines for which tee box each golfer should tee off from, and he agreed that this sounded about right.

A father and son drove up behind us in a cart, so we naturally let them tee off before us so that we wouldn't hold them up, and it would give me time to further explain the other GITCA rules for Jim to quickly ascertain. Jim was excited to be a guinea pig for GITCA as an outsider, and since this was his home course, he was confident that he was going to score well. I explained to him that with our version of the Stableford system, the scoring would be plentiful and that a good time was likely to be had by all. Even though we all hit very good drives, we decided to utilize our first tee mulligans to see if we could improve upon our noble efforts and to let the father-and-son tandem get a little further in front of us. We all basically hit equal drives to our first efforts, so we went to our best ball and hit our approach shots to this raised and very challenging green. Having home course knowledge, Jim hit his ball to the back of the green and was a mere ten feet from the hole for his birdie attempt. Bob also split the center of the green and had no problem two-putting for an easy par and a quick two points right out of the chute. I, unfortunately, found the bunker with my approach shot, and I did very well to secure a bogey and its token point. You could see it in Jim's eyes that he so badly wanted to make this opening birdie and vault to the top of the leaderboard, but alas, his putt came up just short, and he had to settle for a tap-in par to tie Bob with two GITCA points. We were all smiles as we walked off the green, embracing the fact that we had all started the round on a positive note as we all had secured at least a point.

When we all parred the next hole and each of us secured two more points, we were all practically giddy as we looked out on all the beauty surrounding us on this perfectly groomed golf course with the sun slowly beginning its descent over the horizon. Unfortunately, only Bob was able to par the next hole as both Jim and I limped in with bogeys. Hole number 4 is a very short par 3 hole that I reminded everyone might be a good hole to invoke one's par buster. Bob stated that this hole had given him fits in the past and that he was going to save his par buster for the very short par 5 seventeenth hole. When Bob nearly sank his tee shot for a hole-in-one, it was readily apparent that he wishes that he could have declared this hole as his par buster. Seeing how easy Bob had made it look, Jim took the bold initiative to declare this hole as his par buster. Both Bob and I were quick to point out that if in fact Jim did hit a poor tee shot, he still had his roving mulligan to utilize as a contingency plan. This seemed to relax him, and he fired at the pin in a similar fashion to Bob, but his ball ended up about ten feet above the hole. We all knew that this was going to leave for a very precarious putt but that he was now putting for an eagle rather than a birdie due to his invoking of the par buster. I was tempted to utilize my par buster right here as well, but I was not feeling very confident in my irons, so I decided to defer as well. Naturally, my iron shot was pure, and my ball landed a mere fifteen feet to the left of the hole. Since I was away and with nothing to lose, I buried my putt into the back of the cup for an awesome birdie to add a quick four points to my total. Jim then carefully struck his ball so that it came to rest a mere foot away from the cup for a tap-in par buster birdie to add four points to his total as well. Even though Bob's putt was but a mere two feet away, we all insisted that it was no gimme, and he would have to validate his birdie by making this putt. Not wanting to be left out of the birdie bonanza, Bob calmly looked over his putt from all sides before cramming it in to join the birdie brigade and add four points to his total as well. So through the first four marvelous holes, Bob had ten points, Jim had nine points, and I was in my usual spot with a very respectable eight points.

Over the next three holes, Jim with his wonderful course knowledge and Bob simply not missing any shots began to pull away from me as I struggled to get anything going at all. As I recorded two bogeys and a double, Jim and Bob had three pars each to surge out to big leads over my now measly ten-point total. As we entered the short par 5 seventeenth hole, Bob was clinging to a one-point lead over Jim, and he was now a full six points ahead of me. Since I hadn't played this back nine in almost a decade, I was debating whether to utilize my par buster now or to save it for the very short but treacherous par 3 finishing hole. Both Bob and Jim implored me to take it now as this hole was basically a very short dogleg hole that I might actually be able to reach in two. Bob went first, and he hit an okay drive but one that was going to leave him about 240 yards from the green. Not pleased with this effort, Bob reloaded as he promptly declared that this would be his roving mulligan. He stepped up confidently, but he barely improved on his initial effort. Jim went next, and he hit a horrible first drive, so he followed Bob's lead and promptly pulled out his roving mulligan and hit a fantastic drive that left him a mere 220 yards from the green. Knowing that I had nothing to lose since I was trailing by so much and that I had my roving mulligan in reserve, I promptly pounded a drive that left me a mere 200 yards from the green on a hole that, thanks to my par buster, was now an extremely short par 6. Bob, still miffed about his roving mulligan not being much better than his first drive, was determined to make amends by trying to knock his four-wood onto the green from a heck of a long way out. He struck the ball well, but unfortunately, it hit the one overhanging branch, which knocked it straight down into the last gathering of woods lining the right side of the fairway. Seeing the error in Bob's way, both Jim and I decided to smartly lay up so that we had half wedges into the green for our approach shots. Fortunately, Bob found his ball in the woods and was able to knock it out for a nice recovery, but alas, he limped his way home on the hole and ended up with a six for a par buster par and its subsequent two points. Needless to say, he was not pleased that he had wasted both his par buster and roving mulligan and had ended up with such an awful hole. Jim was able to knock his approach shot onto the green, and he two-putted for a nice five to add two points to his total to remain one point behind Bob with but one hole left to play. Knowing once again that I had nothing to lose, I hit my approach shot right at the flagstick, and the ball came to rest a mere four feet from the hole for a nice look at eagle for me. I realized that if I was going to have any chance to be a factor in the competition, I had to sink this putt. I intently studied it from all sides before calmly knocking it in for an awesome par buster eagle to add eight points to my score and vault myself into a tie for the lead with Bob and move one point ahead of a now disbelieving Jim.

I expected Jim to spout that this didn't seem fair, but quite the contrary, he stated that he loves how this system allows everyone the opportunity to be in it until the very end. I had played the hole beautifully, and I had pulled my par buster out at just the right moment to get myself back into contention.

Teeing off first on the last hole, I still had my roving mulligan in my back pocket to pull out in case I totally flubbed my first attempt. Since this is a very small green with severe slopes on both sides, nothing less than a perfectly hit iron shot was going to hold this green. The hole was playing about 115 yards into a slight breeze, so I decided to hit a smooth 9 iron and then pray. Fortunately, the golf gods must have been listening because the ball was hit perfectly and ended up barely coming to rest on the left fringe a mere five feet from the hole. Elated and not wishing to dare piss off the golfing gods, I decided to forego my roving mulligan and be grateful for what had just unfolded. Bob and Jim hit decent shots, but unfortunately, the wind and the slope of the green sent their balls to the right of the green, leaving them with very difficult chips back up the hill to the extremely narrow green. Jim's chip unfortunately would not hold the green, and his ball came to rest right next to my ball. Being the deft chipper that he had always been, Bob knocked his shot to within gimme range for a tap-in par. Jim putted first and showed me the line as his ball came up just short of the hole for a tap-in bogey. Now all that I had to do was make my short birdie putt to secure my unlikely victory. Alas, I missed the putt but made the testy comebacker to tie Bob and finish a mere two points ahead of Jim. We all shook hands and lamented on my remarkable good fortune at the end to storm back and finish in a tie for first place. Bob had clearly been the most consistent striker of the ball all day with Jim a very close second, but unfortunately for them, I was able to hit the big shots when it mattered and to properly utilize my par buster to allow myself to share the victory belt with Bob.

I asked Jim what he thought about GITCA GOLF now that he had been fully indoctrinated. "I absolutely love it!" he exclaimed. "I am going on a golf trip soon, and I know the guys on the trip are going to love the GITCA GOLF guidelines."

Needless to say, I was thrilled that Jim had loved GITCA GOLF, and more importantly, I honestly feel that I have now added a wonderful golfing companion to play with for many years to come. He stated that he loved how the system accentuated the positive while allowing a few liberties that made the game more strategic and infinitely more enjoyable. He is excited to tell his wife about GITCA GOLF in hopes that it will bring her out to the links more than three to four times a year. Knowing what a positive impact GITCA GOLF has had on everyone that I have shown it to, I am quite certain that Jim and his wife are going to be seeing each other out on the links a lot more often. If GITCA GOLF encourages family and friends to tee it up much more frequently, then I am certain that everyone is going to be embracing GITCA GOLF as the standard for how most recreational golf should be played forevermore.

GITCA GOLF Put to the Test by Four Family Members with Huge Dispersions in Their Games

Even though I couldn't be there with them down in balmy Florida on this rather frigid day up north, I was anxious to see how my family members would enjoy all the wonderment of playing GITCA GOLF. In order to properly gauge just how wonderful

GITCA GOLF

GITCA GOLF is at handicapping the field without ever using any tenements of the handicap system whatsoever, you need to appreciate the differences in length and ability among each of my family members.

Todd Peter—Age: 38 Driver Distance: 280 yards 8 iron: 155 yards handicap: 7 black tees 6,863 yards

Darick Peter—Age: 50 Driver Distance: 260 yards 8 iron: 145 yards handicap: 13 blue tees 6,527 yards

Jamie Goodyear—Age: 41 Driver Distance: 230 yards 8 iron: 135 yards handicap: 16 white tees 6,130 yards

Don Marshall—Age: 71 Driver Distance: 190 yards 8 iron: 100 yards handicap: 20 green tees 5,500 yards

So based on these large discrepancies in both handicaps and carry distances among all these golfers, it would seem logical that Don should be receiving quite a number of strokes from each of his fellow competitors and so on down the line, with Todd having to give strokes to everyone in the field. However, if the golf course superintendents have done their job properly and spaced approximately thirty yards between each successive tee box, then unbelievably, all the golfers should be able to stay extremely competitive with one another with no strokes given whatsoever. The beauty of GITCA GOLF is that no one has to bother with giving and receiving strokes because our format doesn't acknowledge handicaps. Everyone starts with zero points, and the golfer who accumulates the most points from their properly designated tee box wins.

The *John's Island West Course* was built in 1988 by Tom Fazio and is one of the most beautiful and challenging courses I have ever played. In fact, I would deem it too challenging for my game most of the time, especially on the extremely windy day with thirty-mile-per-hour wind gusts that my brave family members were battling today. Todd was teeing off from the tips, which are appropriately named the "tournament tees," with the total yardage of 6,863 yards. Darick was designated for the "back tees," so he was gaining over 350 yards to Todd before a single shot had been struck. Darick seemed to like this idea as he fancies himself as nearly as long as Todd. Jamie, who hits about the same distance as me, was playing from the "middle tees," so he was likewise gaining almost 400 yards to Darick's total and over 700 yards to Todd. Don, being the spry young age of seventy-one, fully welcomed the distance advantages that he was getting teeing off from the "standard tees." Knowing these large discrepancies in distances, I was anxious to see how the GITCA GOLF guidelines would hopefully even out the playing field for all the varying competitors' golfing credentials.

Even though I was a thousand miles north of them and working while they all were playing, I had my phone near me so that I could get updates on this truly historic round for GITCA GOLF. This was a true litmus test for the sanctity of GITCA GOLF as four of my beloved family members were all teeing off from different tee markers based on their varying distance capabilities. Todd was the clear favorite, but I know for certain that he had only played this course one other time, and he certainly had never played it before from the tips. Evidently, Jamie was complaining that he should get some strokes, but everyone assured him that the scoring opportunities would even themselves out based on the differences in the length of the hole that they would all have to traverse. While the others had a chance to hit the driving range and warm up, Todd had to sprint to the tee box from his car as he was running late. Not getting a chance to properly get loose seemed to affect Todd's opening few holes as he went bogey, double, and bogey to start. He stated that he was initially overwhelmed by playing from so far back as he hadn't found his swing, and it was difficult initially for him to know where to attempt to land the ball.

After his initial hiccups, Todd seemed to find his groove as he properly invoked both his par buster and roving mulligan to put himself in the lead with twelve points at the turn. Darick, playing from the blue tees, found his groove right away and finished with a strong ten points through the front nine, and he had yet to utilize his par buster or roving mulligan. Jamie and Don both picked the same short par 3 fifth hole to garner par buster birdies as they each finished the front nine with very respectable eight points each. Todd called me excitedly at the turn to tell me that they all were having a ball and that they couldn't believe how close in proximity their drives ended up next to each other as a result of teeing off from the varying tee markers. Obviously, the scores proved that the varying distances that they all had to play from was keeping the match extremely competitive and that anyone could still end up on top at the end.

Since he still had yet to utilize either of his lifelines, Darick was very optimistic about catching and then surpassing Todd. Provided that he loves this course and that he knows it like the back of his hand, Darick knew that he would save his par buster for the very short par 4 sixteenth hole, which can be reached with a great drive. Unfortunately for Darick, Todd's game went to that next level of greatness, and he recorded three natural birdies and finished at one over par for this incredibly difficult final nine holes to make his grand total for the round a very impressive thirty-one points. To go along with his three birdies, Todd's round included seven pars, five bogeys, and three GITCAs. By the time Darick successfully utilized his par buster for a sweet birdie on the sixteenth hole, the white flag had already been raised by him and all the other golfers. Darick finished the round with a robust twenty-three points, which included two birdies, four pars, seven bogeys, and five GITCAs. He was smiling from ear to ear at recording this many points from the blue tees, and more importantly, he saw the inherent beauty that GITCA offers by your round not being tainted by a few horrible holes. Darick's stroke-play score was a ninety, and that included picking up several times after he had recorded a double bogey or worse. Todd's stroke-play final tally was an 81, so under the auspices of stroke play, Todd totally kicked Darick's butt. With the GITCA scoring guidelines, Darick still had a chance to catch up to Todd with some late dramatic birdies. Even though this never came to fruition, Darick still theoretically was in the match with three holes to play. Throughout the round, Darick kept complaining that he shouldn't be playing from way back there, but finishing second in the standings proved that he could in fact play this extremely difficult course from those lofty distances. Finishing with twenty-three points while traversing an extremely difficult course in extremely windy conditions is nothing to sneeze at, and everyone agreed that Darick had played quite well on a majority of the holes he had played. Don and Jaime ended up tied with eighteen points each and were equally elated to tie for the bronze. Both of them admitted that they did not play their best but that they sure felt that they were competitive and weren't overmatched at all.

I have seen Todd play at this really high level several times, and needless to say, it is quite breathtaking to watch a golfing display that is beyond my wildest dreams. To watch your own flesh and blood literally crush a golf ball heights and distances that come close to rivaling Tiger Woods and company is awe-inspiring and intimidating at the same time. It makes you pause and ask yourself, "Why do I even bother trying to compete against that, as I have no prayer whatsoever?" And then you realize that, thanks to the beauty and guidelines of GITCA GOLF, you do have a chance, and you can compete with him as long as he doesn't up his game to the stratosphere the others had to witness firsthand today. But rather than being mad and complaining that they had no chance, the others simply admitted that they all left too many points out on the course today and that if they had played a little bit better, they could have battled him to the bitter end. When I asked each of the golfers to rate one another's performance, they all agreed that Todd had brought his "A game," Darick his "B game," and Jamie and Don their "C games." It is my contention that if each of these golfers had brought their "A games," the GITCA scoring would have been much closer and probably wouldn't have decided a winner until the final putt was struck. The inherent beauty of GITCA GOLF is that it does reward the golfer who brings the highest level of their game to the course that day with the championship belt most of the time.

When you see someone get to that next level of ball-striking, with GITCA GOLF, you revel in their glory rather than being resentful and hope to replicate their scoring bonanza from your own tee box someday. I asked my stepfather, "Aren't you glad that you didn't have to tee off from the black tees with Todd? And also, how fair would the competition have been if you all decided to tee off from yellow tees?"

He responded, "Certainly I can't play from the way-back tees, and Todd would have drubbed all of us had he been able to tee off from the yellow tees. Either scenario would have been no fun for anyone."

So seeing the vast difference in distance among the varying participants, my stepfather as well as everyone else readily saw that playing from the varying tee markers is the only way to keep the game fast-moving and quite competitive. Now I know that in this lifetime, I will never be able to hit my drives over three hundred yards, but that doesn't preclude me from being able to someday post thirty-one points of my own at the *West Course* from my properly designated tee markers. Considering I only posted fourteen points from the white tees the last time I feebly attempted to attack this course, I realize that I have a long way to go with all aspects of my game or that maybe I need to swallow my pride and move up a tee box. I am anxious to move up a tee box and compare my scoring totals as well as my overall enjoyment.

It was a historic day for GITCA GOLF indeed, and I can confidently conclude that it passed the family litmus test with flying colors. Although there were some initial doubts by all, once they settled in, everyone soon saw the hidden beauty that GITCA GOLF provides. Todd's rough start did not ruin his day as he was able to right the ship so well that he went on to record a round of golf that everyone who witnessed will not soon forget. Being the older brother, the always pessimistic big brother Darick overcame his initial skepticism to see all the hidden benefits that GITCA GOLF allots to every golfer who tees it up under this system. He initially complained that he shouldn't be teeing off from way back there until Todd reminded him that he averages over 260 yards with most of his drives. Once he saw that he was significantly longer off the tee than both Jamie and Don, he realized that the blue tees were in fact the proper tee markers suited for his game. Both Jamie and Don were more than content with the GITCA format and felt that they simply left too many points out on the course. They both realized that they simply had to get better with their scoring irons if they want to stay competitive with Todd and Darick under the GITCA format. When everyone hit a decent drive, everyone saw the genius of the GITCA blueprint firsthand as similar clubs were hit into most of the greens by all participants. Even though the handicaps varied greatly, every golfer felt that they had an equitable chance to hit the majority of the greens in regulation. No one felt overwhelmed playing from their properly designated tee boxes, and everyone felt that they had ample opportunities to score well, presuming they hit decent golf shots. The nineteenth hole was equally joyous as the beer flowed freely, and toasts were made all around to each golfer with a tip of the hat going to me for formulating the GITCA GOLF system. Even though I was a thousand miles away, I could feel the camaraderie and good cheer that was enjoyed by everyone. I was overjoyed that they all had finally bought in and saw firsthand all the positive vibes that GITCA GOLF promotes. I am eager to play with all my beloved family members soon so that we all can attack the course from our properly designated tee boxes. I know full well that I cannot compete with Todd and Darick from their respective tee boxes, but playing from the white tees, I have an excellent chance to compete and even beat them from time to time without them giving me any strokes whatsoever. The lesson learned is that we are all pretty decent golfers provided we tee off from our proper tee markers and that the hottest golfer that day will be rewarded for his/her excellent play.

The entire eighteen holes were completed in three hours and forty-five minutes, so all those naysayers who say that everyone playing from different tee boxes would drag out the pace of play was proven dreadfully wrong. Darick initially thought this exact same thing, noting that in this foursome, they were in fact teeing off from four different tee boxes and that this obviously took slightly longer on the front side of the hole. However, I was quick to point out to him that when everyone plays from their proper tee boxes, all golfers should be hitting much more greens in regulation, thus greatly increasing the speed of play for everyone. Provided that this foursome finished in well under four hours proves that point perfectly. Being the devil's advocate, I asked Darick to imagine how long it would have taken for this foursome to finish if they all decided to tee it up from the black tees with Todd. He curtly replied that that would be idiotic and would have taken forever to finish. My point exactly, I reiterated to him, but this is what most foursomes do when they all decide to erroneously tee off from the blue tees together. I then asked him to imagine how ridiculously easy this course would be for Todd if everyone teed off from the yellow tee boxes. We both agreed that he would shoot in the 60s and that no one else would have a chance to catch him. So finally seeing my logic, he agreed that the minute or two longer it took to tee off from the varying markers made perfect sense and overall greatly increased the pace of play and, more importantly, the enjoyment factor for every golfer. All the golfers appreciated viewing the course from the varying tee boxes, and no doubt they all appreciated the fact that only Todd was forced to tackle the course from the tips. As they all watched one another tee off from the varying tee boxes, they all finally appreciated the fact that the varying distances made the game quite fair and equitable for all participants. They all were giddy with the format throughout the round as their double and triple bogeys did not end their hopes for winning the championship. They also liked the fact that no one ever questioned anyone else's reported score as any mark higher than a bogey was simply noted as a GITCA and a corresponding zero on the scorecard. They also liked the fact that no handicap tabulations ever had to be calculated and that the GITCA scoring system was so straightforward and easy to tabulate everyone's running score. Their elatedness gives me hope that the GITCA format will be readily accepted by the rest of the golfing world for recreational play.

    I hope to get these four family members together again for a return trip to this amazing course, but this time, I want them all to move up one tee box from their previous escapade in order to see how the distance affects the overall scoring. With Todd now playing from 6,500 yards, Darick from 6,100 yards, Jaime from 5,500 yards, and Don from 4,800 yards, I guarantee that the scores and pace of play will be much improved, and everyone will have a far more enjoyable round.

The Official GITCA GOLF Team Format Unveiled

December 12, 2016. The temperature was an incredible sixty-five degrees in Cincinnati, Ohio, when we teed off. Naturally, the course was packed to the gills with equally anxious golfers hoping to get in a final eighteen holes before the real winter weather would be upon us. Seeing that the course was jam-packed made us all hopeful for the future of golf, but it dismayed us due to the fact that Randy had to be done by four. Since it was just before noon when we teed off, we all knew that we would be cutting this deadline close and that we might not get to finish all eighteen holes. Nonetheless, we were excited to get in as many holes as possible before the clock struck on all our golfing glory. Since this was a dream foursome, we decided to make it an official GITCA team golf outing in which we would change partners every six holes.

We quickly explained the scoring system to Randy and made sure everyone knew that each golfer's GITCA score would be added together to form the team score for each of the six holes. I reminded everyone about the first tee mulligans but that we probably shouldn't utilize them unless we really hit a bad one since there was a long line behind us. Fortunately for everyone, we all hit fairly good drives, and we were off. I informed everyone that in the GITCA team format where we are changing partners every six holes, no more mulligans are allowed but that each golfer now gets to utilize a par buster during each rotation in order to greatly increase the scoring opportunities for everyone. They all agreed that this sounded fair and that this information would be duly noted. Bob and I were paired together for the first six holes, and this was fortunate for me as Bob came out of the chute-like gang busters. He made a fifty-foot putt on the opening hole to stake our team to an early three point lead over Steve and Randy. Steve was playing from the blue tees, and in a rare moment of poor play, he in fact double-bogeyed the very first hole to put his team in a major deficit right off the bat. This would prove to be Steve's only GITCA of the day, but it proved to be costly as Bob added another birdie on the fifth hole while I added several key pars, and we were able to stave off Randy and Steve's excellent comeback attempt. The final tally was Bob and I a combined twenty-one points to Randy and Steve's tally of nineteen. This was a major upset as both Randy and Steve are far superior golfers to me and are every bit as good, if not slightly better than Bob. The victory definitely would not have taken place without Bob's two birdies, but I was happy to contribute when I did, and I was not too proud to share in this monumental upset of these two golfing legends.

I flipped the tee in the air, and it was determined that Steve and I would be partners for the next six holes. This proved to be a bad pairing for Steve as I was miserable while the other three golfers were nearly unflappable. As we finished off the front nine, Randy and Bibbs had surged out to an 11-to-7 lead, and the white flag was about to come out. We had finished the front nine in a little less than two hours, although it had seemed to take infinitely longer, and we were hopeful that several of the groups would only decide to play nine holes and that the course would then be wide open for us to finish in plenty of time. As we approached the tenth hole, our optimism quickly faded as we saw two foursomes waiting to tee off with two groups still currently playing the tenth hole. Knowing that we were never going to finish our round playing behind all these groups, I quickly jogged over to the starter and asked if we could play the front nine again in order to avoid this logjam. He called over to the gentleman who started us on one, and it was quickly surmised that the front nine was now wide open. Music to our ears, indeed, as we all literally sprinted over to the first tee box to replay the front nine. Now we all would have liked to play the back nine, but it was abundantly clear to all of us that doing so would only lead to major frustration for all of us as we knew that it would be hopeless to try and finish our round before four. We were all eager to get back to the team challenge, and we all had a renewed energy as we did not see any golfers on the first four holes. We all knew that we could now relax and simply enjoy the rest of the round without having to worry about any time constraints. Unfortunately for Steve, my game did not get much better, and Bob and Randy destroyed us by a final count of 23 to 14. Steve had done his part by contributing nine points to our tally, but my play was so sporadic that I only contributed a measly five points. We essentially got our butts handed to us by the continued excellent play displayed by both Bob and Randy.

Steve had played well, but he now stood at 0–2 for his team record with but one rotation left to get on the winning ledger. Certainly, his optimism had to be sky-high as he was going to be paired with the red-hot Bob against Randy and clearly the weakest link, me. True to form, my miserable level of play continued for the next three holes, and Randy and I felt the walls closing in as we trailed by a score of 9 to 5 with but three holes left to play. I quickly reminded everyone that we still had our "par busters" in our back pockets and that the short par 5 seventh hole might be a good hole to utilize it on. We all decided in unison that this would be a great hole for all of us to utilize this extremely valuable lifeline. We all hit excellent drives and great second shots to leave us all within one hundred yards of the pin for our approach shots to this very accessible pin placement. Unfortunately, both Steve and I failed to reach the green with our approach shots, and both ended up settling for "par buster" pars and two points each. Both Bob and Randy had fifteen foot "par buster" eagle attempts, but fortunately for Randy and I, he was the only one to make his putt as Bob had to settle for a "par buster" birdie. So with the eight points secured by his "par buster" eagle to go along with my two-point par, Randy and I had now forged a tie ball game with Steve and Bob with but two holes to play. I still didn't feel like I had contributed much to this team effort so when I was the only golfer to par hole number 8, Randy and I now had a one point lead with but one hole remaining in this dogfight.

Since we had already played the ninth hole, we knew that it was a short hole with a difficult pin placement so that any outcome was possible to decide this match. Bob and I launched our best drives of the day, so we all were likely to get close to the green with our approach shots. Unfortunately for Bob, he got a little too greedy and pushed his hybrid into the pond guarding the right side of the fairway. The pressure was clearly on Steve to have to birdie if his team was going to have any chance, while Randy and I decided to be more conservative and simply play for pars to try and secure the victory. Bob took his drop and was able to get his fourth shot onto the green to give himself a good chance for a two-putt bogey to secure a point. When Steve hit his third shot to within ten feet of the pin, Randy and I knew that we had to secure our pars, or we might in fact lose the match. Randy put his approach shot right into the heart of the green to almost guarantee a two-putt par, while my approach shot landed on the fringe some twenty-five feet from the hole. I was pretty confident that I could two-putt from here, but with the wintry conditions of these greens, a three putt was not out of the question. I carefully studied the putt from all sides before giving it a firm whack, only to see it head straight for the pin and bounce off it and fall straight down into the bottom of the cup for an unlikely birdie to seal the victory for our team. With a single stroke, I had gone from being the goat of the day to the most unlikely of heroes. Everyone else two-putted to make the final tally 24 to 19. This proved to all of us that with the GITCA format, it is never over until the final hole has been played by everyone. Randy and I were trailing by four points through three holes before we came storming back to win by five points and leave our opponents in disbelief. Poor Steve had played excellent golf throughout the round, aside from his opening double bogey, and he was 0–3 to show for his fine play. Steve finished the round with twenty-seven GITCA points, which is not too shabby by any means. My par, birdie finish had allowed me to gain some respectability as I finished in last place with twenty-two GITCA points, but I had played just well enough in two of my three rotations to allow me to go 2–1 in the team format. Certainly, Bob and Randy had burdened most of the weight when I was paired with them as neither of them recorded a single double bogey all day. To have no "GITCAs" in these less-than-stellar course conditions is some excellent golf indeed. Bob was clearly the most consistent golfer of the day as he tallied eight pars and seven bogeys to go along with his three birdies to allow him to finish with an amazing thirty-five GITCA points. Not to be outdone, Randy tallied nine pars and seven bogeys to go along with his birdie and his eagle to finish with an incredible thirty-seven points to enable him to claim the GITCA crown for the day.

What we learned from this format is that the beauty of it is that everyone gets a fresh start as well as a new partner every six holes.

Even if you have a terrible stretch of holes, with the GITCA format, you and your partner can recover in time to secure the victory over your stunned opponents. Even if you are clearly the worst golfer out there, which I clearly was today, you can still ride your partner's coattails enough to win a match or two along the way. By rotating partners every six holes, everyone gets a chance to play with the hottest golfers and the not-so-hot golfers, and may the hottest golfers for that six-hole stretch claim victory. There were never any handicaps to try and figure out as we all clearly knew that Steve's length dictated that he would be playing from the blue tees. Being of similar length to one another, Bob, Randy, and I knew that the matches would be fair with the three of us teeing it up from the white tees. Even though Steve is thirty yards longer than us with his drives and at least a club longer than the rest of us with his irons, none of us felt overmatched playing from our properly designated tees. We all had scoring irons for all our approach shots, the other three golfers were all spot-on with their short irons, while I struggled, to say the least. Overall, I give myself a solid B for my performance as I putted fairly well and did not miss a single drive. My GITCA score paled in comparison to the rest as they were all much steadier than me and hit far more greens in regulation than I did. I simply have to improve my distance control with my scoring irons, and then I am confident that I can compete with these other three exceptional golfers a majority of the time. Overall, I would give the other three golfers straight As, and other than the fact that he made no putt over eight feet, Steve was right there with Randy and Bob. The beauty of the day was that we were playing the game we all love in short sleeves in mid-December in Ohio, and we were having the time of our lives. We all wholeheartedly endorse the GITCA team format and most likely will use this format for the rest of our golfing days.

December 30, 2015. It had rained extremely hard for four days straight, and we all were tired of being cooped up inside as the weather was unseasonably warm in Cincinnati for late December. So with forty-degree temperatures with a wind chill that made it feel like thirty-five degrees, of course, we had to play one more round of GITCA GOLF prior to the New Year ringing in. Randy, unfortunately, was unable to join us, so it was myself, Steve, and recently-turned-seventy-year-old Jerry bundling up as much as we could to tackle Mother Nature as well as our beloved *Circling Hills Golf Course*. We were hoping to get eighteen holes in, but we knew that we were probably going to run out of sunlight, so the starter told us to simply pay for nine holes and then play as many holes after that as we wanted to for free! Steve and I knew that if we really pushed it, we could definitely get in eighteen holes, but it was rather chilly, and we didn't want to push Jerry so hard that he wouldn't enjoy it. Thus, we all decided that we would play thirteen holes under the GITCA format, and may the best golfer win. I reminded Jerry about all the GITCA rules and told him that Steve would be playing from the blue tees while I would be teeing off from the white tees and that he should probably tee off from the yellow tees. Jerry had almost always teed off from the white tees in the past with us, but he clearly did not have the distance he once had, and he excitedly agreed that the yellow tees were indeed the correct markers for him if he hoped to honestly compete with Steve and I. I thought he might rebuke at having to move up to the yellow tees, but he readily accepted the fact that he had no business continuing to try and beat his brains in from the white tees in trying to compete with me. (Just as I have no business kidding myself into thinking that I could readily compete with Steve by teeing off with him from the blue tees.)

The first hole at *Circling Hills* exemplifies the GITCA guidelines to a tee as there is exactly thirty yards difference between each successive tee marker on this relatively flat, straightaway hole that has a very accessible green that is easy to reach in regulation, assuming you hit a decent drive. I aptly reminded Jerry that a mulligan is granted to all golfers on the first tee, but after we all hit great drives, we quickly scurried after all balls without a second thought about teeing up another ball. After hitting his customary 260-yard drive, Steve had but a wedge left to the green on this hole that was playing almost 400 yards from the blue tees. Unfortunately, the wind pushed his shot slightly to the right, so Steve's attempt finished pin-high 5 yards to the right of the green. Jerry had mustered a 200-yard drive right down the middle of the fairway that left him with a 7 iron for his approach shot on this hole that was playing just over 330 yards for him from the yellow tees. Unfortunately, he too just missed the green to the right, so he would have a short pitch shot to try and get up and down for his par on this opening gauntlet. Fortunately for me, I had really tattooed my drive as it had carried over 240 yards, leaving me with an easy 8 iron for my simple approach shot. Knowing that I had more than enough club to get the job done, I swung easy and watched my ball make a beeline for the flagstick before coming to rest a mere eight feet past the pin. Jerry immediately turned to me and asked with all earnestness, "Are you that good now?" Since I hadn't played with Jerry in over a year, I so wanted to lie to him and say yes, but the cold hard truth would be readily apparent to him over the rest of the golfing holes, I was certain. As I rattled my straightaway putt home for a birdie, while both Steve and Jerry had to settle for bogeys, I had jumped to a 4-to-1 lead over both of them as I had made it look rather easy.

Reality quickly set in on the very next hole as I pulled my tee shot way left on this lengthy par 3 and had to settle for a double bogey and the first GITCA of the day, while both Steve and Jerry made great ups and downs for their pars. When we all parred the short third hole, I was leading the pack by one point as I had tallied six points to their five points each. Unfortunately, I bogeyed the next hole, while they both made tap-in pars to leave us all tied with seven points through four holes. I asked Jerry how he liked competing against us from the yellow tees, and he was all smiles! Jerry's smile turned to a permanent grin as he saw that the yellow tees had been moved up at least one hundred yards from where they usually were placed, and he now had a huge length advantage over Steve and I for this already short par 5 hole. He took full advantage of this gift and proceeded to easily par this hole to match Steve's effort, while I unfortunately had to settle for a bogey to now trail each of them by a point. Fortunately for me, I was able to muster a par on the ensuing par 3 hole, while they both struggled to get bogeys, which left us all in a tie. What a battle we all were having as we were all seeing firsthand how the GITCA guidelines had greatly leveled the playing field. We quickly reminded Jerry that we all had yet to use our "par busters" and "roving mulligans" and that there is much strategy to consider on which holes these are best to be utilized on. Steve and I both explained that the short par 5 seventh hole is an excellent hole to bring out the par buster as it is a rather short hole and is easy to reach in regulation. So we all agreed to utilize our par busters. Steve and I played the hole perfectly as we ended up with easy fives for our "par buster birdies" that allowed us to take a two point lead over Jerry as he struggled to make a six and a "par buster par."

Jerry rebounded nicely on the second-to-last hole by making a clutch par putt to move a single point behind Steve and I as we both managed to eke out bogeys on this treacherous hole. So entering the final hole, a rather benign par 5 hole, Steve and I stood at twenty points, while Jerry was right in the running with a total of nineteen points. We all hit decent drives, but we all decided to utilize our roving mulligans, knowing that this was the final hole of the day. We each improved on our opening drives, and our second shots left us all with but a mere hundred yards to this long but extremely narrow green. Unfortunately, Jerry and I both just missed the green with our approach shots, while Steve calmly hit his approach right smack-dab into the middle of the green. When Jerry and I both missed our par putts, Steve was now left with a three-foot putt for the win and to ascertain the crown once again. Being the clutch player that he is, Steve calmly knocked the putt into the back of the hole to once again claim victory. I had managed to barely secure the silver medal by defeating Jerry by a single point, but the real winner on the day was GITCA GOLF as it allowed all of us to be extremely competitive with one another right down to the final agonizing putts. We all are extremely excited to get right back out there in the New Year the very first chance we get. Jerry finally moving up to the yellow tees is a move that was long overdue and will readily allow him to compete with the rest of us as long as we all shall play, which in 2016, I am hoping, is quite often. Now that he has accepted the fact that he should always tee off from the yellow tee boxes, he is going to be as competitive as anyone out on the links. Thus, there should never ever be a time when he feels too embarrassed to try and golf with the rest of us ever again. We all wished one another "Happy New Year" as we resolved to make these wonderful moments happen much more often in the coming year. I can hardly wait for the more magical moments that are certain to come from playing GITCA GOLF with my friends and family in 2016.

Heaven on Earth for Don and Mom

March 1, 2016. Don playing a quick nine holes with his beautiful bride records his second hole-in-one ever! The first person he called was me to tell me of his good fortune and to inquire as to how many GITCA points a hole-in-one is worth? I responded quickly that it is worth twenty points, but forty points if you declared the hole as his "par buster." When he told me that it was hole number 5 on the West Course, I knew that it was indeed his par buster for it is the only easy hole on the entire course. I told him that he would have to put a big forty points on his scorecard so that everyone would be able to clearly see that it was indeed a par buster hole-in-one! What makes the occasion even more special was that he did it in front of the love of his life on a beautiful spring afternoon as the sun was setting! I asked him if he was going to celebrate with some big juicy steaks and some champagne, and he said that I must have read his mind. "But of course," I exclaimed, "these moments are rare and precious, and they need to be celebrated accordingly." I am just so happy that Don and Mom got to experience this joyous moment together and that they could reflect fondly on it for the rest of their lives. I can't wait to go down and visit and see the scorecard with the ace recorded with a big 40 right beneath it. I am quite certain that this nine-hole GITCA score will never be matched again by Don or, for that matter, few others.

For the record, in addition to his forty-point par buster hole-in-one, Don recorded three pars, four bogeys, and a double for a robust fifty points for his nine-hole journey with his beloved bride. The amazing thing is that Don and Mom just decided to go out and play a quick nine holes before the sun went down. No hitting the practice range or putting green ahead of time, just a quick nine before dinner. Who knew that Don was going to post a GITCA nine-hole mark that may not be topped for a very long time? Somebody asked me the other day what the nine-hole GITCA record was, and I said that I wasn't sure. I am sure now, and I am tickled to death that it is my poster child for GITCA GOLF, my stepfather, Mr. Donald Marshall! Don is the epitome of what I hope every GITCA golfer strives for: he has learned that he is definitely a yellow tee player and that he can score quite well most of the time from these markers, he always has a great time out on the links, and he greatly increases the optimism for everyone else in his foursome. In other words, Don has learned not to take himself or golf too seriously, and he cherishes every moment that he has on this earth with his beloved friends and family. If you are ever fortunate enough to golf with this GITCA record setter, I highly encourage it as you too will have the time of your life out on the links. It is my goal for all golfers to adopt some of Don's positive outlook on golf and on life so that the links can be a much more enjoyable place for everyone.

On my GITCA GOLF website, I am going to continually update the record books for lowest nine-hole GITCA scores from each tee marker so that everyone can have worldwide records to shoot for as well as continually trying to best their own personal best score. I am going to have people send me their best GITCA scores, and I will have daily, weekly, monthly, yearly, and all-time GITCA records kept on the website for all to bear witness and then try and best. My goal is to have these records kept by every course around the world so that everyone can try and etch their name in the record book on their own favorite course, whatever that might be. In other words, I would like to have the all-time records from each tee marker on every course from Augusta to your local par 3 course. Everyone loves to see their name listed in the record book from time to time.

March 25, 2016: What a Way to Kick Off Spring Break

Unfortunately, I had to work, so I couldn't join Steve for the 75 he shot with his brother that morning. I was, however, able to meet up with him for a quick eighteen holes at the *Tri-County Par 3*

Course. As I was waiting for Steve to finish up with his earlier round, I got a chance to chip for a solid hour before he arrived. I spent equal time with my pitching wedge and sand wedge so that I felt that I could handle any short shot around the green. Well, it didn't take long for my due diligence to pay off as I got up and down easily on the very first hole with a perfectly executed chip shot that nearly went in. The touch that I had garnered with my short irons apparently found its way into all my full shots, and I hit nearly every iron I struck with great precision. As I made an assault on nearly every pin I saw, Steve innocently remarked, "I have never seen you strike the ball better." Even though this was no more than a casual remark by him, it was a compliment that I won't soon forget. On the rare occasion that I did miss a green, most of my chip shots were impeccable and allowed me to get up and down on the majority of the holes we played. Naturally, Steve was nearly matching me shot for shot, but I still held a one-point lead with two holes to play. We both made incredible up and downs on hole 17, which allowed me to retain my one-stroke lead with only the diabolical downhill eighteenth hole as a climax. Steve had honors, so naturally, he hit a perfectly executed sand wedge that ended up a mere twelve feet below the hole. Knowing that Steve is one of the great clutch putters of all time, I knew that I too would probably have to birdie the hole if I hoped to end the day with top honors. I took out my pitching wedge and hit a beautiful cut that nearly clipped the top of the flagstick before coming to rest on the back fringe twenty-five feet past the cup. I said to myself as I approached this putt, just get it close so you don't end this wonderful day of golf with a dreaded three putt that would likely haunt me forever. I hit the putt the perfect speed on just the line I wanted, and the ball never wavered from the hole. Unfortunately for me, the ball struck the right lip a wee bit too hard and just lipped out, and I had to settle for my par. Being the nice guy that I am and since he had complimented my game earlier, both Steve and I concurred that his putt must be struck firmly toward the right edge of the cup. I reminded him that these greens were still rolling so untrue and that a firm whack to the right edge was definitely his best bet. Knowing full well that Steve rarely missed in these opportunities, I was actually delighted that the ball did in fact hold its line and fell straight down into the bottom of the cup for yet another victory for Steve from the clenches of defeat.

Even though I once again had to settle for runner-up, I could not have been more pleased with my play or the wonderful gamesmanship that had incurred over the seventy minutes that it took us to finish all eighteen holes. For a measly twelve dollars on a very short par 3 course, we once again accrued many magical moments that we are certain will stay with us for the rest of our lives. In addition, I learned a very valuable lesson that practicing chipping and putting will lead to immediate and long-lasting dividends.

As we headed to the clubhouse, I saw a familiar face that was on the putting green with his grandson. I went up and gave him a big hug and exclaimed, "What a wonderful place to play with your grandson."

"Oh, it's a rinky-dink little course that my grandson and I have some fun on," he chimed back.

"Isn't that what it is all about?" I practically shouted out.

"Indeed it is," he shot back, with a twinkle in his eye.

March 26, 2016: Another Beautiful Day in Paradise

It was one of those crisp springtime days when the temperature was slowly climbing from the low fifties to the low sixties with a slight breeze and the sun shining brightly: in other words, a perfect day for some golf. Being that it was Easter weekend and Steve and I didn't want to spend too much time away from the family, we decided that we would see how many holes we could get in at our favorite par 3 course, the illustrious *Little Miami Par 3 Course*. It cost us a mere $6.50 apiece as we scurried out to the open first tee as eager as beavers to tee off on this magnificent day for some golf. There were a few groups several holes in front of us, so we made a pact that we would play each hole at least four times, provided that there was no one waiting behind us. We played two balls on each hole: Steve teed off from the blue tees and then would join me at the white tees for his second ball. I had a slight advantage as I got to tee off from the same tee on each hole, but playing the incomparable Steve, I needed every single advantage I could muster. Just like the previous day, I was hitting most of my irons rather crisply and was finding the center of the green on most of the holes. Steve, however, was pin hunting on nearly every hole as most of his tee shots ended up within a ten-foot radius of the pin on about 90 percent of his amazing attempts. We both were giddy as one shot after another was coming close to tearing out the flagstick. Unfortunately I started to miss a few greens, while Steve continued to hit every single one of them.

About halfway through the round, as Steve had already built up a twelve-point lead on me, I made it known that I was definitely going to have to pull a rabbit out of my hat and record yet another hole-in-one if I hoped to overtake him today for the GITCA title. No sooner had I said this when my next tee shot nearly one-hopped it into the hole. The ball ricocheted off the pin before settling an inch away from the cup. A tap-in birdie is always nice, but I knew that I had to have the hole-in-one and its twenty-point value if I was going to overtake Steve on this magical day. I had a few more shots along the way that threatened to go in, and once again, I gladly accepted my tap-in birdies, but alas, I could never shrink Steve's lead lower than eight prior to the final hole. Alas, we came to the final hole, and I aptly reminded Steve that we both had yet to utilize our par busters. I knew that if I were to somehow get a 2 on this hole, my par buster eagle would give me eight points and would allow me to tie Steve if he somehow got a 5 on this extremely short par 3 hole. When Steve promptly put his tee shot right in the middle of the green, I realized that a four putt was not likely to happen and that I must now make another ace to once again somehow attain victory from the jaws of defeat. I took dead aim, and the ball made a beeline for the pin, and Steve shouted out, "NOT AGAIN!" Alas, the ball just missed the flagstick and ended up a mere eight feet from the pin. We both managed to two-putt for our par buster birdies, and Steve had incredulously ended our forty-hole journey even par with six birdies and six bogeys and twenty-eight pars for a GITCA score of eighty-six points. Even though I still had a puncher's chance entering the final hole, my five birdies, twenty-four pars, and eleven bogeys had left me with a very respectable seventy-nine GITCA points. Not a bad way to spend two hours and a mere $6.50 having an amazing time with my dear friend on this glorious afternoon.

Four Days Later and a Return to Paradise for a Quarter More

Since it was April 1, April Fools' Day, I guess the starter decided to raise the rates to $6.75 to see if it would deter me from playing one of the most enjoyable par 3 courses in the country. Fortunately, I was able to scrounge around my car for another quarter so that I once again could establish some wonderful memories out on the links with my good friend Steve and his son Luke. I had never played with Luke before, but I knew that he had just recently taken up the game as a seventh grader and, in fact, played for his middle school golf team. He was initially nervous playing with his dad and me, but he quickly overcame his nerves and was striking the ball beautifully by the fourth hole. Meanwhile, Steve and I were once again firing at every single pin, and the birdies were dropping at an astounding rate. Steve was coming within a ten-foot radius of the pin on almost every tee shot, but I was the one who was making the majority of the putts. It almost became comical just how good my putting was as nearly every putt I took was finding the heart of the cup. Luke turned to his dad and said, "He putts like a pro." Steve and I both laughed heartily as we knew that, although I am a terrific putter, I certainly am no pro.

We finished the first nine in about forty-five minutes as we had to wait on no one, so naturally, we went inside to pay for another quick nine-hole jaunt around the links. We passed over the money readily because it was $6.75, and it was peace we lacked. Luke relaxed even more on the second nine and even made three pars in a row. Steve and I continued our onslaught on the course as we each had recorded four birdies through the first seventeen holes. I had only bogeyed three holes, while Steve had unfortunately bogeyed four holes. So as we entered the final hole, I had accrued a 39-to-38 lead, and I was clearly letting Steve know about it. Steve had honors and fired a beautiful tee shot that flew right over the flagstick before coming to rest a mere five feet past the hole. Visibly shaken by what had just transpired, I came up just short of the green and was faced with a twenty-five foot meandering putt that would be very easy to three-putt and allow Steve to come out victorious once again. I figured that Steve had about a 90 percent chance of making his putt anyway, so I might as well go for it. I decided to keep the pin in as I knew that I was going to be giving the putt a tremendous whack. I reared back and hit the putt cleanly, and we all watched intently as the putt rammed into the flagstick before falling harmlessly into the bottom of the cup for my fifth birdie of the day to seal the rare victory over my fallen compatriot. Luke made an excellent par to finish his first official GITCA round with a robust fifteen points. Normally, Steve would have been somewhat downtrodden to have lost to me, but all three of us were smiling from ear to ear as we recanted each hole over some ice cream. What a glorious day it had been for all of us. Even more important than my victory was seeing Steve's son fully embrace the GITCA guidelines. He innocently remarked, "Why doesn't everyone play this way? It is so much more fun." That is our mission, I assured him, as I knew that his indelible smile would spur me on to make this great game of golf indeed much more enjoyable for golfers everywhere.

April 17, 2016: Birthday Golf with My Best Golfing Buddies

Was blessed enough to get to tee it up with my best buddies for a quick nine holes on the eve of my birthday. The weather was simply spectacular as it was a balmy seventy-five degrees and not a cloud in the sky. The course was packed due to it being one of the best Sundays to golf all spring, but none of us were in any hurry, and we were going to soak up the sun and our wonderful camaraderie for as long as we could. Since it was one of those rare occasions when all four of us got to play together, naturally, we decided that we would play the team GITCA GOLF format and change partners every three holes. I threw the tee in the air, and Pete and I were paired up for the first three holes against the two best golfers, Steve and Bob. Pete hadn't swung a club in months, so when he stripped his opening drive 260 yards right down the middle, all our jaws dropped. He then followed up his grand opening salvo with a perfectly struck pitching wedge that came to rest three feet from the pin. When he calmly sunk the birdie putt, he and I had a 5-to-2 lead over our archrivals. Our lead and our joy were short-lived, however, as Steve birdied the next two holes to secure the victory for his team. For the next three holes, Bob was my partner, and he played beautifully. But alas, I could only muster bogeys on every hole, and we lost by two points to Steve and Pete. Even though it was my birthday, my friends were pulling no punches, and we were all loving every minute of it. I was not playing very badly, but clearly, these three were playing at a different level than me. Fortunately for me, I got Steve as my partner for the final three holes, and his incredible round of golf continued to amaze all of us. I decided to utilize my par buster on hole number 8, and this proved to be quite an intelligent play as I easily made three on the hole for a "par buster birdie" to add four points to our team total. Steve saved his par buster for the final hole of the day, and he finished in style. He made a four on the par 5 hole for a "par buster eagle" to add eight points to our team score and cement the decisive victory over a speechless Bob and Pete.

    Steve had finished his round at one under par and with a GITCA score of twenty-seven for the nine holes played. He was clearly the gold medalist, and he won with everyone he played with to go 3–0 on the day. Pete finished a distant second with a very nice fifteen point total to edge Bob by a single point. Both of these guys had played some awesome golf. They simply couldn't keep up with Steve's blistering pace. Even though I finished in last place once again with a mere twelve points, I still had an incredible time playing nine holes of GITCA team golf with my dearest friends. We all mentioned once again just how ridiculous it is that we all don't get together more often for these quick nine-hole assaults on unsuspecting courses. For the twilight rate of ten dollars / nine holes, it is a small price to pay for all the wonderful moments we can create in less than two hours. The golf is outstanding, the GITCA games that we play are always exciting, and the memories we create will fill our hearts for a lifetime. What a great birthday treat for me! I can't wait to tee it up with these guys again as soon as possible. As I have but one year left before turning fifty, my motto is, "No more excuses." We all simply have to find the time for a quick nine at least every other week. Life is too short to not spend a good part of it playing the game we all love with our best friends.

Thirty-Eight Holes in Less Than Two Hours

Sure it was only par 3 golf, but for $6.75 and the course basically deserted, it really doesn't get much better than this. It had been a steady downpour two hours prior to teeing off, so only a few brave souls had dared to venture out to the *Little Miami Par 3 Course* on this slightly chilly spring evening. Both Steve and I had to be home by 8:30, so we asked the manager how much it would cost to play as many holes as we could get in before we ran out of daylight. When he said, "Same price. Play as many as you can get in until you can't see the ball anymore." Music to our ears as we both knew that we would be doubling back as often as humanly possible. There was a slight breeze, and the temperature was hovering around sixty degrees, and the greens were damp from the afternoon shower. In other words, the conditions were perfect to attack every pin with reckless abandon. I don't know what came over me, but I got into a zone that I rarely do, where every shot came off the club pretty much just as I visualized. Steve also took advantage of these perfect scoring conditions, but he was no match for my Zen-like state. Nearly every shot I took threatened the flagstick, and I recorded a personal best by hitting thirty-five out of thirty-eight greens in regulation. I am a pretty good golfer from 150 yards on in, especially when I am allowed to attack these holes with scoring irons and the ball teed up perfectly. I managed to record thirty pars, three bogeys, and five birdies, including my par buster, to finish with a robust eighty-three points. Steve also played very well, but he could not match my consistency throughout the round, and he finished with seventy-three points to lose by a full ten points to me. Now since I am clearly not as good a golfer as Steve and given the fact that he beats me about 90 percent of the time, this was a dominating performance that neither of us is soon going to forget.

This last-minute golf outing proved to both of us all the inherent beauty of GITCA GOLF. We played a very short par 3 course multiple times in less than two hours for a nominal fee, and we had the time of our lives. Even though my steady play afforded me a very comfortable lead throughout the round, playing short par 3 holes greatly enhanced the possibility that Steve was going to make a dramatic hole-in-one to snatch victory from the jaws of defeat. He came close on several occasions to seeing this come true to fruition, but alas, it was not to be, and sweet victory was mine to cherish. As we hit our final tee shots into the final and very short hole, the sun was setting over the trees and the horizon, and we both noticed all the beauty of this moment. How fortunate were we to get to play this wonderful game on a beautiful night in the land of the free as the best of friends? We shook hands heartily as we vowed to do this again as soon as possible. I am pretty certain that the circumstances may change the next time around, so I am going to cherish this dominating performance as long as I can.

Steve's Revenge and GITCA Enlightenment for His Brother Dave

After the butt whopping I put on him last time, Steve was more than ready to extract his revenge on me. While I was busy working, Steve was playing nine holes to get ready to put a hurting on his brother and me. Fortunately for me, I picked up where I left off from our previous round as I managed to par the first four holes to stake myself to a three-point lead over both Dave and Steve. I wasn't hitting my drives very well, but my short game was bailing me out once again. I drained two putts over twenty-five feet for par saves that left both of the brothers in disbelief. I knew that it was only a matter of time before they both came out of their doldrums and that my good fortune would eventually run out. When both of them parred the treacherous fifth hole while I managed to double bogey it, they both stood just a single point behind me with four holes left to play.

Steve and I both pulled our drives on the short par 4 sixth hole, and he ended up with a large oak tree blocking his path to the pin. He asked if he should go around or go over it. I said, "Most mortals would definitely go around it and hope to salvage a par. But then again, you are Superman, so what the heck, why don't you go for it?" He took a huge backswing, and the ball arched just over the top of the tree before almost swishing its way into the hole. He had to settle for a tap-in birdie after his once-in-a-lifetime shot. I was so shaken up by what I had just witnessed that I managed to double bogey the easiest hole on the course. Dave managed to par the hole, and suddenly I found myself in my usual spot of being in last place. I was still right in contention, with Steve now holding down the lead with 11 points, Dave now had 9, while I was clinging to 8 and not too happy about what had just transpired. But I thought to myself, *This is the beauty of GITCA GOLF*, as both of the brother's poor starts had not ruined their days and that now they were whistling "Dixie" as the match was as heated as ever.

In fact, just then, Dave turned to me and said, "I used to think that this GITCA GOLF idea was ridiculous, but now I see the genius in it. Nobody cares if I shoot a 79 or a 99, and with GITCA, the matches always seem to be very competitive right down to the final hole."

"Usually," I said, "unless your brother starts flexing his muscle and leaves us all in the dust. The nice thing is that we don't have to worry about bloody handicaps and that as long as everyone tees off from their proper tee boxes, the competition is often fierce right down to the final couple of holes. As great competitors with a ton of pride, isn't that what we should be striving for?"

"I agree," he said. And so it was, I had converted one of my greatest skeptics and doubters to the inner beauty of GITCA GOLF.

When Steve took out his 7 iron and nearly jarred it again on the 177 yard par 3 seventh hole, I asked, "Who am I playing with, Jason Day?" Steve's tap-in birdie on that hole and his wonderful par save on hole number 8 increased his lead to 6 over me and 5 over Dave with but a single hole to play. Since we all had saved our par buster for this short par 5 finishing hole, we realized that we still had a chance no matter how small that sliver may be to dethrone Steve with a miracle eagle. Unfortunately, both of them hit great drives, while my drive snuggled up behind a tree and forced me to punch out and all but eliminate any chance I had to win the title. Both of them hit excellent second shots and found themselves forty feet from the green. My third shot was just behind theirs, so I went for the gusto and naturally overshot the pin, and I was lucky to make a six. Dave, also playing with a desperate sense of urgency, followed me over the green, and he butchered his way to a six as well. Steve naturally made a five to end up beating Dave by seven points and me by eight points. Nonetheless, a great time was had by all of us, and Dave and I had a chance to still win entering the final hole. Alas, it was not to be as the best golfer on the day, Steve, came out victorious once again, and we all cannot wait to tee it up again together as soon as possible. Not a bad way to spend a delightful late afternoon in May with two of your closest friends. Even though I did not win, my heart was filled with joy knowing that I had successfully converted one of my staunchest critics. If Dave can buy in to GITCA GOLF, then golfers around the world should quickly embrace it as well.

Another GITCA Lesson for Dave and Steve to Behold

Steve and Dave seek out courses that they have never played before so that they can add them to the ever-growing list of courses played. With over three hundred courses tallied each, a lot of fine courses have been played, and a lot of fond moments have been accrued along the way. I got the privilege to play with them last weekend at an executive course that none of us had ever played before, and we all shot under par, accumulated a ton of GITCA points, and basically had the time of our lives for nine dollars each. Although the course was bustling, we finished our nine-hole journey in less than ninety minutes. All three of us would describe the round as joyous and extremely ego gratifying. We are all quite certain that we will choose to play this course again and again throughout the rest of our days on this planet.

The next day, the two of them went to play another hidden gem near Columbus, Ohio, that unfortunately only had three sets of tee markers. The blue tees measured over 7,100 yards, the white tees over 6,600 yards, and the only set of forward tees measured 5,700 yards. They decided to try their luck from the white tees given that this seemed like the only reasonable option of the three scenarios. Even though the course was immaculately kept and had great variety, by the end of the day, both of them felt beaten down, and the course had clearly gotten the best of them. They both ended up shooting around 90, so essentially, they spent the majority of the day playing near "bogey golf." Certainly, these were not horrible scores given that it was their first crack at the course and that they were being forced to try and play from distances that surpassed their usual tally by at least 400 yards. Playing bogey golf and not accumulating a lot of GITCA points was no longer something that they were accustomed to experiencing, and thus, the round was not a memorable one. Even though it was a perfect afternoon for golf, both of them were quick to note that the course was basically deserted. It only cost them twenty dollars each to walk eighteen holes, so cost could not be an issue as to why this beautiful course had very few patrons. Curious, I visited the course's website to read the reviews and to peruse the course outlay myself. The pictures of the course looked glorious, and each hole looked to be well-thought-out. Most of the reviews of the course were very favorable, but almost every single person remarked that the course played far too long for their game to surmise. The website posted the last 118 scores played from the white tees, and the statistics were very revealing. The average score was just over 90, and the number of greens hit in regulation was 22 percent. Playing over 6,600 yards, these statistics are actually slightly better than I thought they would be but certainly not averages that would inspire many repeat engagements.

I asked the boys if they would be so inclined to return to this course for another crack at it, given that it only cost twenty dollars, and both of them politely declined. So even though the price was right and the course itself was in relatively great shape, both of these avid golfers emphatically stated that they are in no hurry to ever play it again. My good friends' disdain for this inexpensive and well-kept course should be a wake-up call to every golf course management team in the world. Golf courses around the globe must be made much more user-friendly, if they aspire to have satisfied patrons and repeat customers. Thinking outside the box and encouraging the GITCA protocols would go a long way to ensuring this course's survival and thousands of others just like it. The first thing that I would do to make this course much more playable for all its clientele is to add three more sets of tee markers. Place black tees at the 7,100 yard-range, blue tees at 6,400 yards, white tees at 5,800 yards, green tees at 5,200 yards, yellow tees at 4,600 yards, and red tees at 4,000 yards. By allotting combo tees between all these varying distances, every golfer will have far better scoring opportunities throughout the round. By moving up 500 yards and playing this course from the newly minted blue-white combo tee markers, I guarantee that both Steve and Dave would have far better scoring opportunities and would shoot approximately ten shots better each. They would now view this course as highly playable and would be enthused to return to this venue on a regular basis.

The average avid recreational golfer averages just over ninety strokes per round. It is my hope that by adopting the GITCA guidelines, the national average will drop by at least seven strokes. This would ensure that your foursome takes approximately twenty-eight strokes less per round as you all hit far more greens in regulation and play much more efficiently. The ultimate goal is for all golfers to record a par or a bogey on most of the holes that they play with twenty-seven GITCA points being accrued along the way. This is a far cry from the bogeys and double bogeys that currently take up most of the spaces on the scorecard. If most golfers can average nine pars and nine bogeys per round, then everyone will be eager to repeat this experience as often as possible. This will give many golfers the opportunity to shoot in the 70s on a regular basis as they record milestone GITCA scoring totals. Having ample opportunities to post many breakthrough scores will certainly lead to an uptick in golf rounds played around the world.

May 16, 2016: May Day for Golf

When we found out that the powers that be decided to close the *General Electric Executive Course* after a beautiful fifty-one-year run, Bob and I decided that we needed to start playing our beloved *Woodland Golf Course* as often as possible before it is closed for good. Everyone I know loved playing the GE golf course because it had a great mix of long and short par 3s as well as six wonderful par 4 holes. The course was a great challenge for golfers of all abilities, and all eighteen holes could be traversed in well under three hours—exactly the type of course that makes for a great GITCA GOLF setting and one that I feel was the perfect prototype for how most golf courses in the future should be built. Now I know that this goes way against the grain of the current trend in golf course building where adding as much length as possible to a course is all the rage in order to try and combat all the latest technology, but I truly feel that we need to start catering to the baby boomers as well as the novice golfers in order to keep golf far less intimidating to play. Having short and very playable holes is essential to having some semblance of sustained success and allowing golfers of all ages to feel pretty good about themselves and their golf games. If we can elicit these wonderful feelings throughout the spectrum of golf participants, then I feel that golf has a real chance to see a huge increase in the number of golfers who are passionate about the game. So instead of the higher-ups allowing another one of these "rinky-dink courses" to bite the dust, they ought to be doing everything they can to market the hell out of these wonderful courses that golfers across the board can play quickly and have a perpetual grin on their face as they are playing with family and friends of all ages and abilities. In fact, these golf courses are the perfect marketing tool for getting family members of multiple generations to tee it up with one another and have memories that will last a lifetime for each participant.

As I drove up the hill through the tree-lined gate to our beloved *Woodland Golf Course* on an absolutely perfect May day for golf, I felt as though I was entering the pearly gates of heaven. Certainly, most golfers laugh at the thought of two pretty good golfers playing this extremely short executive golf course, but Bob and I know that we always have the time of our lives out on this tiny but majestic course, which is nestled into just a few hundred acres. It was Bob's birthday, so naturally, I paid the ten-dollar green fee for him, and we were all smiles as we had the course essentially to ourselves. There were a few scant golfers that we saw sprinkled throughout the course but not nearly enough if this course is going to survive for that much longer. Courses of this nature are not going to survive unless something is done drastically in the very near future to remarket all the wonderment that can ensue playing these very short but lovable tracks. Of all the golf courses that Bob and I have played, and there have been several hundred between us, none have elicited more positive memories than this course, which is so near and dear to our heart. We have had so many epic battles here that it pains both of us to try and imagine it ever closing. I told Bob that with the GE course closing, it is imperative that I get the word out about GITCA GOLF as soon as possible so that we can reverse this horrible trend of our beloved short courses closing their doors for good.

In about an hour and fifteen minutes, Bob and I laughed and joked our way around our beloved nine-hole course and, once again, had beautiful moments etched in stone in our hearts and minds. Bob's twenty-point GITCA score, which included five pars, two birdies, and two bogeys, far exceeded my fourteen-point tally, but nonetheless, a great time was had by both of us. I had a chance to make things interesting if I would have knocked in my ninety-yard eagle approach shot on the final hole, but alas, it was not to be, and Bob fittingly won once again on his birthday. I told him to soak this all in as we may not get many more chances to play this wonderful course in the future. We both admitted that this would be a shame for us as well as golf in general and that we must get my book out as soon as possible in order to stem this negative tidal wave that golf is on.

May 21, 2016: More Money Well Spent to Try and Keep Woodland Afloat

The forecast called for rain later in the afternoon, so Bob and I hurried out to play at 2:30 before the rain came. Since there were but two other golfers out on the links, we decided, "What the heck, let's pay four dollars more each and play the nine-hole track twice." The sky was looking gloomy, but our spirits were high as both of us registered tap-in "par buster" birdies on the first hole, and the match and the gamesmanship was on. I played very well throughout the round as my chipping game was spot-on, and I made four birdies to go along with my ten pars and four bogeys to finish with a robust forty-point total. Certainly nothing to sneeze at, and I was all smiles from ear to ear as I enjoyed every last hole on our beloved course. Bob ramped up his game to a level never witnessed by either of us as he recorded eight birdies on his round. Along with his six pars and four bogeys, Bob finished with an incredible forty-eight-point GITCA total, and I am certain that the smile on his face will not vanish for many moons.

Now I know that there are many readers out there who are scoffing at Bob and I for playing such a "rinky-dink" course that we both can overpower, but couldn't the same thing be said about the way the top PGA professionals are dismantling the courses that they currently play with all the latest technology? Nearly every week, you turn on the television, and a handful of pros are shooting 64 or better on some of the most demanding courses in the world. They are hitting their drives so incredibly far that a wedge is all that is needed to fire away at the pins on most of the holes. Now certainly, Bob and I do not possess the length to overpower these PGA tour courses, but as evidenced today, we certainly have the power to shoot incredible scores on much shorter and forgiving courses. As both of us will readily attest, it is quite enjoyable to be putting for birdie on nearly every hole. In our younger days, both Bob and I would kid ourselves into thinking that we could tackle some of the top courses in the country from the blue tees, and we almost always ended our rounds humiliated and frustrated as hell. Like most frustrated golfers today, we simply bit off more than we could chew, and our egos and our self-esteem were left in tatters. Only when we decided to play more forgiving courses and to play from distances that would give us many opportunities for success were we able to finally learn to love golf once again. In fact, we cannot wait to get out and attack these executive courses whenever we get the chance. We know that they are not likely to be crowded and that we will be able to play our round quickly and with ample scoring opportunities. Feasting on birdies and pars sure beats the alternative of racking up a large number of double bogeys or worse on your scorecard. Once my wounds heal from my latest thrashing at the hands of Bob, I am certain that I will call him up once again to try and ease my pain.

June 11, 2016: GITCA GOLF at Its Absolute Finest

It cost us each a mere twenty dollars to have memories that we all will surely cherish for a lifetime. At least I know that I will! Many hurdles had to be jumped in order for the four of us to get the opportunity to spend quality time together out at the beautiful *Majestic Springs Golf Club*. I told everyone that this might be as close as we all get to a golf vacation this year and that we better cherish every second of it. We all agreed that we would and that we would do our normal GITCA GOLF format of switching partners every six holes. Dave and I drew each other as opening partners, and we both knew that we would have a tall task in trying to unseat Pete and Steve during this first rotation. Steve is significantly longer off the tee than Dave, while Pete can usually drive it farther than me if he is on his game. Dave and I are gamers though, so we were not intimidated one iota.

Taking full advantage of our opening-hole allotted mulligans, we all managed to leave ourselves very short irons into this small and severely uphill green. Dave came up just short with his shot, while Steve, Pete, and I surrounded the flag with excellent approach shots. While the three of us all settled for pars, Dave unfortunately could not get up and down, and he and I trailed by a point right off the bat.

The second hole is one of the more controversial holes in the state as it has two forced carries that make using a driver off the tee a very risky proposition and thus leave golfers a very long forced carry to try and reach the green in regulation. As a result of this, ascertaining a four on this par 4 hole is quite a rare feat. Due to this innumerable fact, I made an executive decision that we would make this hole a par 5 and base our GITCA scoring accordingly. This proved to be a very wise decision as only Pete was able to muster a miracle four, while Steve and I were lucky to get fives, while Dave once again failed to record a par. The four of our scores averaged out to a five, so I felt very justified in going through with my executive decision. We all seemed to be much more at ease on the hole, knowing that it would most likely be a three-shot endeavor for almost all of us. I am tempted to approach this subject with the golf architect so that all golfers can have a much more enjoyable time with this hole simply by making it a very short par 5 as opposed to a nearly impossible par 4.

Pete's play sputtered a little bit over the next four holes, while both Steve and I continued to play lights out. In fact, through the first six holes, both Steve and I were one under par, and both of us had accumulated fourteen GITCA points. Unfortunately, Dave continued to struggle, and as a result, our team fell by four points to Pete and Steve. Nonetheless, we all were having one heck of a good time!

The next rotation pitted Steve and I together, and even though we couldn't continue our under-par ways, we did manage to shut down Pete and Dave by an 18-to-14 count. I was fortunate enough to birdie one of the holes to offset my four bogeys and my lone double of the day. Steve also had a few bogeys to go along with his four steady pars to help steer us to yet another victory celebration. Pete and Dave both played pretty steady golf, but they couldn't overcome all of Steve's pars to go along with my birdie. Dave was clearly struggling to reach many of the greens in regulation from the blue tees, while the rest of us had but short irons in our hands for most of our approach shots. It was becoming readily apparent to the rest of us that Dave at least ought to think about joining Pete and I from the white tees the next time we all tee it up on a course like this that does average more than thirty yards between each tee marker.

The last rotation was Dave's last hope for salvation, and he was extremely confident that his brother would help him to finally taste victory. I reminded everyone that during this last six-hole rotation is the only time that the "par buster" may be utilized and that everyone should start thinking about which hole they want to invoke it on. When Pete and I both parred number 13 while Dave bogeyed it and Steve doubled it, we immediately had a 4-to-1 lead on the grim brothers. With hole 14 being just a pitching wedge for all of us, I immediately declared that this was going to be my par buster. Dave had honors, and he declined to invoke his par buster here. Big mistake, huge, as he snuggled his approach shot to within ten feet of the cup. Steve declared that he was utilizing his par buster, and he put his ball within two feet of Dave's ball. Pete and I both declared that this hole would be our par buster as well, and when both of us hit short and right of the green, we had to decide as a team who was going to utilize our team's one roving mulligan. Pete has seen me excel on holes like this, so he naturally deferred to me, and luckily, I did not disappoint. My mulligan never left the flagstick and came to rest a mere three feet below the hole. Pete failed to get up and down, while Steve and Dave both two-putted. When I managed to knock my par buster eagle into the bottom of the cup, Pete and I now owned a seven-point lead that would be very difficult to overcome.

You have to give them credit. They never quit, and when Dave made a par buster birdie on hole 16, that closed the gap down to three. Pete and I played conservative and, I must say, very smart golf on the final two holes to hold on for a four-point victory over the now very grim brothers. We all gladly shook hands and tallied up the final numbers over some cold beverages as the sun was setting. Under the auspices of the traditional stroke-play scoring method, both Steve and I finished the day with matching 78s while Pete recorded a very strong 82 while Dave limped home in last place with an 86. The final GITCA tally was Dave with 24 points, Pete garnered the bronze with a strong 28 points, Steve accrued the silver medal with a strong 33 points, while in a very rare occurrence, I garnered the gold medal with a hefty 37-point GITCA effort. Even though I was extremely proud to beat three of the best golfers and athletes whom I know, I was more pleased with just how steady my play was and how I took advantage of the breaks that I was getting. Certainly, the GITCA guidelines helped my score, but they helped everyone's score as well. Bottom line is that we all had a great time, and the team element was much more enjoyable than the final individual tally. After rehashing the scores, I am going to make a motion that Dave move up to the white tees for our next round together simply for scientific purposes to see how much it affects the overall scoring and team play. The stubborn-headed Dave, who insists on teeing off from the blue tees, is most likely going to finish near the back of the pack, whereas I believe the much-enlightened Dave will find traversing the golf course much more enjoyable from the white tees. I had so much fun with my buddies playing under this GITCA team format I can hardly wait to do it again.

Good Friends, the Power of Karma, and the First Verified GITCA Sasquatch

Desperately in need of a "new" used car, I feverishly searched the internet for weeks on end hoping to buy a halfway-decent car with relatively low miles for less than $8,000. After coming up empty at one used car lot after another, I finally found what seemed like a perfect car for me that happened to be located 220 miles north of Cincinnati. I was all set to take a Greyhound bus up to Akron when my good buddy Steve offered to drive me up there if I would buy him a few rounds of golf. Being that this was a "win-win" for both of us, we headed up north at 6:00 a.m. Saturday morning August 27, 2016. The seller met us at the bank around ten, and by eleven, I was following Steve to an unforeseen golf course in Zanesville, Ohio, in my brand-spanking-new-looking car. The car drove impeccably, and I was so glad that all my due diligence had landed me this fine automobile. I was also thanking my lucky stars that my good friend had saved me from an all-day bus journey and that we now were on our way to play one of *Golf Digest*'s highly rated golf courses. We both were a little apprehensive as we drove through the heart of Zanesville as it is not the most scenic city in America, and we were even a little more apprehensive as we arrived at the course whose clubhouse was basically wedged in between several strip malls. I had gotten a great deal online, so the round was only going to set me back fifty dollars for both of us to play eighteen holes in a cart. We headed out to the first tee, and a magnificent course unfolded before us. *EagleSticks* has many different holes interspersed throughout an ever-changing topography, and playing from our respective tees, we had a ball.

We decided to play each nine as its own GITCA entity, and both nines turned out to be historic! After starting out very slowly on the first three holes, I suddenly managed to catch lightning in a bottle as I birdied three of the next four holes to surge out to what I thought was an insurmountable lead. Both Steve and I only managed to get par buster pars on hole number 8, so I had a three-point lead heading into hole number 9. Steve would have to birdie this 400-yard uphill hole if he wanted to have a chance, while I would have to get a bogey or worse. Naturally, Steve hit his best drive of the day, and when he managed to hit a 6 iron from 185 yards to within twenty feet of the hole with his approach shot, I knew that there was a good chance for him to catch me. After hitting a great drive by my standards, I felt that all-too-familiar twinge in my arm, and I knew right then that this would be my last hole of the day. When I tried to hit my approach shot, a pain worse than I have ever felt shot through my arm, and I picked up and accepted my double bogey, and zero points was put on the scorecard for my GITCA. Normally, I would be rooting for Steve to just miss this putt so that I could have a rare taste of victory over my nemesis, but since he had done me such a great favor, I was honestly rooting for him to make the putt so that he would always remember this day triumphantly. He studied the putt intently and muttered that he better not leave it short. The ball shot off his putter and screamed toward the cup with a ton of mustard. Fortunately for him, the putt was hit dead center, and it struck the back of the cup with such force that it bounced two feet in the air before settling into the bottom of the cup. We both let out a heartfelt cheer as once again Steve had pulled off the improbable. Karma is alive and well, folks, and don't ever bet against it.

I bought Steve lunch as I informed him that I would now be playing the role of his dutiful caddie as we got paired up with a delightful gentleman for the back nine. Harish was a middle-aged

Indian man, and he was an outstanding golfer who played in a lot of amateur tournaments around the country. I informed him that I had hurt my elbow and that I would simply be tending the flagstick and reading putts for whomever wanted my input.

    I took great joy in being a caddie for Steve as it is much easier to tell someone else what to do rather than your own entity, especially when you are caddying for a golfer as good as Steve. Since neither of us had ever played the course before, I would often ride halfway up the hole in the cart to assess our best strategy for attacking the hole. Our goal was to have Steve hitting an 8 iron or less for all his approach shots. Since Steve is so long with his irons and the course is not real long from the blue tees, Steve could hit 4 or 5 iron off most of the par 4s and still have some sort of wedge in his hand for his approach shots since he can carry most of his wedges at least 140 yards. Our collaborative efforts were paying off handsomely through the first five holes as he was even par without ever worrying about making a bogey. On the fifteenth hole, I aptly reminded him that he had yet to utilize his par buster on the back nine, and this might be the opportune hole to do so since it was a "drivable par 4" for him. He didn't want to possibly blow his run of good holes by hitting a driver, but I convinced him to go for it since he still had his roving mulligan on the back side as well. We waited for the green to clear before Steve hit a perfect drive that faded ever so slightly off the bunker guarding the green. Since it was a slight dogleg, we couldn't see where it landed, but we surmised that it must be on the green and that it might be pretty good. As we floored the cart to anxiously see where Steve's ball had ended up, all three of us let out a holler as we saw the ball six inches from the cup! Steve hurriedly stepped up and knocked in his putt for the first verified GITCA "double eagle!" This amazing feat quickly added sixteen points to his GITCA point total, which is amazing, but had the ball gone in for a "par buster hole in one on a par 4," he would have added a cool eighty points to his tally. *Karma is alive and well, people!*

    When Steve followed up this spectacular feat with yet another birdie on number 7, Harish wanted to know if Steve was in fact Superman in disguise. When he shrugged it off that he was just having an exceptionally good day, I stepped in and told Harish that he usually plays at a very high level and nearly always kicks my butt. "Good," said Harish, clearly exasperated, "now I feel a little better." Steve managed to par number 17 before unfortunately bogeying the finishing hole. Seeing what a great green reader I was, Harish asked me to read his ten-foot par putt for him. I am glad to say that he listened well, and the ball followed our intended line perfectly before falling harmlessly into the cup. He let out a yes as he had finally beaten Steve on a hole. We all shook hands as we had greatly enjoyed one another's company. Steve had finished the round 2 over par on a course he had never played before and with a grand GITCA total of fifty points. What a magical day it had been for all of us. I had gotten my wife a great deal on a car, and Steve had played a nearly flawless round. We got back into our respective cars and drove the remaining two hours of our long journey with eternal smiles.

October 13, 2016: A Return Trip to the Illustrious *Dorset Field Club*

Of course, the real reason for the return trip to Vermont was to spend time with my beloved mom and her doting husband, Don. The added bonus to this trip was that I was going to be eating fabulous meals and getting to play a few holes of golf in God's country. I didn't even care what GITCA score I was going to post; I was just excited to get to spend quality time with two of my favorite people in the world and soak it all in.

Even though it was a brisk morning, I decided that I would wear shorts, a hat, and two sweatshirts. There was supposed to be a nine o'clock shotgun ladies' start, but when we arrived at the club, the starter gave us the green light to go on out whenever we were ready as only one foursome of ladies had dared to brave the elements. That was all the invitation that we needed as Don and I jumped in the cart and headed to the first tee like two kids in a candy store. The course was in pristine shape, and there was not another soul on the course other than the course superintendents. The temperature had climbed to a comfortable fifty degrees, and with the adrenalinc pumping, we were both very comfortable in our surroundings. We both hit excellent tee shots, and we were off and running. After less-than-stellar approach shots, we both made well-earned bogeys to secure our first GITCA points of the day, and we were all smiles as we headed to the second tee. I aptly reminded Don about the par buster and that this might be a good hole to utilize it on. He concurred, and he declared it as his par buster and then promptly hit an 8 iron a foot from the hole. He was beaming with pride as he tapped in for a par buster eagle that netted him a quick eight GITCA points to add to his total. I decided to save my par buster for later and was glad that I did so as I overshot the green and was lucky to record another bogey. I continued to struggle over the next several holes, while Don parred the next two holes to open up a 13-to-3 shellacking over me through the first four holes. Unfortunately, we both double-bogeyed the devilish par 5 fifth hole, but Don regrouped and parred the next three holes to build an insurmountable 19-to-7 lead over me with just two holes left to play on the front nine. We both bogeyed the par 5 eighth hole, and I netted only a par buster par on hole number 9 to finish was a measly ten GITCA points to Don's twenty-one. It was a thorough thrashing given to me once again by Don, and neither of us could be more elated. For months, he had been struggling with his game, so to see it all come together for him on his home course in front of his stepson was a joy for both of us to revel in.

After a quick stop into the clubhouse for some delicious hot chocolate, we started a new GITCA game with new lifelines to utilize in our arsenal for the back nine. The sun came out, and the temperature started to heat up, as did my golf game. I was able to capitalize on a hot start and a successful par buster birdie to edge Don on the back nine by a 13-to-12 count. He made a daring charge at me on the final hole, and if his putt would have fallen, we would have tied at lucky thirteen. Don played well on both nines, and his eighteen-hole GITCA tally of thirty-two made a mockery of my twenty-three GITCA points. So overall, Don was the big winner, but I had managed to eke out some semblance of pride with my excellent back nine score. Other than the one group of ladies we saw briefly, we were the only ones out on the course. The weather had turned out to be spectacular, and Don's phenomenal play was inspiring to both of us. He obviously is a big fan of the GITCA system for all its positive aspects and lifelines, and he said that he truly enjoys playing with someone as positive as me. Needless to say, neither one of us can hardly wait to tee it up again tomorrow for more memories that will certainly last us a lifetime.

October 14, 2016: Another Memorable Round at Dorset

Well, the cold front that came through caused a three-hour frost delay. Undeterred by the temperatures hovering right around fifty degrees, we decided that a quick nine holes would be perfect. Seeing that there was a group on hole number 2, we decided to hop on the back so that we would not be held up one iota.

Even though I usually take a mulligan, I hit such a great opening tee shot that I quickly picked up my tee peg as Don moved up to the yellow tees to hit his first tee ball of this glorious day. Unfortunately, Don did not hit a good drive on either of his tee shots, and he was fortunate to record a bogey as I made an easy par to take an early 2-to-1 lead. We both managed to record bogeys on the always difficult eleventh hole.

We then both decided to declare the twelfth hole for our par busters. Unfortunately, the wind knocked down both of our initial attempts and left them well short of the green. We both decided that we needed to utilize our last lifelines each as we hit our roving mulligans. This proved to be an outstanding decision for both of us as we both hit our subsequent tee shots five feet from the hole. We both managed to make our putts for par buster eagles as we high-fived one another as we danced around the green triumphantly. Unfortunately, our joy was short-lived as we both double-bogeyed the treacherous thirteenth hole for our first GITCAs of the day. I, unfortunately, double-bogeyed the next hole as well, while Don made a nifty bogey to level the match at eleven points apiece.

Don then seized the lead on the next hole with an excellent par, while I was lucky to scrape out a bogey. We then matched each other with matching bogeys and pars over the next two holes to enter the final hole of the day with Don clinging to a one-point lead. Fortunately for me, I hit a tremendous drive and an amazing four-wood to get hole high on this finishing par 5 hole. I was able to sneak in a par putt, while Don just missed his par attempt to leave us with seventeen points each for the final tally. A tie was very fitting for our final round of my trip and left us both grinning from ear to ear as we shook hands triumphantly. We headed to the nineteenth hole to sit in front of the fireplace as we toasted each other for our excellent play and memorable day out on the links.

We went home and watched *Good Will Hunting* as Robin Williams reminded us that it is the little things that make life so special. What a great way to end an incredible weekend in Vermont with two of my favorite people in the world. *Golf and life get no better than this*, I thought to myself as I tried to soak it all in.

March 9, 2017: A New Favorite Executive Course

Bob and I had always talked about trying out *Robin's Nest Golf Course*, but we had never gotten around to trying it. We had mistakenly discarded it as just another rinky-dink course. The course doesn't look like much from the road, and the clubhouse is simply a modest shack that serves its purpose. We were excited that they had four different sets of tees so that we could play from various tee boxes on each of our nine-hole journeys. Since it was extremely windy and the conditions of the course were far from perfect, we decided that we would play each hole that was longer than two hundred yards as a par 4. This turned out to be an excellent decision as we both had ample scoring opportunities on almost every hole. I can't remember a time when both Bob and I were striking the ball so well, and we both were certain that I had never hit better pitch shots in my life. Since there were a few groups in front of us and no one behind us, we decided to play two balls each on the last six holes from varying tee markers. It was one of those rare days when everything was clicking for me throughout the bag. Bob was striking the ball beautifully as well, but he trailed me by four points entering the finishing hole on our first nine-hole journey. Since we both designated this hole as our par buster, I reminded Bob that if he eagled this hole and I only birdied it, we would end the front nine in a tie. Alas, we both were left with but ten-feet eagle putts each. Bob insisted that I go first so that he would be putting for the tie if I were to miss. Unfortunately for him, I drained my putt to assure the victory, and when Bob missed his, I had won the front nine 36 to 28.

As we made the turn, the starter told us that no one had teed off in the last twenty minutes and that we could probably play as fast as we wanted. This was music to our ears as we both needed to finish this round quickly before heading back to work. We decided to play only one ball each and that we would play from the tips. Utilizing our over-two-hundred-yard rule, holes 1–4 as well as the finishing hole would all be playing as par 4s for us. Given new life and a fresh GITCA start, Bob promptly birdied the first hole and parred the next five, while I could only manage to par all of them. Even when we both bogeyed the seventh hole, Bob maintained his slim two-point lead over me heading into the very short eighth hole. When Bob pulled his wedge left of the green, I knew I had an opening. The hole was only playing 110 yards into a slight breeze, so I knew that a full pitching wedge would be just about perfect for me. I hit the shot exactly as I visualized, and the ball came to rest a mere three feet below the cup. Alas, my putt hit the lip and spun out to deny me the equalizer. On the final hole Bob and I both nearly drove the green on this now very short par buster par 5. Once again, I hit a great chip that left myself a mere five feet above the hole for yet another eagle. Not to be denied again, Bob putted to within gimme range to secure victory on the back nine. When I was able to successfully negotiate my eagle putt as well, Bob had triumphed over me by a 24-to-22 count. We shook hands triumphantly as we both had secured a victory on our new favorite course.

Now I realize that most people would discard this course as a goat pasture, but to us, it was like a field of dreams. We can hardly wait to bring our other golfing buddies out to experience this short but extremely enjoyable course. Bob and I both agreed that for all future GITCA play, any hole that measures over two hundred yards on an executive course will automatically be deemed a par 4 and any hole over four hundred yards a par 5. Since most clientele who play executive courses are distance challenged, we both feel that this will greatly increase everyone's scoring chances and lead to many more rounds played on these hidden gems. This course suits up perfectly for our GITCA guidelines as there are many bare patches that would make standard USGA guidelines nearly impossible to circumnavigate. Our freedom to lift, clean, and place on a suitable lie makes this course extremely playable and a hell of a lot of fun. It is mom-and-pop courses around the country that will clearly benefit from the GITCA GOLF boom that I have prophesized. Unless more people see the hidden value in these wonderful executive courses, many of them will be forced to close their doors for good. What a shame that would be as many wonderful moments would be missed.

My Dear Friend Pete Just Lost His Father after a Long Battle with Parkinson's

It was to be expected since he had been fighting this horrible illness for over two years, but the finality of it was especially difficult. Anytime you lose a family member, it is hard, but when a son loses his father, it is especially traumatic. A son always wants to make his father proud of him, and one wonders all his life if this all-important goal has been successfully achieved. Being a great teacher, husband, and parent to two wonderful children, I am certain that Pete's dad was forever beaming about his only son.

With the passing of Pete's father, I realized that all my closest guy friends have now lost their fathers. When this suddenly dawned on me, I quickly called my dad and pointed this out to him and let him know that we need to spend a lot more quality time with each other. He concurred, and we made a pact that we would see each other at least once a month for lunch or golf. What any one of my closest friends wouldn't give to be able to have lunch or play golf with their dad just one more time.

March 12, 2017: Pete's Fiftieth Birthday Celebration

It was the first time that we had all seen Pete since his father had passed, so it became a celebration of Mr. Tarnowski's life as well as a coronation of Pete's half century. Since it was a mere thirty-nine degrees when we teed off, we knew that in all likelihood, we would be the only ones out on the course. So bundled in winter caps and two and three layers of clothes, we teed off joyfully. I drew Pete for my partner for the first eight-hole rotation on this glorious *tri-county par 3 course*, so Dave teamed with his brother Steve for what we all knew would be another epic battle. I got off to a sluggish start recording a bogey and double bogey to go along with two pars, and I was hoping that I would not be embarrassed by my buddies on this special day. Little did I know then that I was about to catch lightning in a bottle. I birdied both the seventh and eighth holes to put fear into Dave and Steve's minds, but alas, Steve made a four-foot par putt to hold Pete and I off by a single point. For the next rotation, I was paired with Steve, and we were the favorites since we had played this course much more often than our opponents. My hot streak continued as I recorded six pars and two more birdies over the next eight holes to allow us to stay in the match. Unfortunately, Steve was suddenly the weakest link out on the links, and we ended up losing by two points as Dave drained a birdie putt on the final hole to seal the victory. Pete was happy to be on the winning side for the first time all day, and his play was steadily improving with each swing. With two younger kids at home, it is rare for Pete to get out with us very often, so we all were cherishing this wonderful day out on the links with our best buddies.

Dave and I were partnered together for the last ten holes, and all of us were now playing lights out. My unbelievably spectacular play continued over these holes as I recorded nine pars to go along with a par buster birdie to end my round with an incredible fifty-seven GITCA points. This allowed me to edge Steve by a mere point to garner the gold medal for the day. The birthday boy, Pete, received the bronze with an outstanding forty-nine GITCA points, while Dave brought up the rear with a very respectable forty-five

GITCA points. So even though I had ended the day 0–3 in the team competitions, I had barely garnered enough points to come out as the top GITCA dog for the day. The rest of them all ended the day 2–1 in the team competitions, so everyone felt like winners at the end of the day. In reality, we all were the true winners as we had the golf course to ourselves on this spectacular day, and we all struck the ball extremely well. No doubt we all will remember Pete's fiftieth birthday celebration for the rest of our lives. I can't wait to do this once again when I turn fifty next month. No matter what the final GITCA tally is, I will be the real winner simply playing the game I love with my closest friends.

March 19, 2017. Bob and I decided to take Dave and Steve to our new favorite course, *Robin's Nest*. The weather was a balmy forty-five degrees, so of course, we all were excited to play Bob and my new discovery. I was anxious to see if Dave and Steve would enjoy playing this course as much as Bob and I had the previous week. Being the competitors that they are, they both arrived about a half hour before Bob and I to get a feel for the putting surface. Everyone was expecting to only play nine, but I reassured everyone that we would finish eighteen holes in less than two hours since barely anyone else was out on the course. We each paid our fourteen-dollar green fee for the eighteen holes, and we were on our way. Bob and I paired up to battle the brothers for the first six-hole rotation, and I was glad to say that my excellent play continued from the previous week. I had five pars and one birdie, and Bob played just well enough for us to edge the brother tandem by a single point.

Dave and I then teamed up to have an incredible seesaw battle against Bob and Steve. We were all tied heading into the twelfth hole, but fortunately for Dave and I, we both made excellent pars to edge our compadres by a single point. Once again, I had been rock steady as I recorded five pars to go along with a single bogey to secure eleven points for our team. Everybody else recorded four pars and two bogeys each to record ten points each.

We were all set to do battle for our final rotation when Dave was suddenly called away for a minor family emergency. Dave hated to leave while the competition was so close and extremely fierce, but we all assured him that we would pick up this battle again next weekend. Thus, Steve, Bob, and I decided to go mano a mano for the last six holes. Naturally, Steve started out with a par to secure the early lead over Bob and I, as we both bogeyed the thirteenth hole. When both Steve and I parred the next four holes and Bob could only scrape together two pars to go along with two bogeys, Steve had secured ten points to my nine and Bob's seven with but two holes left to play. Alas, Steve bogeyed the seventeenth hole, while Bob and I both made pars so that now I was tied with Steve, and Bob trailed us both by two points with our "par buster hole" still left to finish off the afternoon in style. Number 18 is a par 4 hole that only plays about 210 yards from the way-back tees. Being that we were all utilizing our par buster, this final hole was now an extremely short par 5. I went first and struck a perfect three-wood that made a beeline for the flagstick. None of us could really make out where my ball had come to rest, but I knew that it had to be pretty darn close. Bob also hit his tee shot up near the green and was in all likelihood putting as well. Steve unfortunately just missed the green to the right with his 5 iron tee shot, but we all knew better than to ever count Steve out of a hole. When we got up to the green, I was excited to find that my ball had come to rest a mere eight feet below the cup. Knowing that I had a relatively easy putt for double eagle, Steve pulled off one of the greatest chips of his life and nearly holed his own shot for a double eagle. Bob hit a great first putt as well, and both of their eagle putts were conceded. It was now left up to me to try and make history and record my first ever GITCA double eagle. I gave the putt a firm rap, and it raced to the hole and hit the back of the hole with a terrific thud. Unfortunately, the ball hit the back of the cup and popped out, leaving me with a tap-in eagle and a tie ball game with Steve. Although Bob had barely lost to both of us, we all declared ourselves winners for getting to spend this perfect afternoon with our friends on this wonderful, short, but awesome course. When we tallied up all the GITCA points for the eighteen holes, it turned out that I had edged Steve by yet a single point for the second week in a row. Anytime that I could edge out Bob and Steve, I would gladly take it, but I was more excited for this new hidden gem that we all discovered and that I was striking the ball as well as my much more accomplished playing companions.

There are still two weeks left in March, and I have already played golf ten times this year. I am well on my way to reaching my goal of playing fifty times this year. Out of the ten times I have played, all but three rounds have been played on par 3 or executive courses, and I have had a ball every single time out. Playing with my buddies at any venue is fun under the GITCA format, but we all have learned that the shorter courses allow us to play many more holes and have a much higher likelihood of recording high GITCA scores. Since we often get in many more holes, the one or two bad holes that we have are often quickly forgotten as we move on expediently toward our next great scoring opportunity. Many of these courses are in pretty rough shape as spring has just recently sprung, but none of us seem to mind as we continue to score with a reckless abandon. Having a set rotation where we rotate partners during the round allows all of us to play with everyone and creates harmony throughout every partnership. If someone is struggling through a certain portion of his round, then he can start anew during the next rotation and simply forget about his prior shortcomings. Each golfer gets three chances to record a victory as well as being crowned overall GITCA champion for the day. I have been fortunate enough to be declared the GITCA champion the last three times out, which is definitely a first for me among this fine company. I am so excited to be striking the ball so well, but I am even more pleased with how each match is ultra-competitive following the GITCA format. Everyone is having a blast under this format, and we all are getting so much better in recognizing the best ways to invoke the GITCA lifelines. It has been fun finding these off-the-beaten-path "mom and pop" golf courses, and they have proven to be the perfect venue for our GITCA competitions. It is all our hope that GITCA GOLF can not only save many of these golf courses but also realistically help them thrive forevermore.

I relish these times out on the links with my beloved friends. I used to be in awe of them, and I always felt like my game didn't stack up to theirs. Following one brutal golf trip when I had played particularly poorly, I came to a crossroads about whether or not I should give up golf forever. My dear buddy Pete encouraged me to stick with it and to simply practice harder and smarter. With his encouragement, I persevered, and today, I can confidently say that through the auspices of GITCA GOLF, I can fiercely compete out on the links with any of my golfing buddies. Just think how many wonderful moments I would have missed out on had I given up the game for good that fateful day. I can hardly wait to tee it up again with my friends and family every chance we get. Thank you, Pete, for believing in me and restoring my confidence. I look forward to many more epic battles with you and all our golfing buddies. No one outside of our realm really cares what scores are posted, and oftentimes, we don't either. But thanks to GITCA GOLF, all our souls are satiated every time we hit the links.

A Quick Nine Holes before Watching the Back Nine at *the Masters*

April 9, 2017. A day that will long be remembered for Sergio Garcia and the rest of the golfing world as he finally, as he won his first grand slam tournament by winning the Masters in a sudden death shoot-out over Justin Rose. To make it all the more special, he did it with his fiancée right there and millions of golf fans around the world rooting this great champion to victory on what would have been his hero Seve Ballesteros's sixtieth birthday. Alas, the golfing gods sometimes do smile favorably upon us all from time to time. Perhaps even more special than the victory was the class and great sportsmanship demonstrated freely by both Justin and Sergio as they competed tooth and nail against each other in an almost match-play-like atmosphere. The whole afternoon was spellbinding and left us all with an even greater appreciation for what a marvelous game golf truly is.

Prior to witnessing all this wonderful drama, Steve, Dave, and I had our own epic battle that not a soul witnessed nor cared about the outcome. But the three of us sure did as we battled it tooth and nail down to the final putt of the day. The wind gusted on and off throughout our nine holes up to 30 miles an hour or more, but we all hung tough, and I held a one-point lead over Steve and a two-point lead over Dave as we headed to uphill par 5 finishing hole at *Glenview East*. Naturally, we had all saved our "par buster" for just this occasion as the hole plays less than 500 yards from the blue tees and even shorter from the white tees where I was teeing off from. We all hit fairly good drives, but none of us had a chance to reach the green in two. When I slightly topped my 4 iron, I left myself with a 150-yard tee shot that was playing straight downwind. As both Steve and Dave left themselves with short pitch shots for their third shots, I knew that I must pure my 6 iron to try and maintain my lead. I hit the purest 6 iron of my life, and the ball made a beeline to the flagstick. When I arrived at the green, I realized that I had hit the shot too pure, and it had carried all the way to the back fringe. I now faced a thirty-five-foot putt that had a severe slope to it. I hit a decent putt, but it kept running by the hole, leaving me about nine feet for my par buster birdie attempt. Steve pitched on and calmly two-putted to get in the house with a par buster birdie. Dave's pitch left him about ten feet above the hole for a slick putt that would earn him a par buster eagle and the victory if he made it. He made a bold stroke, but unfortunately, the putt missed high and right. Now all the pressure was squarely on me. If I made my putt, I would secure the victory and win the gold medal. However, if I missed, Steve would claim victory, and Dave and I would tie for the silver. Now I am certain that both Sergio and Justin felt more pressure as their putts on eighteen were to win the Masters, but at that moment, this putt felt equally monumental to me. I visualized the putt intently from all sides and then trusted my body and my stroke. The stroke was true, and the ball never left the hole as it tumbled harmlessly into the bottom of the cup! Once again, a thrilling victory for me over my dear friends made possible by holing the last putt on the final hole of the day. Now my victory did not garner me the attention or fame and fortune that Sergio earned for himself on this wonderful day for golf, but I felt equally proud that my nerves of steel had come through for me just as they had for the newly crowned Masters champion.

    I am sure that there have been many moments when Sergio had doubted himself in whether or not he was ever going to win a major championship, just as there had been many moments over my golfing career when I felt like throwing in the towel. Today's triumphs for both of us would never have been made possible if we had simply given up on ourselves. I will cherish my victory today over my much better golfing companions because it proves to myself that I do have what it takes to compete and sometimes defeat my dear friends whom I idolize on and off the course. I am certain that we all will tee it up again within a week or two, and rest assured, they will be ready to exact their revenge on me. All I can say to them is, "Bring it on!" I know no matter what the outcome, we all will have the time of our lives.

Easter Weekend 2017: One of the Best Weekends of My Life

Not only did my children make it home from college for Easter weekend, my beloved sister Katie decided to throw an amazing fiftieth birthday party celebration for me. All my dear friends were invited, but many could not come due to their own family gatherings. Those who could not come were kind enough to send me the most heartwarming cards that I will cherish all my life. The fifty or so people who were able to make it made it a celebration that I will remember forever. As many of my lifelong friends gave wonderful speeches and toasts to me, I was almost speechless as to how blessed a life I had lived for my first half century. I have the most wonderful friends and family a person could ever have as all of us are quick to point out just how fortunate we all are. None of us take anything for granted, and we are all quick to pick one another up whenever one of us has to deal with misfortune. As I looked around the room and soaked in all this wonderful kinship, I realized that what makes all my friends and family members so special is that they are truly beloved by everyone else. None of them have any pretentiousness whatsoever, and they all are truly salt-of-the-earth human beings who would gladly give you the shirt off their back. I have learned so much from all of them, and I am hopeful that I have passed on these wonderful traits to my own children. The most important thing in the world is true friends. Most people are lucky to have one dear friend in their lifetime. I am fortunate to call several dozen my beloved friends. I can approach any of these dear friends any time of the day and pour my heart out to them, and they feel the same security in doing the same to me. There is nothing in the world more precious than this. If you are fortunate enough to have true friends like this, never ever take them for granted!

Following a wonderful church service and brunch with my in-laws, Steve and I managed to meet up on this glorious Easter afternoon for a quick jaunt around the *Little Miami Par 3 Course*. For the first time in a long time, I managed to beat Steve to the course and had a few moments to work on my short game. Just getting a feel for my touch seemed to loosen me up and build up my confidence as I unleashed a barrage on nearly every pin I looked at. Poor Steve didn't have a chance as he once again got a case of the shanks. I ended up beating him by ten GITCA points over the twenty-seven holes that we played in a little over an hour, but if I had made a few more putts, it would have been much worse. Nevertheless, due to the par buster being brought out on the final hole, Steve still had a chance to hit a walk-off hole-in-one for forty points to snatch victory from me. Alas, he shanked his par buster attempt, while mine just missed going in the hole. Now hitting a hole-in-one on the final hole would have been icing on the cake for this spectacular weekend for me, but nonetheless, I left the course fully satisfied with my golf game, and my heart filled with joy over how truly blessed I have been throughout my life. I wouldn't trade my beloved friends and family members for all the tea in China. I have lived a life far greater than most people ever get to live, and I am never ever going to take anyone or anything for granted. I am going to continually shower all the special people in my life with a barrage of love and let them know every day just how much they mean to me.

April 23, 2017. Pete was able to join us at the last moment, and we are all mighty glad he did as we had one of those great GITCA golfing days that none of us will soon forget. It was a slightly overcast day, but the course was filled with many patrons on this beautiful spring Sunday at *Glenview Golf Course*. We had secured the last tee time of the day, so we knew that no one would be pushing us on any of our shots and that we could double back and play some extra holes if time allotted. The round started out smashing for all of us as we all parred the first three holes. None of us could recall a time when we all had begun a round with all of us even through the first three holes. Unfortunately, I was the one who ended the streak with a bogey on the fourth hole, while those two continued with their consecutive par streak. I turned the tables on them as I made a great par on the fifth hole, while they each had to settle for bogeys. Since there was now a logjam in front of us and not a soul behind us, we decided to double back and play holes 4 and 5 again. We all parred them both, so through our first seven holes played, we all stood even with thirteen GITCA points each. We had each missed some makeable birdie putts, but none of us was complaining with how consistent we all were striking the ball. The sixth hole was playing into a strong breeze, and all of us were fortunate to end up with bogeys. The seventh hole was playing downwind, and I was the only one who managed to make a par. Steve settled for a bogey, while Pete recorded the first and last double bogey of the day. Sensing that he was about to lose to me for the fifth consecutive round, Steve summoned all his might and promptly hit a laser beam shot that ended up two feet from the hole on the par 3 eighth hole. He tapped in for birdie, while Pete and I managed to eke out our pars.

So we entered the last hole with Steve clinging to a one-point lead over me and a three-point lead over Pete. Naturally, we all had saved our "par buster" for the final hole of the day, so this match was still anyone's ball game. We all hit decent drives, but this hole was playing directly into a howling wind. After hitting decent hybrid clubs, we all had just over a hundred yards to the pin. I went first and unfortunately overshot the green with my 9 iron. Pete and Steve both found the putting surface with their approach shots, so now I was going to need a miracle to have a chance to secure the gold medal. I took out my 9 iron and formed it to my body like a putter. The ball came out of the rough perfectly and made a beeline for the hole at a wonderful pace. Agonizingly, it slid just past the cup, and I had to settle for a "par buster birdie." Pete now had a chance to secure the victory if he could make his "par buster eagle" putt to add eight points to his total. If he were to make his putt and Steve were to miss his opportunity, then Pete would be crowned the champion of the day. He hit a good putt, but alas, it slid by on the amateur side, and Steve was able to calmly two-putt to secure the gold belt once again. The final tally was Steve with 23 points, me with 22 points, and Pete with a strong 20-point effort.

We all noted that Pete was a mere few inches away from securing the victory, and this was only his third time out all year. Both Steve and I had already logged over twenty rounds apiece, so for Pete to be within an eyelash of us speaks volumes as to the type of athlete he is and also to the beauty of the GITCA format, which gives ample opportunities to come from behind and steal the win. Some people believe that the "par buster" is too gimmicky, but I insist that it keeps everyone relevant right up until the final putt has been holed. I hate playing out the string in stroke play when it is readily apparent that I have little to no chance of catching my opponent who is several strokes in front of me. With the GITCA format, there is such a bonanza of points available that most participants have a chance to win entering the final hole or two. Usually, all that we ask for as competitors is to have a chance at the end to be victorious. GITCA usually provides these opportunities in spades, and almost everyone leaves the course feeling that they had a chance to win over the final few holes. We all were so glad that Pete was able to get out and join us and compete with us until the very end. We called Bob after the round to tell him about all the fun he had missed. He was sorry that he wasn't able to join us, but he was playing with his young granddaughters and was having the time of his life. "Not all of life's precious moments occur on the golf course!" he noted. We all agreed, but this was one of those rare and precious rounds that neither Pete, Steve, or I will soon forget.

May 13, 2017. Steve and I decided to go at it one more time at the *Little Miami Par 3* on this glorious afternoon for golf. There was barely a cloud in the sky, and the course was in perfect shape. We managed to hit the course at the perfect time as there was barely another soul on the course. I had arrived early to work on my putting, and it didn't take long for my diligence to pay off handsomely. We decided to play two balls on each hole since there was no other golfer obstructing our play, one from the blue tees and one from the white tees. From the first tee shot until my last, I was on fire with every iron in my bag. I got a birdie on one of my balls on the first six holes, and I built up a huge lead over the flabbergasted Steve. Fortunately for him, Steve managed to birdie the sixth hole, but I answered with yet another birdie on the eighth hole to stretch my lead back up to an incredible fifteen points with but two holes remaining. We both proclaimed our last tee shot of the day to be our "par buster," and when I almost drained mine, I had but a kick in for a "par buster eagle" to secure a twenty-two-point beatdown of my fiercest rival. On this incredible day, I had managed to record a par buster eagle to go along with seven birdies, seven pars, and three bogeys for an incredible fifty-three points. Steve had not played that badly as he recorded two birdies, seven pars, and nine bogeys to finish with a quite respectable thirty-one points. Steve was clearly disheartened, but I told him that most likely, he would return the favor to me in the very near future. You never know what is going to happen in golf, and it was simply one of those days when everything went my way. Even as one-sided as this round was, Steve still had a chance to win on his final shot if he had made a "par buster hole-in-one" for forty points. The beauty of GITCA GOLF is that each participant still has a chance to win if they are fortunate enough to pull off a miracle shot. I did it to Steve on this very same course, so if he was to duplicate my feat, I would obviously tip my hat to him as we both would have a round to commiserate about for the rest of our lives.

 The absurdity of playing with handicaps would have come to the forefront today as Steve is a legitimate five, and I am about a sixteen. Not only would I have beaten Steve straight up by thirteen strokes, with handicaps, he would have had to give me an additional eleven strokes. So with golf's magical bullet of invoking handicaps, I would have emerged victorious over my rival by a mere twenty-four strokes! That sounds fair to me, until someone decides to break my thumbs. This is the main reason why I detest handicaps. No one knows what is going to happen on the golf course on any particular day, and that is what makes it the greatest game of all. I was six under today during this incredible round on an extremely short course. Tomorrow, I may shoot twenty-five over on a much longer and/or extremely challenging course. I have no idea how I am going to play, and I love the fact that I might get into a zone and not have to worry about the repercussions that may ensue from playing the round of my life. How ridiculous that a stated handicap should prevent me or anyone else from being able to shoot a round for the ages.

A 16 Handicapper Shoots Even Par and Lives to Tell about It

Following my dismantling of Steve, my next biggest rival, Bob, wanted to see if I was really playing as well as advertised. We decided to meet at *Circling Hills Golf Course* on this spectacular day for golf. Bob strode to the first tee box and hit a very nice 230-yard drive right down the center of the fairway. He then looked dumbfounded as I proceeded to hit the greatest opening drive tee ball of my life. When I hit the ball right off the sweet spot, the ball seemed to carry forever before ending up a full fifty yards past Bob's well-struck drive. Both balls were center cut, mine just happened to be a half a football field closer to the green. While Bob had to hit a 7 iron to reach the green, I was left with nothing more than a three-quarter gap wedge to safely find the putting surface as well. It wasn't a great shot, but I was so happy that I hit a decent approach following one of the greatest drives of my life. So often, I will follow up a career effort with a worm burner, so I was tickled to death to find the green as we both were happy to start the day with easy tap-in pars. I told Bob that I had learned a lot watching him play smart golf for decades, so now I was going to finally follow his lead and simply try and hit the center of the green and gladly take my pars.

What followed over the next three hours was sheer blissfulness as I hit almost every fairway and green in regulation. Bob was playing very well also, but I was clearly dialed in once again. I never tried to force anything as I was simply taking what the course was giving me. I took plenty of club and aimed for the center of the green on almost every approach shot. For perhaps the first time in my life, or the second time in a week, I actually looked like I knew what I was doing, and I was hitting the shots almost exactly as I planned. Both Bob and I kept waiting for me to come crashing down to earth, but alas, it never happened. I recorded twelve pars to go along with three birdies and three bogeys to finish at even par for the day. Not bad for a 16 handicap. So I guess with my handicap, my net score would be a 56 for the day! Certainly, if we played with handicaps and I was playing with new golfers for the first time, they would never buy into the validity of my stated handicap.

My final GITCA tally was thirty-nine points while Bob posted a very respectable thirty-four GITCA points. In fact, on most days, Bob's four over par total would have won him top honors, but not on my best day of golfing ever on a regulation-length course. Even though he had only lost by five GITCA points and four strokes, Bob told me he felt like he had just gotten run over by a steamroller. If I can play anywhere near today's effort for the rest of my career, I will gladly take it. Even though most of my drives were only about 230–240 yards, playing from the white tees allowed me to have an 8 iron or less for most of my approach shots. Granted that I had played about 300 par 3 holes in the last couple of months, I am now very confident with my scoring clubs. My friends are now a little taken aback by my newfound consistency, but they are so happy that I am now getting so much joy from golf. They remember all too well my years of eternal frustration with this game and my never-ending quest to try and be able to compete with them. Even though I have discovered the holy grail for the moment, I know all too well that I could lose it in an instant. I am simply going to try and harness these good swing thoughts as long as possible, and I am going to soak in all the blissfulness that comes from competing with and beating my beloved friends from time to time.

Bob's Birthday Celebration and a Round for the Ages for Both of Us

Since it was Bob's fifty-eighth birthday, naturally, I was treating, and I wanted to make the round memorable for both of us. We returned to the now infamous *Robin's Nest Golf Course*, and what transpired over the next two hours was nothing short of astonishing. Bob was more determined to dethrone me from my recent incredible run, but I was not quite ready to relinquish my crown even though it would be fitting for Bob to win on his birthday. Since turning fifty, I haven't lost, and I am pretty certain that I am well under par since embarking on the back nine of my life. If Bob was going to beat me, he was going to have to play lights out. We decided that we would play a separate nine-hole GITCA format for each nine holes played and also include an overall GITCA champion for the day. Right from the start, the match was fierce as both Bob and I were striking every single shot with pinpoint placement. In fact, through the first seven holes, Bob had recorded six pars and a birdie to surge ahead of me by three points. Undeterred, I birdied the eighth hole to put the onus back toward Bob. Naturally, he answered with a birdie of his own to retain his three-point lead entering the final hole on the front side. We both had saved our par busters for this short par 4, which now conveniently became an extremely short par 5 for both of us. We both hit excellent tee shots that just missed the green. Fortunately for me, I was able to putt my second shot, while Bob was forced to hit a delicate bump and run to a downhill pin placement. Unfortunately for Bob, he ran his shot eight feet past the hole, while my noble attempt ended up about four feet past the hole. When Bob just missed his eagle attempt, we both knew that a make by me would give me an eagle and a front nine victory over the birthday boy. I studied the putt from all sides before knocking it right into the heart of the cup for a 25-to-24 front nine victory. Miraculously, Bob had finished the front nine three under par to my one under par, but I had secured the victory, thanks in large part to my "par buster eagle" on the final hole.

We had made the turn in just about fifty minutes, so Bob grabbed a quick bottle of water, and we headed back out to start a new GITCA battle on the back nine. The back nine was just about a carbon copy of the front nine as Bob recorded six pars to go along with three birdies to post an incredible twenty-four points once again. I was not nearly as consistent as Bob, but fortunately for me, I was able to post four birdies, three pars, and two bogeys to salvage a tie with him for the back nine. Bob had an excellent chance to win the back nine and, in fact, win the day on the last hole, but he just missed a four-foot putt that would have netted him a par buster eagle and the victory. It would have been extremely fitting to see Bob knock that putt in on his birthday, and many people out there are wondering why I didn't give it to him, but Bob would never accept a four-footer for the victory. Even with the near miss, both Bob and I had one heck of a time out on the links. For a mere twenty-eight-dollar total, I was able to treat my dear friend and myself to a round of golf neither one of us will ever forget. We finished in less than two hours, we had the course basically to ourselves, and Bob posted a bogey-free round that included six birdies and almost secured him a victory over his beloved rival. I can't ever remember a time when both of us had struck the ball so well for nearly the entire round as we both looked like we knew what we were doing.

I asked Bob after the round, "Do you think any two golfers in the world had as much fun out on the links today as we did?"

"Absolutely not, my friend. This was about as good as it gets!" We shook hands heartily as we congratulated one another on our round for the ages.

Three Days Golfing in the Sunshine State

Since I was obviously playing the best golf of my life prior to arriving in Florida, I was very excited to see how my assault on my far easier Ohio golf courses would translate to the far-more-difficult tracks down at John's Island, Florida. Even though I knew that I was playing as well as I ever had, the difficulty of these Florida courses had haunted my memory for years. This was especially true of the legendary *West Course* where I managed to post a near-record-low five measly points the last time I attempted to navigate this extremely difficult course. Clearly, the course had gotten the best of me the last time around, so I had extremely low expectations prior to teeing off. I figured that if I were fortunate enough to bogey every hole, I would leave the course extremely content.

Don was also coming off some of his worst rounds of golf ever, so he had extremely low expectations as well. When we saw that it was forecast to rain for most of our round, our expectations became that much lower. We arrived at the course as the second tee time of the day, but the single who teed off prior to us was already five holes ahead of us. So the course was wide open, and our expectations were to try and simply mark on most of the holes that we were attempting to navigate. Don managed to start well by bogeying the first two holes, while I recorded back-to-back double bogeys to pick up on this course where I had left off last time. I righted the ship a little bit with a great bogey save on the third hole, while Don unfortunately recorded his first double bogey of the day. We both felt a little discouraged as we both double-bogeyed the par 5 fourth hole, but we both got some redemption of the short par 3 fifth hole as I recorded a "par buster birdie" while Don settled for a "par buster par." The rain began to come harder as we limped into the clubhouse with a mere seven points each at the turn. We retreated inside as a lightning delay caused us to wait out the storm as we licked our wounds. We thought about ordering a beer, but it was still only nine in the morning. Perhaps we needed something even stronger, but we decided that we needed our full wits behind us if we were going to exact some revenge on the course over the final nine-hole segment of our journey. Fortunately, we both played some of the best golf of our lives as we both managed to mark on every single hole that we played on the back nine. The rain had stopped, the sun had come out, and we both looked like we knew what the heck we were doing. We both managed to record a total of fifteen points each on the back to allow us to end the day tied with a very robust twenty-two points on one of the most difficult courses that I have ever attempted to play. Since it was now ten thirty in the morning, we both decided that our fine play warranted us a mug of these ice-cold suds. We toasted each other as we decided to try and replicate our performance tomorrow same bat time, same bat place.

Fortunately for Don, he was able to replicate his strong performance the next day as he continued to mark on nearly every hole to record another excellent score of twenty-one GITCA points. I struggled all day around the green and felt fortunate to record a mere thirteen GITCA points. Nonetheless, Don and I toasted each other as we decided to tackle the much more forgiving *North Course* the next day. Mom decided to join us for the front nine as she was just coming off a severe rotator cuff surgery. As a result, she would only hit a few short irons on each hole as Don and I battled it out for the GITCA crown. We had a few extra minutes prior to our tee time, so we hit the range to warm up. Coming off my horrendous round the previous day, I needed to hit some good range balls to try and rekindle some much-needed confidence. Fortunately for me, I had the best range session perhaps of my life as I hit every iron crisp, and I was nailing every single driver and five-wood I attempted right down the middle and long. The weather was a lot hotter today on this glorious morning, and the course was fairly crowded for this time of year. Mom was hitting some decent shots in her rehab effort as she watched both Don and I play some incredible golf. We both marked on every hole on the front, and I was fortunate enough to come away with a 13-to-11 lead at the turn.

Mom decided to leave after the front nine, and Don and I decided that we would jump on the front nine again since there was now a logjam on the back nine. In this hot of weather and taking pull carts, we decided that we didn't want anything to delay our hot streak. So we returned to the scene of the crime, and the excellent golf continued for both of us. Don marked on every hole but one to add twelve more points to his GITCA total. I, on the other hand, struggled over the final few holes and was fortunate to add ten more points to my GITCA total. Once again, Don and I managed to forge a tie with twenty-three GITCA points each. We both left several golden opportunities slip through our fingers, but we both were ecstatic at just how well we both had played for the majority of the round. Our decision to repeat the front nine was a wise one as we only had to wait on the ninth hole for the golfers to finish in front of us. If we had tried to venture on the back, our round would have taken about an hour longer, and we would have been eternally frustrated and, as a result, probably would not have scored as well. We had managed to play the entire round in just about two hours and forty-five minutes, and now we had the entire rest of the day to frolic in the ocean and poolside. What an incredible day it turned out to be! I am so glad that it didn't take us five hours to play our round of golf as we would have missed out on the rest of the day's wonderful adventures. We ended the day with some cheap wine and some marvelous pizza. We toasted each other for these three incredible days as we look forward to all reuniting up in Vermont in the fall to try and create even more wonderful memories.

Twenty-Seven Holes in Our Newly Discovered Golfing Paradise

Perry Park Golf Course in Warsaw, Kentucky, is like "paradise found" for me and my golfing colleagues. It is definitely off the beaten path, and in fact, most of the people who stay there are guests enjoying a golf trip at this spacious resort. All three nine-hole courses are slightly different, and we played all twenty-seven holes in just under six hours. The nice thing about the resort is that it has five different tee markers, so everyone can choose a distance that they can rack up a lot of great scoring opportunities.

We changed partners every nine holes, and we all played extremely well, and the matches were all very competitive right down to the ninth hole in each contest. Steve ended the day undefeated as he was the most consistent golfer throughout the day. Bob finished with the silver medal as he played beautifully from tee to green but unfortunately struggled on a few of the greens. Dave nabbed the bronze medal by beating me by a mere two points, but I had a phenomenal time nonetheless. All of us had many excellent scoring chances, and we all marked on a majority of the holes played. Steve ended the day with an incredible 58 GITCA points, Bob tallied 55,

Dave 49, and I brought up the rear with a robust 47 points. The weather was a perfect seventy-eight degrees with low humidity, and we all cherished every minute that we were out there. We all feel as though we have discovered a hidden gem, and we are all excited to make many return trips to this wonderful golfing mecca.

HOLE NUMBER 17

What Defines a Good GITCA Score?

Obviously, determining a good GITCA score is predicated by how many holes you play. The more holes you are able to get in, the higher your GITCA tally should obviously be. I like to define GITCA scoring as the golfer versus the golf course in a match-play hole-by-hole situation. Clearly, anything worse than a bogey and the golf course wins that hole. Whereas a par or better on a hole means that the golfer has triumphed and can bask in all the glory of his/her wonderful hole. Getting a bogey on the hole is declared a stalemate, which is clearly better than a loss for each of the combatants. Being able to salvage a bogey on a hole and its subsequent point is often a clear moral victory for a golfer playing a particularly difficult hole or after he/she has hit an errant shot or two. It is my contention that every time you mark on a hole, it is far better than receiving a big fat zero. So enjoy escaping the hole with some semblance of pride, and pat yourself on the back for once again avoiding the dreaded GITCA label.

With this being the protocol, equaling the number of GITCA points to the number of holes played should be declared a decent round and an overall stalemate. Hopefully, with all the GITCA lifelines provided, you can better this watershed mark most of the time, but unfortunately, you may subject yourself to very difficult courses that occasionally kick your butt. These are okay to challenge yourself with from time to time just to keep your ego in check, but I personally like to play a course that doesn't overwhelm me most of the time. If my buddies and I are playing a course that we can handle and we are marking on most of the holes, then rest assured, everyone is going to have one hell of a good time. However, if we choose to play a really challenging course, then everyone must readjust their contentment levels to appreciate attaining a bogey on most of the holes played. With the course slope rating being very high for your entire foursome, points are going to be at a premium for everyone. As a result, fewer points will be accumulated by all participants, and hence, the competition should still be ultracompetitive right down to the final hole or two. In other words, the course is likely to kick everyone's butt, so learn to play for bogeys on most of the holes, and you will probably be in contention for top GITCA golfer at the end of the day.

My general rule of thumb is that for an eighteen-hole round, any golfer who accumulates a GITCA score around twenty-seven has had a heck of a day and is most likely going to be in contention for top honors. Any golfer who has a score hovering around twenty-seven points for eighteen holes has most likely attained a score of par or bogey on most of the holes played. With this being the case, a score of around 13 or 14 is considered a very good score for a nine-hole round. By throwing in all the GITCA lifelines, your chance of attaining these totals is obviously greatly enhanced. Take advantage of these opportunities, and you are most likely going to be filled with contentment at the end of your round. If it is difficult for you to attain these point totals on a consistent basis, then by all means move up a tee box or choose to play combo tee markers to greatly enhance your chances of attaining higher GITCA tallies. It boggles my mind to see foursome after foursome teeing off from tee markers that offer them few opportunities to reach most of the greens in regulation and then complain that golf is too frustrating for them. Do yourself and your foursome a favor and finally swallow your pride and move up a tee box so that you can finally hit a large number of the greens in regulation. By finally being able to play from distances that give you ample opportunities for success, you and your buddies are much more apt to post good scores far more often as well as garnering much more satisfaction out on the links.

Two Tickets to Paradise

As I was heading to play golf with Steve and Bob, Eddie Money's classic song "Two Tickets to Paradise" came on the radio. Naturally, I cranked it up and sang along as I began to contemplate what really constitutes "paradise." Does it have to be the perfect setting? Are there margaritas flowing? Who in my life needs to be there for me to conclude, "Aha, this is paradise?" Over the next ninety minutes out on the golf course, paradise was indeed found!

When we got to the course, we were shocked to find the course packed, and our hearts sank when the starter said that everyone needed to be off the course by three for a shotgun outing. He said that we could play as many balls as we wanted, and he would simply charge us the nine-hole rate. That was music to our ears as we knew that we could get in at least sixteen holes from the various tee markers as long as we weren't holding anyone up. We were indeed the last golfers whom he allowed to tee off, so we decided to play a ball each from the blue tee markers as well as one from the white tee boxes. Even from the blue tees, the first hole is a drivable par 4. When we all hit our drives onto the green and we all made our putts for eagle, we immediately sensed that this indeed might be a magical day. From the white tees, the hole plays as a long par 3, so when we all made tap-in pars, we all left the first green with ten GITCA points in our back pocket. When both Bob and Steve went birdie-par on the next hole as I went par-bogey, they surged to a lead that looked very daunting. I was undeterred, however, as I knew my ball-striking was very good and that I simply wasn't making enough putts. Over the next ten holes, I quickly remedied that as I began to sink almost every putt I looked at.

We entered our last hole of the day all tied, and we all had yet to pull out our "par buster." This drivable par 4 now became an extremely inviting par 5, thanks to the par buster. We surrounded the green with our drives, and we all chipped on to within ten feet. It was readily apparent that whoever made their putt was going to at least tie for the championship and that if we all made it, we would all tie. Steve went first and left his eagle attempt on the front edge. We waited ten seconds for it to fall in, but alas, it never did. I was fully expecting to make my putt, so I was disheartened when it failed to fall in the left edge. Now all the pressure was on Bob to make his six-footer to secure the victory or miss and leave us all tied on this glorious August afternoon. Unnerved, he calmly knocked his putt into the back of the cup to secure the hard-fought victory. He was naturally delighted to win, but both Steve and I were so pleased with our own ball-striking that we all celebrated our fine play. We all finished the seventeen holes well under par, with Bob accumulating fifty-three GITCA points to beat both Steve and I by four points. As we shook hands, we all were hard-pressed to remember a time when the three of us had ever struck the ball so well at the same time.

I politely asked, "Is there three golfers in the world who enjoyed themselves out on the links today more than we did?"

They both stated, "Absolutely not!"

So maybe we had discovered what "paradise" truly is. Certainly, we weren't playing a course the likes of Pebble Beach or Augusta, but we had about as much fun as anyone can have out on the links. The competition was fierce right down until the final putts of the day, and not one argument was had. We all embraced this wonderful opportunity to experience golfing nirvana with our beloved friends, and we accomplished this amazing feat in less than ninety minutes. As we headed off the final green, we all looked at our watches, which said 2:58 p.m. "Damn, we could have played that par 3 hole one more time," I jested. Maybe I would have hit a walk-off hole-in-one to make the day even more memorable, but I knew that I would remember this moment for a long, long time. We had completed seventeen holes in eighty-eight minutes, and we all had ample scoring opportunities in which we all saw many of them through to fruition. So for a mere nine dollars each, we were all quite certain that we had found heaven on earth.

Ran My Proportional Golf Equations by My Math Gurus to Get Their Input

I was so excited to run my golf equations by Steve and Dave because they are both math whizzes who used to be actuaries. At first, they both couldn't believe what I was telling them, but they both double-checked my math, and we all came to the same conclusion that the best golfers in the world are teeing up at least two tee markers in length from what they should be proportionately speaking in relation to the distance most amateurs are trying to play. Since both of them insist on playing from the blue tees most of the time, I reminded them that they really should be teeing off from the green tees if they want to get a true sense of what the PGA professionals feel like on almost every hole out on tour. We couldn't resist putting our theory to the test as the three of us got out for a quick nine holes on our beloved *Glenview Golf Course*. Steve and Dave moved up two sets of tee markers to the green tees, while I put my ego aside and teed off from the red tees so that we could experience playing from distances comparable to what the PGA professionals encounter each week. Even though we rarely played the course from these close-in distances, it didn't take us long to discover that this simple thirty- to forty-yard advantage on almost every hole was paying dividends with all our scores. Instead of having to hit driver on every par 4 and par 5, we now brought our fairway woods and hybrids out of the bag so that we could greatly increase our chances of hitting almost every fairway and subsequently nearly every green in regulation. On some of the shorter holes, we were able to drive on or near the green to set up several makeable birdie opportunities.

I ended up winning the day as I was able to record seven pars, a birdie, and a "par buster birdie" to finish with a robust twenty-two points for the nine holes. Both Steve and Dave finished with twenty points each as we combined to record a "pro-like total" of twenty-four out of twenty-seven greens hit in regulation. Since we had no one in front of us and we hit so many greens, the three of us traversed the nine holes in less than eighty minutes. Dave quipped, "That was almost too easy!" I then asked him when was the last time he ever heard a professional golfer leaving the course saying that the set up was way too easy. "Never," we all exclaimed as we headed to the clubhouse to check our math and relish in how much better we all were feeling about our scores and our golf games. We all now have renewed confidence that we are actually much better than any of us realized and that for a majority of our golf outings, we are actually playing a much more difficult game than the professionals do proportionately speaking. Take that, Tiger and company. We are not as bad as we previously were led to believe. Playing the game from distances that are proportional to yours, it is not nearly so daunting a task to make at least a bogey on nearly every hole we play.

We all got home in time to watch the Solheim Cup. What a wonderful display of golf by everyone involved. Although the American golfers were triumphant in most of the matches, the high level of golfing mastery put on display by both teams was a sight to behold for golfers around the world to celebrate. Not only was the skill level as high as any I have ever seen, the camaraderie and genuine sportsmanship among all the combatants left no doubt as to the sport of golf being the true winner on this glorious day.

Watching a Record-Setting Display and Loving Every Minute of It

Bob and I returned to *Robin's Nest* on a spectacular late Sunday afternoon as the sun was setting, and we literally had the course to ourselves. These sublime conditions were a far cry from the driving rainstorm we had played this course in a week earlier, and Bob made certain to capitalize on these pristine conditions. He birdied the first four holes to get a huge lead on me, and he never let up the entire round. I was striking the ball extremely well also, but Bob was keeping the ball below the hole and was sinking nearly everything he looked at. Whenever he did miss a green, his chips and pitches were spot-on as he got up and down all day long. My chips were not up to his wonderful display, and as a result, I found myself fourteen points down entering the final hole of the day. We both had saved our par buster for this very drivable par 4 finishing hole, but neither of us had saved our roving mulligan for this occasion. I knew that my only chance was to drive this now very short par 5 hole and make my putt for a "par buster double eagle" and garner the sixteen points in a desperate attempt to tie or overtake Bob. Unfortunately for me, Bob had other ideas as he nearly drained his tee shot, which would have given him an incredible "par buster hole-in-one" on this par 5. Had his tee shot found the bottom of the cup, it would have netted him an incredible eighty GITCA points and would have given him a GITCA eighteen-hole scoring record that might never be broken.

    I hadn't played badly, and I still lost by a record deficit of twenty-six points. Bob finished the round at seven under par, and I am sure that there are many out there scoffing at us playing this "rinky-dink" executive course and tearing it to shreds. Now seven under par is an incredible score for any golfer, but I am currently seeing pros shoot rounds in the low 60s almost every day on the PGA Tour. Now I don't see any of them complaining that the course was too short or too easy for them. But as I noted earlier, even though they are playing from distances way farther back than most of us could handle, they are essentially playing courses that are over 1,000 yards shorter than what they are capable of handling. If the greatest golfers in the world don't mind playing courses from distances that they are quite capable of overwhelming, then why should us rank amateurs apologize for playing on courses that clearly boost our ego and overall golfing esteem? As my buddies and I have demonstrated for the last four years by applying the tenets of GITCA GOLF, there clearly is nothing wrong with giving yourself ample opportunities to achieve sustained success out on the links. Not only is it less maddening, it is downright exhilarating! I highly recommend that everyone in your foursome move up one or two sets of tee boxes your next time out, and you all can thank me later. Once everyone becomes acclimated to playing up, there will be many good looks at par or better on nearly every hole you play. Doesn't this sound a lot better than scrapping out a double bogey or worse on most of the holes you play? By having short irons in your hands for most of your approach shots, most of the greens will be hit in regulation, and as a result, you all will be recording record-low scores and playing a heck of a lot faster and no doubt whistling Dixie throughout your round. Once GITCA GOLF becomes the new norm, everyone will be moving up, playing faster and better, and having infinitely more fun than they ever thought possible out on the links.

Revenge

    Having been thoroughly embarrassed my last time out by Bob's incredible record-setting round, I was more determined than ever to try and keep up with him. I went to the putting and chipping green four days in a row, and I finally figured some things out. I was feeling so cocky that I even suggested that we return to the course Bob grew up on, the beloved *Neumann Golf Course*. Not wanting to lose my newfound putting and chipping revelations, I arrived at the course a half an hour before our tee time. By the time Bob had gotten there right before our tee off, I was filled with confidence and eager for redemption. Naturally, I three-putted the first green for a bogey and, once again, found myself trailing. Bob's lead proved to be short-lived as I played lights out the rest of the round and won by a 36-to-30 GITCA count. My putting was excellent, and I only had to chip a few times as I hit sixteen out of eighteen greens in regulation. I was thrilled as this course had always given me so much difficulty in the past even though it is not a long course by any stretch of the imagination. In fact, from the white tees, the course now only measured 5,300 yards. (I feel that this is a brilliant move as most golfers I know who play this course are baby boomers or older, so moving all the tees up on this course is going to keep their clientele feeling great about themselves and their games.) Now on most courses, this yardage would constitute the green tees, but Bob and I had always played this course from the white tees, and we both were excited to see how low we could go. Fortunately for me, I had done my homework ahead of time and realized that I could leave my driver at home. I teed off on most of the holes with my three-wood and three-hybrid, and I didn't miss a fairway. I had scoring irons in my hands for nearly all my approach shots, and as a result, I was finding the middle of the green on almost every hole. Bob brought out his driver on most of the holes as he was intent on bringing this course to its knees. Although this proved to be fruitful on several holes, it got him behind the eight ball on many others. It also didn't help his ego that I was hitting it past his driver with my three-wood on many holes. I was just trying to hit the ball solidly down the middle of the fairway all day, and I think not trying to overswing really helped me find the sweet spot on nearly every shot. It finally dawned on me that this is the same philosophy that the professionals adhere to when they say that they usually only swing at about 70 percent capacity.

Now that I know that the professionals play from tee markers where they don't have to swing all out, I adopted their philosophy on this shorter course, and it worked like a charm. I am convinced that if I play many rounds from distances where I don't have to swing "all out," my ball-striking and my scoring will improve immensely. If I am striking the ball pure and scoring a lot better, then rest assured, I am going to be having the time of my life out on the links. Bob certainly knows this as well. He was just intent on trying too hard to produce another record-breaking round. As we all know too well in golf, a hot streak unfortunately does not last forever. Bob shook my hand and congratulated me on my excellent round. "I learned from the best," I told him as we vowed to get out again as soon as possible.

The Perfect Round

Bob and I both had hectic schedules, but we both agreed that we had just enough time to play a quick eighteen holes at our beloved *Robin's Nest*. We got there just before the afternoon rush, so essentially, we had no one holding us back from playing at a very brisk pace. Without a single practice putt, chip, or full shot, both Bob and I played the round of our lives. From the very first tee shot until the final putt of the day, we both played flawlessly. Every tee shot was hit right on the screws, and we both went flag hunting as we both racked up incredible GITCA scores. The weather was around seventy degrees, and there was barely a cloud in the sky. We felt like Tom Watson and Jack Nicklaus once again as our match came down to the final two putts of the day to determine the winner. When I missed my five-foot birdie putt that would have clinched the victory, it was all up to Bob to make his four-foot putt to secure the victory. As I watched him intently line up his putt, I thought to myself, *It doesn't really matter if he makes this putt or misses it.* I have done all that I could to win, and I have played flawless golf in front of my beloved friend. We both have struck the ball as well as we ever have, so in essence, we both should declare the round a rousing success regardless of whether he makes the putt or not. Alas, he missed to the left, leaving me with an incredible 49-to-47 GITCA victory. We both shook hands heartily as we both realized that it doesn't really get much better than this.

The Real Reason We All Play Golf: Escape from Reality

As Bob and I arrived at our beloved *Circling Hills Golf Course*, we noticed that the course was packed on this beautiful fall morning and that everyone besides us was over seventy years old. We both were excited to see so many senior citizens golfing as we felt like we had stumbled on to a remake of *Cocoon*. I knew exactly why they were all out here, but I wondered aloud if Bob did. "Why do you think that they are all out here on this nice but slightly chilly morning?" Bob had no answers, so I quickly enlightened him. "They are so excited to get out of the house and get away from their nagging spouses!" In addition, this is about bonding and letting the competitive juices flow once again. Most of these golfers are lifelong friends, and they know how precious these days out on the links with their beloved friends are. How many more days this year do you think that they are going to be able to leave their houses and enjoy the sunshine and all this wonderful camaraderie? The bigger question is, How many more chances in their lifetimes are they going to be able to repeat these treasured moments? None of us are getting any younger, and certainly, the length of our shots isn't getting any longer. We need to take advantage of every opportunity that we are blessed with and never miss a chance to live life to its fullest. Golf, for all these wonderful souls, is therapy. Now these guys are clearly embracing each moment and having a great time, but I wonder how much more magical all their time spent on the links would be if all of them learned to embrace GITCA GOLF?

Bob totally concurred with me and added, "They might never go home!"

Reveling in seeing these older golfers embrace the game with passion, Bob and I were more inspired than ever to play well and embrace our special time out on the links. I don't know if it was just the inspiration we needed or what, but both Bob and I played as well as I can ever remember. Each of us only had one or two shots that didn't turn out exactly as we imagined as we both posted unbelievably great scores. Even though the course was literally crawling with golfers, we finished the nine holes in an hour and forty-five minutes, and Bob emerged victorious with twenty-three GITCA points to my nineteen, thanks to his "par buster eagle" on the seventh hole. I made a valiant charge at him at the end, but my eagle putt on the final hole failed to drop. Even though I hadn't won, we both were smiling from ear to ear. The ball-striking by both of us had been superb, and the bantering and camaraderie that we experienced were something that filled our hearts with joy. It was as though God himself was looking down on us and pointing out that this is what life is truly about. Hopefully, Bob and I will still be playing golf often when we are senior citizens and embracing life as the golfers we witnessed on this remarkable day. I told Bob that these special moments are what life is all about and that we need to make the most of them whenever we get the chance. Certainly, we are all "busy" with life's other responsibilities, and certainly, there are many more important things that should be at the top of our priority list, but we must make time to get out with our friends from time to time in order to lift our spirits and soothe our souls. "Sunday afternoon, the weather looks promising," I said with a twinkle in my eye.

One's Handicap Can Vary Greatly Based on Varying Courses, Conditions, and Tee Markers

Knowing my own game like the back of my hand, I would say that my actual handicap would vary greatly depending on what course I am playing on and what yardage I am playing from. If I am playing a par 3 or executive course, I would dare say I am around a 3 handicap. On the other hand, if I am playing a true championship course from the tips with a slope rating over 140 with lightning-fast greens, I am probably a 25+ handicap. Whereas if I was allowed to move up to the blue tees on this extremely challenging course, my handicap would probably drop a few strokes. Certainly, a few more would be knocked off if I was permitted to tee off from the white tees. Playing from the yellow tee markers, I would almost certainly be a single-digit handicapper. So trying to tell other golfers what my actual handicap is would vary greatly depending on the condition and length of the course that I was playing.

The all-pro wide receiver Larry Fitzgerald just won the Pebble Beach Pro-Am, and he constantly had to defend his stated 13 handicap all week long. Most of the spectators in attendance swore that he was playing much closer to a 5 handicap and that he was essentially cheating the system. Instead of basking in all the glow of playing some of the best golf of his life on one of the greatest golf courses in the world, Larry had to constantly answer questions about the legitimacy of his handicap. I believe you, Larry, and let no one put asunder your glorious week!

Fortunately, we don't have to worry about all these variables with GITCA GOLF as I know exactly where to tee off from, and I start every round with zero points just like everyone else. No one ever questions the legitimacy of my stated handicap because I never have to answer that question. I simply tee off from the white tees and play straight up against everyone else teeing off from their properly designated tee markers. At the end of the round, the golfer with the most accrued GITCA points wins fair and square with no questions asked. I would be honored and thrilled if Larry Fitzgerald ever wants to join me for some GITCA GOLF at any venue of his choosing. He would tee off from the blue tees and I the white tees, and may the golfer who accumulates the most GITCA points be declared the undisputed winner.

A Return to Reality Brings about Some Much-Needed Insight

Following so many triumphant and glorious rounds with my compatriots, I was destined to fall back to earth sometime, and when

I landed, it was with a tremendous thump and blow to my ego. I had played so many wonderful rounds in a row that I was now taking for granted just how great my ball-striking had been. I was so excited to show Randy and Jerry my newly found golfing prowess that I arrived at their home course an hour early in order to hit some range balls. Their home course is *Miami View Golf Club*, and it is a spectacular layout with an incredible practice facility. I paid the modest guest fee of twenty-five dollars walking for nine holes and then headed to the driving range in hopes of fine-tuning my game prior to my buddies' arrival. The range balls were free and unlimited, which are magical words to my golfing budget, so I was intent on hitting as many of them as I could in an hour. Naturally, I started with my wedges and worked my way down to the driver. Right from the get-go, my swing was feeling forced and labored. Now the forty-mile-per-hour wind gusts certainly didn't help, but my magic in a bottle had suddenly left me, and my shots were going every which way but the direction I intended. The more balls I hit, the worse my swing became. With our tee time approaching, I headed to the putting green to get a feel for the speed of the greens prior to my colleagues' arrival. The greens were running at least an 11 on the stimpmeter, so this only added to my overall anxiety and trepidation.

As we got to the first tee, I was overcome with panic as I saw that this par 4 hole was playing over 456 yards from the white tees into a monsoon. The pressure to perform under such scrutiny obviously got the better of me as I proceeded to post an eight on the very first hole. Bob's heroic seven garnered him no GITCA points as well, and we both were less than pleased with our auspicious starts. To further tighten the screws, I followed up my opening snowman with a triple bogey on the 430-yard par 4 second hole. I was ready to leave the course right then with my tail between my ears and hightail it out of there, never to return. On a day that had started with such high enthusiasm and hopes, it now had turned suddenly sour and into an epic embarrassment. I could now empathize with Sergio Garcia on the eight over hole that he had recently recorded at the Masters, but the difference was that he had never lost faith in his ability. I was now starting to question everything from my golf swing to my manhood as I literally tore apart this golf course. I did manage to right the ship a little bit during the final seven holes with a couple of pars and bogeys, but the damage had already been inflicted, and the scars would be there for some time. Since we basically had the course to ourselves on this extremely windy day, Jerry suggested that we play nine more as long as we all were out there. I made up some lame excuse as to why I couldn't because I didn't want this carnage to continue.

    I took the scorecard home with me, and I hung it right next to the scorecard from my best round ever. I wanted it to be a reminder to me of just how quickly one can lose one's confidence out on the golf course. I knew that this embarrassing outing was a great lesson for me to empathize with the eternal frustration that a majority of golfers deal with on a majority of their outings. As I perused the scorecard, it immediately dawned on me that this wonderful golf course has set up its constituents for failure a majority of the time that they tee it up. Now certainly the golf course powers that be didn't intend to do this on purpose, but nonetheless, the course is set up for good scores to be rarely posted. Similar to *Terrace Park Country Club*, *Miami View Golf Club* doesn't have black tee markers. As a result, both of these clubs have their blue tees playing over 6,600 yards and their white tees measuring over 6,300 yards. According to my GITCA guidelines, this is too far for their patrons to have to negotiate and hope to score well a majority of the time. In addition, both courses have their greens running very fast, which makes them much harder to hold and leads to far more putts per round on average. Certainly, both of these courses have bought into the misled macho golfer mystique of the eighties when everyone was trying to make their course harder and more dramatic than the next. It seems as though every course is afraid of their golfing venue not being challenging enough for the scratch golfer or professional. Once again, these courses are intent on trying to cater to less than 1 percent of their clientele! Is it any wonder that most golf courses around the world are struggling to stay afloat? Certainly, there are many courses that are trying to make themselves out to be so difficult that the top golfers will tip their cap to them as being a formidable challenge, but in the meantime, 99 percent of the rest of their patrons are banging their heads against the wall in utter frustration. This Neanderthal mindset needs to change immediately if these great golfing treks hope to stay afloat and add new clientele.

My recommendation to these two great golfing establishments and countless others around the globe: make your courses much more user-friendly! The first and most important thing that you can do is to add another set or two of tee boxes. Put in black tee markers where your blue tee boxes currently sit and then simply put the blue tee markers where the white tee markers currently sit and repeat this process all the way through the various tee markers and allow combo tee boxes so that golfers have eleven different distance options. Even if the course doesn't have the means to add another forward tee box, the easy fix is to simply throw out some red tee markers in the middle of the fairway and make the course much more user-friendly for every single one of your patrons. The second-easiest solution is to not cut the greens so close so that they are more receptive to approach shots and much easier for most people to putt on. Once again, these courses might get some initial flak from the old warhorses intent on protecting the sanctity of their beloved golf course, but in the end, you will have far more satisfied patrons by making your course much more user-friendly. Not only will the scores be better, but the pace of play and overall mood of all the golfers will be much better. The small number of constituents that used to brag about the severity of their home course will now be drowned out by the rousing number of patrons who are enjoying themselves far more on their newly fangled, much more golfing-friendly venue. By making the game much more enjoyable for the vast majority, the number of patrons should steadily increase rather than slowly dwindle down. The increased revenue should allow these courses to stay open and prosper for many years to come.

June 30, 2018: The Beauty and Wonderment of GITCA GOLF Was on Full Display

Steve, Pete, Bob, and I got together on the links for only the second time all year, and we were like little kids on Christmas morning.

Bob had never played *Majestic Springs*, so the other three of us were excited to show him one of our favorite courses, and we all knew that the competition would be fierce. I figured that Steve would naturally play the back tees, which measure over 6,400 yards, and the other three of us would tee off from the markers one set up, which measure almost 5,900 yards. But Steve had just played from the tips his previous time out in which he shot a 73, and he wanted to see if he could in fact break 70 from our tee box. In order to make things GITCA fair, the rest of us should have moved up one more tee box, but we all said, "What the heck. Let's all tee off from here and see how the chips fall." Steve and I were paired up for the first six-hole match, and his prodigious length gave him a decided advantage over the rest of us. I didn't mind since he was my partner, and it was actually my birdie on the sixth hole that clinched the victory for Steve and I. Even though Steve had hit every green in regulation, he had three-putted three times to keep the competition exciting right down to my birdie-clinching putt.

Pete and Steve were partnered up for the next six-hole jaunt, and Steve's dominant length on the two par 5s allowed the two of them to escape with a one-point victory over Bob and I. We had our opportunities, but alas, I recorded no points on either par 5 to doom our chances. Bob played very well as he was matching Steve in recording GITCA points, but in the end, we missed some golden chances. Nonetheless, the competition was heated, and the banter was flowing freely.

With the two of them playing the best golf and Pete and I both leaking oil, the final match might as well have been the Soviets versus the Americans in the 1980 Olympic hockey as they were the prohibitive favorites. Being the gritty, gutty competitors that we are, Pete and I never backed down as we both made "par buster birdies" to take a three-point lead heading in to the final hole of the day. Naturally, Steve had saved his par buster for this final hole as he nearly drove this three-hundred-yard par 4 finishing hole. With our backs clearly against the wall, Pete and I managed to scrape in with a bogey and par, respectively, to tie our much-more-heralded colleagues. Even though it was a tie, it clearly felt like a win for us. Handshakes were given all around as we all remarked what a wonderful day and competition we had all been fortunate enough to participate in.

Pete had struggled somewhat throughout the round, and he clearly stated that playing the GITCA format and starting new matches every six holes had allowed him to keep his enthusiasm going throughout the round, while playing a stroke-play format would have caused him to throw in the towel at the turn. Steve kept track of the stroke-play tallies, while I kept the GITCA totals for everyone. Even though he putted poorly throughout the day by his standards, Steve still recorded a 75 and tallied 32 GITCA points to claim the gold medal. He also ended the day 2–0–1 in the three competitions to also garner those honors. Bob and I essentially tied as he recorded an 81 to my 82, while I beat him 28 to 27 in GITCA points. Pete finished with a respectable 86 while recording 25 GITCA points, so a wonderful day was had by all of us. With even a moderate putting day, Steve clearly would most likely have broken 70 and wiped us all out. His length gave him a decided advantage on about eight or nine holes and thus led to much better scoring opportunities throughout the day. While the rest of us were hitting 8 irons in for most of our approach shots, Steve was like a magician as he hit most of the greens in regulation with nothing more than a wedge for most of his round. It was clearly neat to see someone dominate a course like that, and no doubt, the rest of us would have had as many great scoring opportunities if we too had moved up and played the course from one tee box farther up. Next time, we all will do so, or we will once again regulate Steve back to the tips. We can hardly wait to reunite this fabulous foursome and imbibe on GITCA GOLF once again.

Sadly, the Four of Us Never Golfed Together Again in 2018

Life got in the way, and the four of us never got out again as a foursome the rest of the year. As the author of this book about capitalizing on all the precious moments that we have to make with our beloved friends out on the golf course, this is simply unacceptable. We are all at different stages in our lives with varying priorities, but to only reunite once during the calendar year for a round of golf is inexcusable. We all know that playing as a foursome under the pretenses of GITCA GOLF is certain to be one of the highlights of our year. There simply is no excuse as to why we didn't all make a concerted effort to make it happen more often.

May Day 2019: The Quintessential GITCA Round

The wind was howling at over twenty-five miles per hour, and the greens had recently been aerated, but that didn't dampen our enthusiasm as Bob and I battled it out on our new favorite course: *the North Trace of Fairfield Greens*. This wonderful nine-hole course is only 1,885 yards from the tips. It has no bunkers and very few trees to stifle one's round. The course is located on Augusta Boulevard, so you know that it is a sacred place indeed. This was our fifth time playing this short but fairly well-kept course, and we all feel that it is the perfect GITCA course as there is approximately 30 yards between each tee box. For our first nine-hole trek, Steve always tees off from the blue tees and Bob and I from the white tees. For our second time around, we all tee off from the forward yellow tees in order to give us all ample opportunities to score extremely well coming home.

Since it was just Bob and I today and we both had been playing really well, we knew that it would most likely be a knockdown brawl until the very end. Provided that there was a strong wind at our back on the first tee, both Bob and I decided to invoke our par busters right off the bat. When Bob drove the green and was able to secure an easy par buster eagle to my par buster birdie, he had forged to an early four-point lead, and he kept adding to it throughout the front nine. By the turn, he was up an incredible thirteen points, and he showed little sign of letting the lead slip. I started to fire at every pin, but I could only cut his lead to nine entering the final two holes. Since we both had already used up our par busters, it was going to take a miracle for me to catch up to him. Fortunately for me, sometimes, God answers your prayers as my birdie-eagle finish to Bob's bogey-par finish allowed me to escape this unforgettable day with an unbelievable tie. Bob had outplayed me for most of the day, but when my drive on the uphill 228-yard par 4 finishing hole almost went in, I somehow had managed a much-deserved draw. Registering twelve points over the final two holes had secured this dramatic finish and would not have been possible under the guise of normal stroke-play scoring methods. So for a mere nine dollars each, Bob and I both enjoyed eighteen unforgettable holes in less than two hours. Certainly, the pros would never subject themselves to putt on aerated greens, but somehow, Bob and I managed as we both ended the day at even par. While most traditional golfers might mock us for playing these less challenging courses from easily traversed distances, we dare anyone to have more fun than we had out on the links today and nearly every single time we tee them up following the GITCA guidelines.

My Long-Awaited Introduction into *Topgolf*

I had heard about how fantastic the Topgolf experience was for everyone who had tried it, including my own children, but I had never had the privilege until last weekend. First of all, I was blown away at how crowded the place was on a Friday night. We had to wait over an hour for a hitting bay to clear, but the wait was well worth it as my dear friend and his boys and I had the time of our lives. Each of us hit two balls to various targets, and then it was next man up. We tallied our scores together as a group each round as we tried to post the best total score possible. The boys were intent on hitting driver or three-wood on most of their attempts, while my buddy and I hit every club in the bag to the various targets. We all enjoyed some food and drinks as we tried to better our team total score each round. The laughter and the banter were grand as we continually spurred one another on to find our chosen targets. For one magical round, it all came together for us as we posted a much better score than our other attempts. Hitting off the pristine mats or off the tee, all of us found our groove as most of our attempts landed near the chosen targets. We high-fived one another with each successful attempt, and we playfully harassed one another about the shots that greatly deviated from the chosen target zones. A few blisters developed, but this special night would long be remembered by all of us. I can't wait to get back home and take my family there so that a similar magical time can be had by all of us as well.

Transitioning from Topgolf to a Real Live Golf Course

My friend's boys were so excited from the joyous time we had at Topgolf that they wanted to know if I could take them golfing on a real course for the first time in their lives. Seeing all their enthusiasm from the previous night, I thought that this would be a great litmus test to see how they would fare on a real course under the GITCA guidelines. Being in Chicago, the cost for the three of us to play nine holes was rather steep, but it was well worth it as we had a round that none of us are ever likely to forget.

After rather feeble first attempts, the boys both hit decent drives with their first tee mulligans. Since I nearly drove the green with my initial attempt, I decided not to take a mulligan. We located both of their drives, and then I went about showing them how to properly "fluff" their ball so that it was sitting up for a nice clean hit. They weren't the greatest of hits, but both boys managed to end up about fifty yards from the green. Since the driving range and Topgolf were all they knew, they both were intent on swinging as hard as they could with a 3 iron or more. I told them that all they needed was a smooth pitching wedge from where they were in relation to the green, but *smooth* is a relative term. Both of them swung with all their might, and one attempt found the roof of the house located directly over the green, while the other one's ball landed in the adjacent swimming pool. Fortunately, no damage was done, and the owner did not come out and scorn us. I pulled out my sand wedge and gently landed my ball on the green a mere five feet from the hole. I missed the birdie putt but made an easy par that greatly impressed both boys as they both ended up with doubles for a very promising start.

Once they got a feel for the various clubs and how to better control their distances, a magical time was had by all of us. Although they had double bogeys or more on a majority of the holes, they both managed to secure a few well-earned bogeys, and each of them almost made a par on the final hole of the day. The boys were amazed at how easy I made it all look as I finished one over par as I bagged two birdies to go along with three bogeys and four pars. Securing nineteen GITCA points for nine holes is not too shabby playing a course that I had never seen before with rental clubs and balls that were as hard as a rock. The boys were amazed at my level of consistency but bragged that they would soon be beating me. I look forward to that day, and I am so excited that they have caught the golfing bug and have been properly indoctrinated into the wonders of GITCA GOLF. Even though they both finished with a mere four GITCA points each, they both are extremely confident that their totals are soon going to skyrocket. The key, I told them, is to try and master their short games, especially their putting, which they can work on for free. I am thrilled that they are so excited about golf now, and I can hardly wait to go home and indoctrinate my own children into GITCA GOLF on a real live course as well.

Neumann Golf Course Becomes the Precursor for Golf Courses Everywhere

Having played *Neumann Golf Course* many times in the past, I was pleasantly surprised to find that they had moved the white tee boxes up from their usual tee-off areas. Since we had always played the white tees in the past, Bob and I didn't think anything was that unusual until we both recorded even par scores for the front nine. Now both of us were striking the ball extremely well, but neither of us had ever hit almost every green in regulation before. As we totaled up the scorecard, we both were startled to discover that the course had simply added black tees where the blue tees had been and simply moved everything forward one tee box. I guess they figured that if people were too stubborn to move up to tee markers that were a color that they were not used to playing, they would simply move the varying tee marker designations up themselves. *What a genius concept!* Knowing that humans are creatures of habit, the golf course management team simply moved the tee markers up so that no golfer would have to leave the comfort zone of the tee box color that they had always been associated with playing. Even though the white tee markers had been moved to where the yellow tee markers had always been, the clientele didn't seem to mind as they continued to play from the same color tee boxes that they had played for most of their adult lives. Knocking three hundred yards in distance from where they had almost always played from certainly made the scoring conditions much more favorable for everyone as Bob and I could readily attest. As we continued to play well and post respective scores of 73 and 75 and GITCA scores of 37 and 35, Bob and I felt a sense of contentment on the course that unfortunately most golfers miss out on. Knowing that we no longer had to hit shots that were out of our comfort zones to score well, both of us played exceedingly intelligent golf as we both made going low look and feel extremely easy.

Obviously, the rest of the patrons were catching on as well as I could never remember the course being this crowded with senior citizens. Most of these baby boomers were teeing off from their customary yellow tees, which had replaced the red tees and measured a mere 4,500 yards. Since they had always associated playing from these designated tee markers, there was no embarrassment in playing the course from this now very playable distance. In fact, most of these golfers were playing golf as though they had just found the fountain of youth. The scores and the enthusiasm were palpable as these senior golfers were obviously enjoying the heck out of themselves and their new lease on their golfing lives. I was quick to point out to Bob how much more fun all these golfers will have once they are introduced to GITCA GOLF. We both acknowledged that they will soon be having more fun out on the course than they ever dreamed possible. The scores will be much better, and there will finally be an end to all the unnecessary arguing and bickering. This is how the golden years of your golfing life should be spent: scoring better than you ever dreamed possible and having as much fun as you can remember with your lifelong friends.

Bob and I were quick to note that we had never before seen this wonderful old muni in such phenomenal shape. The greens and fairways were pristine, and all the bunkers had ample amounts of fresh sand. Since the profits made from the course were far exceeding its previous output, the management team had enough capital leftover to put money back into the course upkeep. So the lesson learned here is to make your course far more playable and in great shape such that the demand to play it never wanes. If you have enough satisfied customers, the word of mouth about the playability of your course will attract new golfers from near and far. Nobody cares that they are playing a course that will never be rated in the top 100. All they care about is getting out and having as much fun as possible with their friends on a very forgiving course that allows a grand time to be had by most of its patrons. We used to only play this course once or twice a year, but now that it is in such great condition and the scoring opportunities have been greatly enhanced, I am certain that this will become a staple in our golfing rotation. What course doesn't want satisfied customers who are eager to play their course much more frequently?

    I believe that most golf courses around the world will learn from Neumann Golf Course's pioneer efforts and simply add another set of tee markers and then move every tee marker up one place in line. Doing so will get rid of much of the humiliation factor by keeping everyone in line with their trademarked tee box color designation. By knocking three hundred to five hundred yards off everyone's challenge, the scores will be much better and the frustration levels kept to a minimum. The old guard will be pleasantly surprised with every golfer's improved proficiency, and the number of rounds played at each course should at least double. Golfers playing the course for the first time are likely to be so thrilled that they are apt to return and bring their buddies back to a place that brought them so much solace.

    Certainly, moving the white tees up gave both Bob and I a huge break that allowed us to hit two clubs less into every green from our normal protocol. Hitting our various wedges into these now-very-receptive greens made scoring a relative breeze for both of us. I was able to hit thirteen greens in regulation, which meant that obviously I had thirteen birdie putts. Disappointed that I could only manage to make two of them, I was nonetheless ecstatic that I had tap-in par putts on most of the holes. I did manage to make a fifteen-foot birdie putt on seventeen that helped secure the victory, and I only three-putted once. Bob and I were feeling really good about ourselves and our games until we watched many of the PGA golfers shoot in the low 60s at the Wyndham Championship. We quickly realized that there is still a huge difference between our games and the professionals, but we are now very content to know that we have the ability to shoot near-par golf if put in the right circumstances.

This round of golf was definitely my most satisfying round of golf ever because I had hit nearly every shot exactly as I had planned. I was no longer gripping it and ripping it and hoping that the ball would end up in a good place. I was carefully calculating which club to hit off the tee to leave me in a favorable spot for my next shot. Obviously, this new way of playing was very satisfying as it allowed me to successfully execute most of the shots as I had visualized. Of course, this novel way of playing golf was only made possible by my mind being put at ease that I no longer had to hit career shots in order to successfully navigate my way around this very playable course. The golf course management team had given us the opportunities to be successful, and we passed the majority of their tests with flying colors.

Compare all these positive vibes with all the disdain we had for several of the other courses that had thoroughly triumphed over us in the past. Now the only difference between some of these courses and Neumann is that these other courses had set most of their clientele up for a long and miserable day. Looking back on it, Bob and I had only a slim chance to ever be successful on these long and arduous courses as their white tee boxes were stretched out to over 6,300 yards. That is over 1,000 yards longer than Neumann from the white tees and is almost assuring failure for any average golfer who tries to conquer it from those obscene distances. They are adding an average of 55 yards per hole for their constituents to try and tame over our beloved Neumann Golf Course. It doesn't take a rocket scientist to discern that 99 percent of the patrons are going to have a much more positive experience testing their metal on the shorter and far more forgiving track. Certainly, shooting near-par golf on the much harder track would be even more amazing, but the probability of most average golfers achieving this would be highly unlikely. After many years of trying to achieve the latter and being extremely frustrated, I have finally decided that I much prefer the easier and shorter venues. My likelihood for success is significantly enhanced, as is my mood throughout the round. By putting ourselves in positions to succeed, my golfing foursome has a blast nearly every time we are fortunate enough to hit the links. We are excited for you and your foursome to give GITCA GOLF a try so that you too can enjoy playing golf more than you ever imagined.

My Stepfather and I Put the Neumann Protocol to the Test

Don and I decided to move up one full tee box from our usual spots as we tried to conquer the diabolical *West Course at John's Island* from about 650 less yards than normal. Thus, before we had hit a single shot, the course was going to play an average of thirty-five less yards per hole and would hopefully be infinitely easier for both of us to try and traverse. Instead of having to rear back and try and hit the ball with all our might, both Don and I will be able to swing free and easy and hopefully find the sweet spot and the putting greens much more often and in far less strokes. After a sluggish start, we both were able to settle in and record far more greens in regulation than we ever had before on this brutally hard course. Following the GITCA guidelines exactly, we each were able to record eagles with our "par busters," and I nearly had a pair of hole-in-ones. We marked on nearly every hole, and we easily finished the eighteen holes in less than two and a half hours. Filled with excitement at just how well we both had played, we decided to play another nine holes as we basically had the course to ourselves. Don was hitting his drives so well that he had a 7 iron or less for a majority of his approach shots. Since we both are pretty proficient with our scoring irons, we both had our balls coming safely to rest on most of the greens we attacked. As a result, putting for birdie was becoming the norm for both of us, and this was clearly unchartered territory for Don.

Playing from their usual tee boxes, Don and his usual golfing buddies are hard-pressed to reach many of the greens in regulation. Even though they all are usually equipped with the latest golf gear and golfing tips, it is highly unlikely that any of them are going to experience any sustained success trying to attack this difficult course from these distances. As we perused the scorecard, both Don and I agreed that it would be nearly impossible for anyone in his foursome to reach the green in regulation on ten of the eighteen holes from the distances they were being asked to try and conquer. So right from the start, Don and his cohorts were being set up for a less-than-satisfactory experience. What should be a fun and enjoyable round with your colleagues filled with laughter and banter will soon give way to many long faces and grumpy tirades. The only difference between heaven on earth for these golfers and eternal hell is a mere 650 yards. Don and his golfing buddies must decide if they want to spend the twilight of their golfing careers in misery or ecstasy.

The simple solution for this wonderful course is to simply add one more set of tee markers that can be played from 4,400 yards for those new, old, and in-between golfers who lack authority with most of their golf shots. Now golfers of any age or gender who are distance challenged can once again take on this beast of a course and maybe, for the first time in their lives, actually enjoy playing it. Don and his peer group will then feel less auspicious about having a fair battle with this course from 4,800 yards since it would no longer be the most forward of the tee markers. Once the clientele gets comfortable following all the GITCA protocols, it is highly probable that every single member of this outstanding club will enjoy playing golf more so than at any other point in their golfing career. The only thing preventing golfers everywhere from playing faster and with far more enjoyment is oftentimes their selfish pride. Are you going to spend the next year of your life continuing to be eternally frustrated out on the links, or are you going to relish playing golf with those closest to you from parameters that allow for many great memories?

THE FINAL HOLE

Tragic Passing and the Reevaluation of Our Priorities

Just two weeks ago, Bob, Steve, Dave, and I teed it up for what none of us knew would be our last time all together out on the links. We all played with one another for six holes and then rotated partners following the GITCA team competition protocol, and a splendid time was had by all. Naturally, I had a chance to win the match, for Dave and I had I made a ten-foot par buster eagle putt on the last hole. Alas, the putt veered left at the last moment, and we all congratulated one another on another well-fought match. "We will get them next time," Dave stated emphatically as we all shook hands for what would turn out to be the very last time.

I always presumed that Dave and I would play hundreds of more rounds together over the next thirty or so years. Tragically, at age fifty-five and what seemed like the prime years of his life ahead of him, Dave had a massive heart attack and was unable to pull through. He leaves behind a loving wife and three wonderful school-age children whom he cherished with all his heart. All of us are in shock as Dave was one of those guys whom you felt like would outlive us all. He was an avid sportsman and was in seemingly excellent health. Always the competitor, Dave wanted to beat your brains in no matter what activity you were engaged in. He took great joy when he did triumph over us, especially when he could turn the tables on his younger brother, Steve, at golf. This didn't happen often, but the last time they played together, Dave stomped Steve by nine strokes and fifteen GITCA points. It was the largest defeat for Steve in their storied rivalry, and he remarked that he had never seen Dave hit the ball better or with more gusto.

Dave's passing has left all of us heartbroken. The only saving grace is that Dave's memory will live on in all our hearts. He wore his emotions on his sleeve, so those closest to him all knew just how much he cherished all of us. His family and friends never doubted his love or his loyalty as he was always quick to point out how lucky and blessed he was to have all of us in it. I personally will miss his competitive edge and banter as well as his quick wit and zest for life. He has inspired me to love my own friends and family even more and to no longer take even one second for granted. I am going to live each day to its fullest and never stop reaching for all my dreams. Dave would want it no other way.

Honoring Dave the Best Way We Know How

Dave's funeral was a wonderful celebration of his life. The place was packed as friends and family from all over the country came to honor and pay their last respects to a man who had continually inspired all of us. Dave's son, brother, and pastor all gave very moving eulogies that made us all realize just how fleeting life can be and that we must make the most out of every day and every moment while we still can. Seeing Dave's son display such grace under fire filled my heart with contentment knowing that Dave would be filled with enormous pride. It then dawned on me that I had lost a beloved friend and golfing partner, while his beautiful wife and children would be spending the rest of their lives without their beloved soul mate. Tears began to well up as I thought about how fortunate a life I have had. I am hopeful that my wife and children are fully aware of just how much they mean to me. It is my goal to continually shower them with as much love as I can while going the extra mile to make certain that Dave's family never forgets how much he loved all of them.

The next day, Steve and I decided to honor Dave in the best way that we know how: by playing as many holes of golf as possible before the sun went down. The entire round had an entirely different vibe than our normal escapades as we both talked freely about Dave's legacy and that this should be a wake-up call for all of us to continually strive for excellence in all our pursuits. Dave's presence was definitely felt throughout this very cathartic round as both Steve and I recorded eight birdies apiece on this wonderful executive course that the three of us had played so often together. Fittingly, it came down to the last putt on the last hole as my putt to even the match came up an inch short. A handshake and hug followed as we both turned to the heavens to acknowledge our fallen brother. Hopefully, there will be many more of these wonderful rounds to follow. I am quite certain that neither one of us will ever take any of them for granted.

December 26, 2019: The Final Round of the Decade

Dave, Steve, Bob, Pete, and I were all convinced that someday, one of us would be able to post a ten under par score on one of the executive courses that we all love to play following the GITCA guidelines. I certainly didn't think that it would take place during my last round of the decade, and the smart money would not have been on me to be the first to accomplish this momentous feat. I am clearly the least skilled of the aforementioned golfers, and I am certainly the shortest hitter of this distinguished group. Dave certainly must have been looking down on me from above as almost every shot I took followed the exact path that I had visualized. In fact, my opening tee shot on the short par 4 almost dropped for a hole-in-one. The short tap in eagle putt was followed up with a "par buster eagle" on the very next hole. My final hole of the day was a short par 3 that I nearly had a walk-off hole-in-one on. The entire round was magical from start to finish. Bob played well enough to beat me on most days as he fired a solid three under par round as he accumulated forty-nine GITCA points, but he could only sit back and laugh as he had a front-row seat to the greatest scoring round of my lifetime. The temperature was a record-setting sixty-three degrees in Cincinnati a day after Christmas as I posted an eighteen-hole personal best score of sixty-three GITCA points. I had recorded 3 eagles, 5 birdies, 9 pars, and 1 bogey. I jokingly told Bob to now refer to me as 3591, which is close to my home address of 3593. When we added up the totals and discovered that I had indeed achieved a ten under par score, we both high-fived each other with jubilance as we both pointed to the sky to salute our dear friend Dave once more. I wish that Dave could have actually been here to witness my improbable feat firsthand. I wish even more that he could be present for his wife and children for the majority of the rest of their lives. But life must go on without Dave and many other beloved friends and family members. It should be our top priority to make the most out of each and every day in order to honor their love and devotion.

I feel like Roger Bannister when he became the first runner to break the four-minute mile. I am certain that all my friends will soon join me in the ten under par club now that I have broken that seal. I am confident that thousands of other golfers around the world will also be able join me in this exclusive club once they fully embrace the GITCA guidelines. Why should under par golf only be reserved for the top 1 percent of golfers? Following the GITCA doctrines allows all golfers ample opportunities to record the best scores of their lives. I certainly could never break par playing from the blue tees or farther back on any of the championship courses that I am fortunate enough to play, but playing from distances that allow me to have a scoring iron in my hand for my approach shots certainly allows me to occasionally post some incredible under par scores. I will never be mistaken for a professional golfer, but thanks to adopting the GITCA bylaws, I have a chance to post scores that might make some of the pros envious. I am so thankful that I have chosen to adopt GITCA GOLF for the rest of my golfing career, and I implore all of you to do the same.

Making Golf More Enjoyable and the World a Better Place Begins with Us

With Tiger Woods tying Sam Snead's all-time tournament victory total at eighty-two, I think he has awakened the next generation to just how good he really is. I truly believe that recording one hundred victories is within his grasp if he can average three wins a year for the next six years. In no other sport could a player dominate as he approaches fifty, but I am fully confident in Tiger's amazing ability to hit tremendous shots with every club in his bag. Golf must take advantage of Tiger's reawakening by having a reboot of its own.

If golf is going to see a revival in its popularity, then everyone must get on board with the GITCA golfing revolution. Number 1, recreational golfers need to take themselves much less seriously. Unless you are a professional golfer or one of the top amateurs in the world, no one really cares what score you shot or where your handicap currently stands. The key to golf blissfulness is to play with your good friends and family members and to lighten up on the traditional golfing rules that should only be strictly followed by tournament-level golfers. By embracing the guidelines set forth by GITCA GOLF, golfers everywhere are going to have far more positive experiences out on the links with their beloved colleagues. I am not going to guarantee multiple hole-in-ones or albatrosses or overall scores of par or better, but the likelihood of achieving many of the aforementioned things is much more likely when GITCA GOLF is fully embraced. Just imagine how much more fun you and your foursome are going to have as you are likely to triple the number of greens you hit in regulation. Naturally, the scores and the pace of play will be greatly improved as well as your overall spirit. Secondly, the golf course management teams must get on board and adapt to the GITCA protocol by making their golf courses much more user-friendly for the majority of their clientele. If the majority of courses offer far more opportunities for everyone to post decent scores, the demand to play those courses will rise exponentially along with the profits.

Change is inevitable. Golf must learn to think outside the box and adapt to alternative ways of playing, or the game will slowly die. Technology has made the game infinitely easier for everyone to find the sweet spot much more often and launch the ball straighter and farther than ever before. The final step to enticing more people to get out and play and to keep them playing is to make the game far more user-friendly. By putting the GITCA bylaws into play, every golfer now has a chance to be successful almost every time out. Armed with the latest and greatest technology and playing from tee boxes that give them ample opportunities to succeed, most golfers will now score far better than they ever believed possible. Rather than the golf course winning almost every time out, GITCA gives you numerous chances to achieve success on a majority of the holes that you are fortunate enough to play. Instead of being depressed when you finish your round, following the GITCA GOLF guidelines will allow you to have far more uplifting moments out on the course. Once everyone reaps all the benefits of transitioning to GITCA GOLF, every golf course in the world should experience a much higher volume of happy patrons.

I think that most golf courses of the future will be nine-hole executive courses with multiple tee boxes and very few bunkers and trees. Many of these ventures will have lights so that epic rounds can be played for extended hours each night. Every hole over two hundred yards will be played as a par 4, so there will be numerous chances for great scoring opportunities by everyone in your foursome. Every starter will encourage each group to finish in ninety minutes or less so that everyone can enjoy their golf and the rest of their day or night as well. By being able to lift, clean, and place, every golfer should have near-pristine lies and should be able to hit many of these greens in regulation. You may not ever record over 90 percent of the greens hit in regulation for a round as Tiger, Annika, Phil, and I have, but you certainly are apt to shoot much better and have one heck of a good time nearly every round you are fortunate enough to get out and play.

The ball is now figuratively and literally in your hands. Are you and your foursome going to stubbornly stick to the mostly unsatisfactory way in which you have always played, or are you ready to finally embrace the wonderful world of GITCA GOLF? It is high time that you join the GITCA GOLFING revolution. Don't waste one more golden opportunity to have the time of your life out on the golf course. Learn to follow the GITCA GOLF guidelines so that everyone in your group can have far more positive moments every time they tee it up. It will not take long for everyone to get on board and be far more enthused to repeat this amazing experience on a regular basis.

So the bottom line is that everyone needs to get out and try GITCA with their friends and family, even if it is just for a quick nine holes. I guarantee you will have more fun than you ever thought possible playing golf, and at the very least, you will have spent quality moments with the most important people in your life. Remember, it doesn't have to be a long or expensive course either to enjoy all the wonderment of GITCA GOLF. Go find a local par 3 or executive course, and follow the GITCA guidelines that I have presented, and prepare yourself to have the time of your life. To waste just one day sitting at home in front of the television when you could be out golfing with those closest to you is a shame. To do this repeatedly is unacceptable and tragic. I can guarantee that on your deathbed, you won't lament the fact that you didn't get to watch more TV, but you certainly will be filled with regret at all the wonderful opportunities that you missed getting to spend more quality time with your beloved friends and family. None of us know how many of these golden opportunities we have left. So dust off those clubs, and invite those people closest to you to join you in playing GITCA GOLF every chance you get.

We may not have the power ourselves to change the world, but we can certainly make it more enjoyable for those closest to us. Once we acknowledge just how blessed our own lives have been due to the sacrifices of so many others near and far, it becomes readily apparent that we need to pay it forward by going out of our way to make things brighter for everyone around us. There are many people around us who are quietly suffering without anyone knowing it. A simple phone call, lunch date, or round of golf is often just the remedy to reconnect with those important individuals in our lives. If we can inspire those around us to see the world in a more positive light, all our lives will be that much brighter. Once we see all the good that can come from reaching out to those closest to us, the next step is to make things better for those less fortunate in our community. Volunteering, mentoring, or donating to a cause are ways in which we can give back, which enrich so many lives, including our own.

Making the world around us a much more habitable place will bring hope and light to where once there was only despair. At the end of the day and at the end of your life, you will have solace in knowing that you have made the world a much better place simply by giving all that you can to those less fortunate. For my final summation, I have come to embrace the fact that GITCA ultimately stands for Gratitude Inspires Truly Courageous Acts. Count your blessings daily as you muster up the courage to move confidently in the direction of fulfilling all your dreams while inspiring others to do the same. Whose life, other than your own, are you going to significantly improve today?

"Each person on this planet is here for a purpose… That purpose is to care for other people and to help this world become a better place through service to others" (Gary Sinise from his book *Grateful American: A Journey from Self to Service*).

ADDENDUM TO *GITCA GOLF*

"The trouble is you think you have time."

—Buddha

My grandfather-in-law passed away August 28, 2018. He was a decorated World War II hero, and he was a true hero to all his friends and family members as well. For the last four years or so, I had been promising myself to get down to Nashville so that I could take him golfing and show him all the wonderment of GITCA GOLF. He has been one of the great inspirations in my life, and I have modeled my golf enjoyment and the GITCA premise around his positive outlook on golf and life. Alas, I never got the chance to fulfill one of my dreams: for four generations to experience all the grandeur of GITCA GOLF together. Even though he was ninety-four, his mind was always sharp as a tack, and I took it for granted that he would essentially be around forever. Life got in the way, and I never took the time to go down and see him before he passed. Fortunately, I was able to speak with him several times before he passed to tell him how much he meant to me, but my dream of golfing with him and shaking his hand after the round never came to fruition. I am saddened that I will never get to hear his voice again, but his words of wisdom and love will continue to fill my heart with joy forevermore.

Don't let this happen to you! No longer say to yourself that there will be plenty of time to do all the things that you want to do with your loved ones. Call them up right now and plan your next get-together. Spend an afternoon golfing, and then go have a memorable meal together. Turn off your phones so that you can really tune in to one another without interruption. Unfortunately, we let far too many of these precious moments get away from us until it is too late. Don't let missed opportunities haunt you for the rest of your life. Take action immediately to make your family and friends your top priority. You and those closest to you will be eternally grateful that you took the time to do so.

ABOUT THE AUTHOR

With the help of a degree in psychology from Vanderbilt University, Kelley Peter has played and coached nearly every sport under the sun. As a tennis teaching professional for the last several decades, he is always in search of ways to help his clients improve and enjoy the game more. By constantly thinking outside the box and tapping into the mental side of performance, he has helped thousands of athletes to excel. After many years of trial and error, Kelley has found a way to make golf much more enjoyable for the masses.

Please visit Gogitcagolf.com for information and updates.
Author Photo by Ken Munson

CPSIA information can be obtained
at www.ICGtesting.com
Printed in the USA
BVHW072041010321
601385BV00002B/81